MW00849955

THE GREATEST COMEBACK

Also by John U. Bacon

Let Them Lead: Unexpected Lessons in Leadership from America's Worst High School Hockey Team

Overtime: Jim Harbaugh and the Michigan Wolverines at the Crossroads of College Football

The Great Halifax Explosion: A World War I Story of Treachery, Tragedy, and Extraordinary Heroism

Playing Hurt: My Journey from Despair to Hope (with John Saunders)

The Best of Bacon: Select Cuts

Endzone: The Rise, Fall, and Return of Michigan Football

Fourth and Long: The Fight for the Soul of College Football

Three and Out: Rich Rodriguez and the Michigan Wolverines in the Crucible of College Football

Bo's Lasting Lessons: The Legendary Coach Teaches the Timeless Fundamentals of Leadership

America's Corner Store: Walgreen's Prescription for Success

Cirque du Soleil: The Spark—Igniting the Creative Fire that Lives within Us All (with Lyn Heward)

Blue Ice: The Story of Michigan Hockey

THE GREATEST COMEBACK

How Team Canada Fought Back, Took the Summit Series, and Reinvented Hockey

JOHN U. BACON

Collins

The Greatest Comeback

Published by Collins, an imprint of HarperCollins Publishers Ltd

First edition

HarperCollins Publishers Ltd
Bay Adelaide Centre, East Tower
22 Adelaide Street West, 41st Floor
Toronto, Ontario, Canada
M5H 4E3

www.harpercollins.ca

Library and Archives Canada Cataloguing in Publication

Title: The greatest comeback : how Team Canada fought back, took the Summit Series, and reinvented hockey / John U. Bacon.
Names: Bacon, John U., 1964- author. | Description: First edition.
Identifiers: Canadiana (print) 20220271321 | Canadiana (ebook) 20220271364
ISBN 9781443464086 (hardcover) | ISBN 9781443464093 (ebook)
Subjects: LCSH: Summit Series (Hockey) (1972) | LCSH: Team Canada 1972 (Hockey team) | LCSH: Hockey—Tournaments—Canada—History.
LCSH: Hockey—Tournaments—Soviet Union—History.
Classification: LCC GV847.7 .B33 2022 | DDC 796.962/66—dc23

Printed and bound in the United States of America
22 23 24 25 26 LBC 6 5 4 3 2

To my Canadian grandparents,
Wally and Helen Graham, who made sure their grandson
had skates and hockey books.

To my parents, George and Grace Bacon,
who drove me to rinks at five in the morning.

And to my wife, Christie, and our son, Teddy,
whom she now takes to mini-mites.

My love of the game starts with them,
and I hope it will spread to others.

Contents

PART III: BECOMING A TEAM OVERNIGHT

PART IV: AGAINST ALL ODDS

Author's Note

I got lucky.

Developmental psychologists tell us we can remember historical events when we're about seven or eight years old.

I turned eight in July of 1972. My timing couldn't have been better.

Two months later I started squirt hockey, the first year you could play back then, right when the Munich Olympics and Summit Series had begun. My best friend's dad, from Owen Sound, Ontario, had played goal on Red Berenson's team at the University of Michigan. His son Scott and I played hockey together (my Canadian mother and grandfather had started me skating at three), and when Team Canada went to Moscow, we would dash home from school to catch the end of the last four games on CKLW, channel 9 out of Windsor, Ontario. And like everyone else who watched those games, I'll never forget them.

I played hockey through high school before joining the senior leagues, where I still play. I also coached hockey for a dozen years, then became a sportswriter, covering the NCAA men's hockey finals, the Stanley Cup Final, and the Winter Olympics. I've written hundreds of articles and 12 books on hockey and other subjects, but I'd only written about the Summit Series as it pertained to other events. I had never considered writing a book about the event itself.

But in 2017, when I visited Toronto on a book tour stop for *The Great Halifax Explosion*, a young man named Jason Chan asked me if I'd like to talk with Pat Stapleton, a stalwart defenceman on Team Canada, about doing just that. Naturally I was intrigued. Over the course of many phone calls and a few meetings with Pat and other Team Canada alumni, he and his teammates decided to trust me with their remarkable stories and pledged their support for this project.

I should note, however, that this is not an "official history" of these players, the team, or the Summit Series. While the players, coaches, wives, and others involved in the series gave me unequalled access, including seemingly unlimited interviews, my work was not subject to their approval, and I am responsible for this version of the Summit Series story. I felt strongly that if this book were to be credible, I had to be able to pursue the truth as best as I could wherever it led, without fear or favour. It's a credit to the Team Canada alumni's integrity and confidence that they wholeheartedly agreed and never interfered with my work.

It helped that we shared a similar perspective on the historic event—specifically, that it shouldn't be boiled down to one goal or one game, but told from the *team's* perspective. It wasn't one player who came back to beat the Soviets, but a team—one that had become so unified that almost all of them say they are as close to their Team Canada teammates as they are to the National Hockey League players they worked alongside for years.

To those ends, it was vital that I talked with as many of them as possible. Of the 22 players who got into at least one game against the Soviets and were still living when my work started, I interviewed 16 of them, along with three of the seven who didn't play, plus Harry Sinden, Alan Eagleson, three wives, several journalists, and others, like Wayne Gretzky and Mark Messier, who shared first-hand memories. These interviews ran from one to four hours and included at least one follow-up conversation.

The vast majority of the quotes in this book come from the 350 pages of transcripts collected from those interviews. In most cases I note where others were derived, except where multiple sources had the same quote—from press conferences and the like—in which case the source is not noted. As a rule, when I use the present tense—"says," "recalls," etc.—it indicates that the quote comes from my interviews, while the past tense signals that the speaker said it at the time, whether to a reporter or in their own book.

Sadly, I did not get to talk with Tony Esposito before he passed away in 2020. Unless otherwise noted, all quotes attributed to "Esposito" are from Phil, who talked with me for four hours.

While dozens of authors have written about the Summit Series and produced a number of great books, many of which I've cited herein, no one has been granted such thorough access to the broad spectrum of people involved. They gave not only their time but also their trust, transparency, and candour—elements that will be obvious when you read their thoughts on the series. For that reason alone I hope the contributions of those I interviewed will allow this work to stand as one of the principal books on the subject.

Like I said, I got lucky.

Foreword

BY MARK MESSIER

Hockey has always been a big part of our culture, even the way we think about ourselves. Everything in Canada seems to be tied to hockey.

Going into the Summit Series, we Canadians felt a lot of pride, and a lot of pressure. Our position was simple: we were the greatest hockey nation in the world, and we felt that was being questioned.

In 1972, every hockey fan and most Canadian kids were intrigued by the Russians and their prowess in international hockey. They won everything—the World Championships, the Olympics. But I don't think anybody thought it was going to be much of a challenge for our best players, who'd never competed against the Soviets before.

I certainly didn't. My dad didn't. But we all couldn't wait to witness it. The impact the Summit Series had on me compelled me to write four pages on it in my book, *No One Wins Alone*.

There was some concern about our players' conditioning, because they had just started their preseason. Unfortunately, you can't rush conditioning in a week or two.

We already knew the Russians were training year-round, but

nobody thought that was going to be a hindrance to our domination. We admired their team, but hey, they were trying to take what we thought was rightfully ours: the title of the world's greatest hockey nation.

The first four games, the whole family watched in our home. I remember the incredible anticipation getting ready to watch our country's greatest players on one team. The opening ceremony, at the height of the Cold War, showed what a big event this was for Canada. I was just feeling really proud of our players, seeing how amazing our NHL stars looked with the maple leaf on their jerseys. They were bigger than life. It felt great to be a Canadian.

The outlook quickly changed, and that just added to the tension. When you see the Russians go up 4–2 in the second period, it hits you: this might not be as easy as we thought, and maybe we're in for a long, hard series. In the third period the Russians' conditioning just seemed to take the game over, and they walked away, 7–3.

I know a lot of Canadians were distraught, but I don't think that would describe my dad's reaction. He was just impressed, *really* impressed, by the Russians: their skill, their athleticism, their conditioning, and even their focus. You could not help but respect their puck control, the way they circled back in the neutral zone, and their cycling on offence, waiting for the right chance. They were playing a completely different kind of hockey than we'd ever seen before. There's just no way anyone who loved the sport could not say they were watching a beautiful style of hockey.

It became apparent very quickly what we were up against. It was our NHL All-Stars in far from peak condition, trying to come together as a team, against a highly conditioned, unified team that had been together for years.

When you see this team of All-Stars, some of the best players the game has ever produced, struggling against the Russians, it goes to show how important it is for hockey players to feel connected to each other, especially their linemates. Without that knowledge and chemistry, you don't have the synergy that's required to win at the highest levels.

As a kid I was enthralled by it all. I couldn't wait for Game Five, but people forget we had to wait two weeks for the next game! The games in Moscow were all in the afternoon for us in St. Albert, Alberta, so we ran home from school to watch them.

Before Game Five they had another ceremony, and everyone remembers Phil Esposito tripping in the introductions, right on his backside. He absorbed that moment with so much grace. You have to be confident, really confident, to play that off the way he did. Shit happens to everyone. It's what you do with it that matters. He brought poise and humour, when few could have pulled it off.

In Game Five we blew another lead and lost 5–3. We kept coming out strong in almost every game, getting a good lead—then losing it. We were obviously a great team, but you put this tournament in December or even better in March, when everyone's ready, and maybe we're not losing those leads.

It takes months of hard work and preparation for your body to reach peak condition, and unfortunately the Canadians just didn't have time for that. Their brains were saying yes, but their bodies were saying no. I think even by the *end* of the tournament, they were still playing at about 75 percent of their capacity. Really, they were playing on sheer guts, determination, emotion, and pride, while their bodies were catching up.

The Russians' gamesmanship off the ice was legendary, but it might have backfired. There's always a way to win without poking the bear too much. When you're pushed too far, and your pride is challenged, that becomes a rallying cry. That's what happened in this case. Everyone just got so fed up with all the off-ice nonsense that it acted as a catalyst. Every championship team ultimately finds the motivation that brings everyone closer together.

And that's exactly what happened here. In Moscow, the mind games provided the spark that galvanized the Canadians. We came back and won Game Six and Game Seven—Henderson was outstanding—and now everyone's watching. This was the original Can't Miss TV.

The whole thing just reached a crescendo—from a hockey standpoint, from a coaching standpoint, from a PR standpoint, from a national pride standpoint. Everything was pulled into this last game. All the chips were on the table. There was so much riding on it, so much drama leading up to it, so many crazy events that had taken place that you couldn't *not* be watching.

My fifth-grade teacher rolled in a TV so we could all watch the final game, and this was happening all across Canada. They say more Canadians watched Game 8 than the moon landing three years earlier. Well, there weren't any Canadians landing on the moon, but even if there were, I still think the hockey game would have edged it out.

It was all coming down to this. At this point, nobody could be sure of the outcome. I don't think we could say we were favoured to win that game, but I think everyone was still surprised that we fell behind 5–3 going into the third period. Still, I don't think anyone had lost hope.

Canadians have always prided themselves on being resilient and able to overcome adversity. Well, this was a classic example of how a team had to stick together. I can only imagine what it must have been like for them in a country so different from ours in every way. It really must have felt like they alone were in enemy territory.

We could all sense the surge coming, even before we scored the final goal. You could feel the momentum had swung when we tied it up, 5–5, and it felt inevitable that someone would score.

And then it came. I'll never forget the play coming out of the corner, how Esposito got the puck to the net, and how Henderson was able to bang in his own rebound.

The whole thing was just an incredible display of pride and grit and determination. Not only to come back again and again and again, but to finish the job the way they did. The Canadian pride was in full bloom. I had uncles who were in the air force, and we'd all heard stories about World War II. I know this wasn't war, but this was as close as we would get. To see it live, to *feel* it, to see your heroes, and this incredible effort fighting for Canadian pride—an *unapologetic* pride, so rare for us—we will never forget it. This was the first time kids my age really felt the full magnitude of Canadian pride.

But the Russians had a huge impact on me, too. I taped my stick like Kharlamov, just the tip, and copied the way he taped his shin pads and even the way he shot the puck. I patterned parts of my game on the Russians. I loved how stoic they were, how disciplined they were, how focused. Those were traits I wanted.

When I teamed up with Wayne Gretzky, we were just 18 years old, and we both admired the Russians. When one of us made a nice play, the other would say, "That was very Yakushevian of you!" Glennie Anderson, on my line, man, he *really* respected the Russians. We were all changed by that series.

Over the years we've done events with the Summit Series guys, and late at night, when we're by ourselves, the conversation always turns to those games, and there's a healthy respect. Everyone can look back and see how important it was for the game of hockey.

Win or lose, the Summit Series elevated the sport.

—Mark Messier

THE GREATEST COMEBACK

Introduction

Team Canada opened the Summit Series as one of the most heavily favoured teams not merely in the history of hockey, but in the history of sports.

Just about every Canadian fan, journalist, player, and coach expected the greatest hockey team ever assembled to crush its untested opponents, eight games to zero. Team Canada's leaders were so certain of victory that they invited 35 players, two full teams' worth, to their training camp in Toronto, and promised all of them that they would get into at least one game. Anticipating little competition from the Soviets, they figured they could use the older players for the first four games in Canada, then let the younger players mop up the last four games in Moscow.

But that, of course, is not how it went.

If Team Canada's training camp was relatively relaxed, the atmosphere surrounding the team certainly wasn't. In September of 1972, Quebec's separatist movement was still making headway, and Cold War tensions could not have been higher—politically, militarily, and athletically. But then, that was why they set up this unprecedented hockey series in the first place. As one TV executive once joked, he could get great ratings for a kayaking race as long as it pitted a North American against a Russian.

That explains the intense global interest in a chess match, of all things, between American Bobby Fischer and Boris Spassky, the Soviet Union's world champion. Held in Reykjavík, Iceland, "the match of the century" ran from mid-July right up to the start of the Summit Series. The Munich Olympics, which started on August 26, focused on the battles between East and West, including the controversial men's basketball final between the USA and the USSR.

"The tension over the Fischer–Spassky chess match, then the Olympics, and then you had this hockey series—my God!" exclaims Mark Mulvoy, who covered the Summit Series for *Sports Illustrated*, helped Ken Dryden compose his account of it, and later became the magazine's editor-in-chief. "You consider all that, and September 1972 has to be one of the greatest months in the history of sport."

For decades the Canadians' supremacy over the sport they had invented was so complete that, from 1920 through 1952, they could send their best amateur teams to the Olympics and World Championships and win all but three of the sport's first 18 international gold medals (not including 1947, which Canada boycotted). But when the upstart Soviets took 10 straight international gold medals between 1963 and 1972, Canadians had had enough and sought to reassert their dominance over their national sport.

"Because Canadians are not loud or boastful," says Wayne Gretzky, "sometimes people don't realize we have such great pride, especially in the sport we invented: hockey. Even as an 11-year-old, I knew we hadn't sent our best players to play in the international tournaments. Like everyone else, I wanted to see the Soviets against our best players, the NHL All-Stars. I was *thrilled* when they finally announced it. It was like waiting for Christmas."

After the Canadians and Soviets agreed to play four games across Canada, then four in Moscow, Canada's hockey leaders formed Team Canada, the first squad ever to feature the country's best players—all of them NHL stars. Sixteen of the 35 players would become Hall of Famers, and years later, 13 would make the list of the NHL's 100 best players, making this easily the most talented team ever assembled in the history of the sport to that time, and perhaps ever.

"All those years, we really had no idea what the Soviets had been up to," says Team Canada's starting goalie, Hall of Famer Ken Dryden. "But we'd find out soon enough. And by the time we did, it was almost too late."

On Saturday, September 2, 1972, in front of a standing-room-only crowd at the Montreal Forum, the Soviets humiliated Team Canada—and really, the nation itself—with a 7–3 drubbing as shocking as it was complete. The headlines were apoplectic. The *Globe and Mail* announced, "Canada mourns hockey myth."

The Soviets skated better, passed better, and were in far better shape than the Canadians, and they proved the first game was no fluke by winning three of the first five games. The vaunted NHL stars could muster only one victory and one tie against those three stunning losses—all against a team that had never played against Canadian professionals before, let alone beaten them. It got so bad that fans in Vancouver booed their national team before, during, and after the Soviets rode to a convincing 5–3 victory in Game Four.

After Team Canada lost the first game in Moscow, their 1–3–1 record with only three games remaining meant Team Canada had to win them all—and in Moscow, on a wider, unfamiliar rink, surrounded by soldiers wielding AK-47s, and ruled by international referees who seemed equal parts compromised and incompetent, sparking stick-swinging fights among the players, a Canadian agent, and Soviet soldiers. Off the ice the Canadians had to surmount every logistical obstacle the Soviets and the KGB could throw at the coaches, the players, and even their wives.

The Canadians would have to do all this while cutting through years of animosity and mistrust they had built up playing against *each other* in the NHL, a league designed to foster hatred among rival clubs. They had to become a real team almost overnight, while figuring out how to stop a Soviet team that employed revolutionary strategies they had never seen before, forcing the Canadians to concoct a new style of hockey in just a few weeks, one that would transform the sport forever.

And if that weren't enough, they would have to withstand the pressure of the world watching the Cold War play out on a Russian rink, with more Canadians watching the final game than had watched the first men land on the moon three years before.

Team Canada did all these things well enough to win each of the three remaining games by a single goal. The experience had the power to create lasting friendships among the players, lifelong memories for the fans, and a new-found national pride that persists to this day.

For all these reasons, Hall of Fame defenceman Brad Park told me, "This was the greatest comeback in the history of sports."

This story explores the trials, tribulations, and ultimate triumphs of Canada's best hockey team, but it's more than a hockey story. It's about overcoming bitter feuds to forge a hard-earned team spirit and inspire heroics against long odds and almost inhuman pressure—a month so unforgettable that the men who played in the series consider it the highlight of their storied careers, the fans who witnessed it still regard it as one of the highlights of their lives, and the nation that produced it was forever changed.

"I remember it like it was yesterday," says Gretzky. "That series had such an incredible impact on the sport. It made the Edmonton Oilers possible: our European players, our fast, flowing style, the passing game—that all came out of the Summit Series. And I think it's a two-way street: Europeans became more physical, playing more of the hard-working, hard-nosed style we played. And that's what sports are all about, isn't it? Learning from each other, and getting better—and that's what that series did, all over the world.

"I'll watch the whole series, all eight games, again this summer, like I do every summer. It was so special—the greatest hockey ever played, in my mind.

"Blood and sweat, man. Blood and sweat."

PART I

The Set-Up

PART I

The Set-Up

1

"TO COPY IS ALWAYS TO BE SECOND BEST"

Whatever surprises the Summit Series had in store, the first might have been the biggest when Team Canada and the Soviets simply agreed to play this unprecedented series. Their paths to Montreal could not have been more different, going back to the dawn of the sport itself.

Two hundred years ago the Industrial Revolution drew farmers to the cities and created something we now take for granted: the weekend. Between 1860 and 1910 the British filled those weekends by inventing 70-some sports, including most of the major games we play today, from soccer to cricket, rugby to darts—not to mention golf and tennis, which predated that productive period. On this side of the Atlantic, the United States introduced baseball, football, and basketball—although it was a Canadian, Dr. James B. Naismith, who invented the latter in Springfield, Massachusetts, on December 21, 1891.

But no one questions that Canada gave birth to hockey and owned the sport for almost a century.

After the sport evolved from stick-and-ball games like bandy, shinny, and hurling, Canada's Indigenous people put the game on ice, and some college kids in Montreal took it from there. On

March 30, 1875, a group of McGill students and friends organized the world's first indoor hockey game at the Victoria Skating Rink. They used a chunk of wood for a puck, and two flags planted eight feet (2.5 metres) apart for the goals, but the sport's inherent excitement and violence were baked in from the start.

"Shins and heads were battered," the *Daily British Whig* reported, "benches smashed and the lady spectators fled in confusion."

Reporters would write similar stories about the Summit Series' Game Eight 97 years later.

Years after the sport had spread to the United States and Europe, the Canadians were still so far ahead that they could afford to send the winners of the Allan Cup, awarded annually to the nation's top senior amateur team, to the Olympic and World Championship competitions and dominate all comers.

In 1920, two years after the NHL had finished its inaugural season, Canada sent the amateur Winnipeg Falcons to the Olympic Games in Antwerp, Belgium, where they won their three games by a combined score of 29–1 to claim the sport's first gold medal. For decades Canada continued to funnel its best players to the NHL, and send its top amateur teams from the country's distant outposts—including the Trail Smoke Eaters, Saskatoon Quakers, and Port Arthur Bear Cats—to represent Canada overseas.

The Canadians consistently crushed the Europeans, despite having to play under international rules that prohibited checking in the offensive zone and referees who penalized the Canadians for playing a tougher style than the Europeans. The International Ice Hockey Federation (IIHF) also allowed European countries to form national All-Star squads, in contrast to Canadian teams composed of local bands of full-time firemen, factory workers, miners, and lumberjacks.

Still, the Canadians had little trouble winning 15 of the sport's first 18 international gold medals they played for between 1920 and 1952. If the annual World Championship had started when Olympic hockey did instead of in 1930; if World War II hadn't eliminated seven tournaments; and if Canada hadn't boycotted the 1947 Worlds over anti-Canadian rules and policies, it's a good bet Canada would have won 15 more gold medals, for a 30–3 overall record. But even that mark doesn't quite do justice to the Canadians' domination of the sport.

The Canadian national team's three losses prove the rule and foreshadow what Team Canada would be facing in 1972.

Canada's first setback occurred at the 1933 World Championship in Prague, Czechoslovakia. After winning the Allan Cup, the Toronto National Sea Fleas' coach stepped down so that Harold Ballard, who would later become the despised owner of the Toronto Maple Leafs, could take over. In the final a team of Massachusetts college students scored an overtime goal to upset Ballard's Sea Fleas, 2–1.

The 1936 Winter Olympics, hosted by Germany, saw Canada finish second again—sort of. In its previous international tournaments, Great Britain had relied on Canadian military officers and exchange students—still British subjects at the time—to win two bronze medals. For the 1936 Games, however, the IIHF ruled that all British players had to be British-born.

Enter a man named John "Bunny" Ahearne, a travel agent who never played the sport but somehow became secretary of the British Ice Hockey Association, then named himself team manager. The year before the 1936 Olympics, he scoured the Canadian countryside for the best amateur players who happened to have been born in Great Britain, then managed to pressure, wrangle, and finagle the various officials to permit Great Britain to field a team on which nine of the 13 players had been raised in Canada, and finally worked similar magic to twist the tournament format to his advantage. The Canadian, American, and French delegations all threatened to boycott over Ahearne's shady but not quite illegal machinations, but none of their protests stopped Great Britain from winning its first and only Olympic hockey gold medal—the only one Canada missed between 1920 and 1952.

"Getting those [Canadian] players was typical of Bunny's shrewdness," says NHL Players' Association founder Alan Eagleson, who quarrelled with Ahearne decades later. "He knew he could get them passports in five minutes. He was a charming, charming guy, but with enough deviousness to get what he wanted."

Ahearne's reliance on Canadian-raised players to win the gold medal didn't prevent him from holding a lifelong bias against Canadians—one that would resurface after he rotated between vice-president and president of the IIHF from 1951 to 1975.

The Canadians suffered their third international loss in the 1949 World Championship, when the Czechoslovakian All-Star team defeated the Sudbury Wolves, 3–2—the first warning that the Europeans were starting to learn this game.

The bigger threat to Canada's hockey supremacy would come not from Prague but Moscow—though no one would have believed that in 1949. In the 1920s and '30s, while the Canadian amateurs were still lapping the best from the U.S. and Europe, the Soviets hadn't even put their skates on yet. But in 1946 an unorthodox, supremely confident visionary named Anatoli Tarasov started a tiny lab outside Moscow that would soon produce Canada's first real rivals.

While the Canadian game had evolved organically from pond hockey to the NHL, Tarasov's game was a premeditated response to the Canadian style, built from the ground up, not for fun but solely to catch the Canadians as swiftly as possible.

According to Ken Dryden and Roy MacGregor's excellent *Home Game*, Tarasov and a group of young Muscovites built their country's first artificial rink, a compact slab of ice 30 feet by 25 (9 metres by 7.5), without walls, a roof, or boards, in a children's park—a facility easily surpassed by countless backyard rinks Canadian parents had been freezing for their kids for decades.

Armed with only a few tattered rule books, and the knowledge that he could never catch the Canadians in his lifetime if the Soviets tried to beat the Canadians at their own game, Tarasov often said, "To copy is always to be second best."

Tarasov did not waste time trying to outmuscle, outrush, or outshoot the Canadians—all losing bets. If it came down to individual talent, Tarasov knew even a squad of miners from Sudbury, Ontario, had more star power than he could muster. Instead, his players would train more and skate better than their Canadian counterparts, and eschew individual play for selfless teamwork. In the process, Tarasov had created the perfect model for Soviet socialism, one enthusiastically supported by government leaders.

Tarasov also commanded his players to use the whole ice sheet, which is hard to cover if you're not as fit as the Soviets. That's one reason why Russian teams often got their goals at the ends of shifts and periods, when their foes were gassed, and they had a knack for scoring them in bunches.

Tarasov's experiment received a boost when he discovered an amazing athlete named Vsevolod Bobrov. Bobrov had left school at 13 to work in a factory, fought in World War II, then became one of Tarasov's first hockey players at the children's park. He quickly established himself as the country's best hockey *and* soccer player, scoring five goals in three games for the Soviet soccer team at the 1952 Helsinki Olympics before devoting himself to hockey. Despite persistent knee pain that several surgeries could not fix, Bobrov led his hockey team to seven national titles, scoring 254 goals in 130 games.

In 1954, a mere eight years after Tarasov launched his program, Tarasov felt they were finally ready to make their debut at the World Championship.

═

THE Canadians arrived in Stockholm determined to make a statement, too. The year before, the president of the Canadian Amateur Hockey Association (CAHA), W.B. George, had led Canada to a boycott of the 1953 World Championship.

"Every year we spend $10,000 to send a Canadian hockey team to Europe to play 40 exhibition games," he told the press. "All these games are played to packed houses that only enrich European hockey coffers. In return we are subjected to constant, unnecessary abuse over our Canadian style of play," all complaints the Canadians could make almost two decades later. In fact, Canada has hosted the IIHF senior World Championship exactly once, in 2008.

So in 1954, when the Canadians returned to the tournament, they intended to reaffirm their hold on the sport. Problem was, no one wanted to burn $10,000 to spend a week in a penalty box across the ocean. According to Michael McKinley's *It's Our Game*, the Allan Cup champion Kitchener-Waterloo Dutchmen declined the invitation, as did the Ontario Senior B champions *and* the runners-up. Canada had to settle for a Senior B semifinalist, the East York Lyndhursts, a suburban Toronto club sponsored by Lyndhurst Motors, a car dealership.

The Lyndhursts were good enough to win their first six games by a combined score of 57–5, including an 8–0 whitewashing of defending world champion Sweden. That left the Soviets, who had won five games but tied Sweden, 1–1, which tempted the Canadians to think they would storm to yet another title. But Tarasov's crafty players outskated and outpassed the Canadians to cruise to a jaw-dropping 7–2 victory. The tournament's best forward? Bobrov, a name that Canadians would relearn years later.

The *Montreal Herald*'s Elmer Ferguson described the loss as "a national calamity, a national humiliation and a mortifying experience."

But it came with a silver lining: even Canadian fans started paying attention to the World Championship.

From 1963 to 1972, the Soviets then rattled off 10 straight Olympic and World Championship crowns, and did not lose to any Canadian team in either competition for 11 years.

By 1964, the Canadians were battling a three-front war against the Soviets, the IIHF, and the International Olympic Committee (IOC). At the 1964 Winter Olympics in Innsbruck, Austria, Canada put together its first bona fide national team of its best amateur players, including defenceman Rod Seiling, led by Father David Bauer.

Canada entered its final game of the seven-game round robin with a 5–1 record against the 6–0 Soviets. With the gold medal on the line, Canada lost, 3–2, to finish in a three-way tie for second place with Sweden and Czechoslovakia. According to the total-goals tiebreaker, Canada would get the bronze medal. But when the Canadians walked into the medal ceremony, they learned that Bunny Ahearne had changed the tie-breaker formula and they would get nothing.

"We didn't get *kinda* screwed," Seiling says today. "We got *completely* screwed—and it still grates on me. In a few minutes we go from playing for the gold to finishing fourth. How can that be? In the middle of the game, they changed the rules. That's how. It's a shame. It never should have happened."

In April of 2005 the Canadian Press reported that the IIHF agreed it had made a mistake in 1964 and voted to award the Canadians their bronze medals—then it backed off two months later out of fear the move would set a precedent.

═

THE speed of the Soviets' stunning rise caught Canada's hockey cognoscenti off guard, but they still refused to take the Soviets seriously. After all, the thinking went, the Soviets were pitting their very best players against a bunch of Canadian carpenters, insurance salesmen, and autoworkers. Nobody confused Kitchener-Waterloo's Dutchmen with Montreal's Flying Frenchmen.

But this logic contained two central flaws.

First, it underestimated the quality of the teams representing Canada. In the 1950s virtually every boy in Canada grew up playing hockey, then had to make one of only six NHL teams, which took a total of 90 skaters and six goalies. Countless great American Hockey League (AHL) players and Allan Cup champions, who would be millionaires today, couldn't earn a decent living playing the game.

Second, the Canadian critics compounded their error by assuming the European competition must not have been very good, either. Because so few Canadians had first-hand knowledge of Soviet hockey, it was easy to scoff at a Soviet victory over the Galt Terriers from what is now Cambridge, Ontario.

But those who *had* seen the Soviets with their own eyes came away with a very different impression. In 1957 Frank Mahovlich was one of the first NHL players to see the Soviets live when they played the Whitby Dunlops, captained by a young man named Harry Sinden, at Maple Leaf Gardens. They beat the Soviets handily, 7–2, but as Mahovlich recalls, "You could tell these guys were doing something right. They were playing a different game than we were. You suspected even then that they were on to something.

"Scotty Bowman tells a great story. He was coaching a Junior A team, the Ottawa-Hull Canadiens, and they won the Memorial Cup. In 1957 they played the Moscow Selects in Montreal. They lost, 6–3, but Scotty wasn't worried because a few nights later they were going to play them again in Ottawa in an odd, egg-shaped rink, so he figured they'd crush them. They lost, 10–1! Scotty couldn't figure it out, so he asked them, 'How did you know how to bounce it off the boards so well?' They said, 'We got the floor plan and put up boards in our rink to simulate it!'"

The Canadians might not have been watching the Soviets, but the Soviets were certainly watching them, and would go to any length to beat them.

The Canadian teams saw even less of the Soviets after the CAHA protested the IIHF's double standard on amateurism, which allowed the Soviet Union to pay its players full-time salaries under the guise of military service, while forbidding Canada from sending junior and semi-pro players who had received modest stipends. The Canadians retaliated by boycotting international competitions from 1970 until 1976, which made it that much easier to ignore the Soviets' rise.

And why shouldn't they? In the spring of 1972, just two months after the Soviets took their third straight Olympic gold medal in Sapporo, Japan, Czechoslovakia snapped the Soviets' 10-year international winning streak at the World Championship—and who the hell were the Czechs?

Even Frank Mahovlich, far ahead of his Canadian peers in seeing the Soviets' rise, could only be so impressed. After the Americans upset the Soviets on their way to winning the 1960 Olympic gold medal in Squaw Valley, California, the New York Rangers called up their goalie, Jack McCartan. When McCartan played the Maple Leafs, Mahovlich lit him up for four goals, accelerating McCartan's exit from the NHL. If McCartan was good enough to beat the best Soviet players, how good could *they* be?

Because the NHL brass didn't think the Soviet players were very good, they failed to see that the Soviets' methods were better—*much* better.

2

HOCKEY PUCK DIPLOMACY

Gary Smith was bored.

On yet another ice-cold Moscow morning in 1972, the young Canadian diplomat was mindlessly sipping his coffee when he noticed an unusual side story in *Izvestia*, the official Soviet state newspaper. He sat up straight.

The paper's sports editor, Boris Fedosov, was writing about setting up some hockey games between the Soviets and the Canadians—and not the usual pack of firefighters, either, but the NHL's best. Smith knew Fedosov would never write such a column without the support of the Soviet officials who could make it happen.

Well, Smith thought, this could be interesting. The timing was right, too, with the Cold War at its peak and competitions in everything from basketball to swimming to chess substituting for actual war. Far better for East and West to settle their scores with hockey sticks than nuclear missiles.

Smith set up a meeting with Fedosov, who backed up his eye-opening column, followed by another with the head of Soviet hockey, Andrei Starovoitov, who confirmed their official interest. Satisfied, Smith sent the message up the chain of command to

Ottawa, where they decided to put the recently formed Hockey Canada in charge of negotiations. And that's when things really started happening.

Alan Eagleson was one of the few who wasn't surprised, because he was there when they first hatched the idea six years earlier. A high-powered attorney, Eagleson's life changed dramatically in 1966, when he negotiated a contract for a rookie phenom named Bobby Orr, managed to pry Carl Brewer out of a bad deal with the Toronto Maple Leafs, and helped settle a labour dispute with the AHL's Springfield Indians by getting the legendary owner, Eddie Shore, ousted. These successes catapulted Eagleson into a bigger role: the first executive director of the NHL Players' Association.

That same year, according to Roy MacSkimming's excellent account, *Cold War*, Canadian government officials broke precedent and got involved with the national hockey program for two reasons: they were tired of losing, and of hearing that Canadian players were hooligans overseas—so contrary to Canada's image. In 1969 they created Hockey Canada to support youth hockey and develop a bona fide national team. Simple enough. But how to do it?

When Eagleson travelled to the 1969 World Championship—incredibly, the first to allow bodychecking in all three zones of the rink, and the last the Canadians would enter until 1977—he watched the Soviets crush the Canadians, 7–1 and 4–2. "Eagleson tried to pass off the defeats as meaningless,'" *Sports Illustrated*'s Mark Mulvoy reported. "'Our team is hamburger,' he told a Swedish official. 'Our NHL players would destroy all the teams here without any trouble.'"

No one knew if his second point was true, but the first wasn't. As Eagleson acknowledges today, about half the players on that Canadian team would make it to the NHL, including Hall of Fame goalie Ken Dryden.

"The Swede stared at him and shook his head," Mulvoy wrote. "'But this is the world championship,' he said, 'and your players have CANADA on their sweaters. We all think these are your best players. They should be.' Right then Eagleson pledged the total cooperation of the Players' Association in the hope that a team of NHL All-Stars, or the Stanley Cup champions, would be able to play the Russians for, well, the championship of the universe."

Getting the U.S., Sweden, Finland, and Czechoslovakia on board was easy. Merely getting the Soviets to meet proved almost impossible. After lots of last-minute cancellations, and the Soviets' insistence they would meet only with NHL president Clarence Campbell, Eagleson decided to rephrase his request, explaining that Mr. Campbell represented the owners, and he represented the workers. With the ask framed in Marxist terms, the Soviets agreed to meet in Moscow on April 8, 1969.

The Canadian ambassador to the USSR, Robert Ford, told Eagleson he needed to arrive with a typed letter. But where could they find a typewriter on a Sunday? Eagleson got lucky. The Metropol Hotel, where he was staying, also housed an Air Canada office manned by Aggie Kukulowicz, a tall, effervescent man with smiling eyes and a prominent proboscis. In his first game for the New York Rangers in 1953, he scored a goal—and didn't score another in his next three games, his last in the NHL. After playing 556 games in the high minors he worked as a baggage handler for Air Canada, until they discovered he spoke German, French, Polish, Czech, Ukrainian, and Russian. Suddenly he was translating for everyone from heads of state to hockey coaches. He hit it off with Eagleson that week, starting a partnership that earned Kukulowicz the nickname "the Henry Kissinger of Hockey."

"He was just a happy guy who seemed to know everyone, and everyone knew him," Eagleson says. "When we were leaving for a plane, I'd send him down a half-hour earlier to say goodbye to everyone, because that's how long it took. He said 'fantastic!' four times in a sentence, so we called him 'Mr. Fantastic.' But he was as tough as any man I'd ever met. One time a guy tried to steal his wallet in a parking lot in Toronto, and I don't know if the guy had a knife, but Aggie didn't care and just whacked him. Down he went."

Mr. Kukulowicz retrieved his wallet from the stranger, who declined to protest, and then calmly walked back to his car.

With the help of Mr. Fantastic, Eagleson composed a pitch to Tarasov and Starovoitov, who were intrigued but worried that playing the pros would cost them their Olympic eligibility. Eagleson reported to the CAHA: "This is going to take a while."

The next year, 1970, Canada seemed to be making real progress. The IIHF had picked Winnipeg to host the World Championship—the first time Canada would do so—and permitted nine professionals from lower leagues to play for Canada. But at the 11th hour, IIHF president Bunny Ahearne changed his mind.

"The agreement was reached in the fall," Eagleson says, "then at the last minute he said, 'No, no, you can't do it. Everyone else would be deemed a pro.' Which was bullshit, but it served Bunny's purpose. He often went out of his way to create rules that were adverse to Canada. Someone should have had a long talk with Bunny to get to the bottom of his anti-Canadian bias. It was ridiculous, and it hurt the game. You'd think he'd care about that."

In protest, Canada disbanded its national team, based in Winnipeg, and rejected the World Championship, which Ahearne moved back to Europe.

In 1969, MacSkimming reports, a Saturday newspaper supplement called *Weekend* magazine asked its readers if they would want a five- or seven-game series between the Soviets and the reigning Stanley Cup champion. Almost 40,000 readers responded, with an incredible 99.1 percent answering yes. One wonders if 99.1 percent of Canadians could agree on anything else. In 1971 Prime Minister Pierre Trudeau raised the subject with Soviet premier Alexei Kosygin.

"Ironically," Mark Mulvoy wrote, "one of Canada's few sympathizers was Russia. 'It became boredom for us to play in the world championship once the Canadians left,' said Georgi Rogulski, deputy chairman of the Soviet Sports Committee. It was time for the Soviets to move up to a different level of hockey, a level with the professionals . . . and learn from them."

The Soviets also feared the progress being made by the Swedes, the Czechoslovakians, and even the Americans. At the 1972 Sapporo Olympics a team of American amateurs, including 16-year-old Mark Howe, took a surprising silver. The Soviets were hearing footsteps. They even pushed out the father of Soviet hockey himself, Anatoli Tarasov, when he had the gall to ask for a modest pay raise after his 10th straight world title, installing his protégé, Vsevolod Bobrov, the two-sport star who had led the Soviets to their first World Championship in 1954.

After Smith read the column in *Izvestia* in 1972, Hockey Canada representatives met with the Soviets in Prague, which happened to be hosting the World Championship from April 7 to 22, 1972. In the midst of their talks, on April 12, the Czechs tied the Soviet squad, 3–3, casting doubt on their new coach, Bobrov, and giving the Canadians even less motivation to take the negotiations as seriously as they should have. During the Cold War, Eastern and Western nations haggled over just about everything, from the formation of the United Nations Security Council to the clocks in chess matches. Nothing was too big or too small. Therefore it's surprising how readily Hockey Canada capitulated on so many points.

The biggest was the first: the series would start on September 2, before NHL teams had even arrived at training camp. Thus, the Canadians had agreed to play a series with no preseason, no regular season, and no qualifying rounds. Unlike virtually every other serious competition, the final would start on opening night—but then, few Canadians thought this would be a serious competition.

They would also swap NHL rules for international rules; hire American IIHF referees in Canada and European referees in Moscow, instead of NHL referees; and use the international system of two officials to call penalties instead of the NHL system of one referee and two linesmen. What seemed trivial to Hockey Canada in April of 1972 would loom large five months later—but by then it would be too late.

Some points were simple: they would play one game each in Montreal, Toronto, Winnipeg, and Vancouver, and then four games in Moscow. But even this says something: none of the Canadians gave any thought to breaking tie games or a tied series.

"To their credit," Eagleson recalls, "I got a call from Hockey Canada, telling me they're getting close to a deal, so you better get over to Prague quickly."

Eagleson didn't have to be told twice. But when he arrived in Prague, after a five-hour delay at the border, the Canadians had just signed the agreement.

IIHF president Bunny Ahearne was "astonished when he learned about the proposed series," *Sports Illustrated*'s Mulvoy wrote, "and he mumbled the usual threats about Olympic ineligibility to the Russians. The Soviets ignored him. Realizing he was too late to prevent the games, Ahearne then volunteered to make the announcement that they were to be played."

"When I showed up," Eagleson recalls, "Bunny had just held the press conference, announcing an eight-game series. The deal was done! The nitty-gritty was the refs, and that would come back to bite us in the ass. In fairness, we all thought we could have *no* refs and still win! I never would have accepted those rules—but then, I would have made it a seven-game series, and we would have lost!"

Harry Sinden, who would soon be named Team Canada's coach, believed there were more nefarious reasons why Hockey Canada rolled over in the negotiations. "They needed the money from the series," he said at the time. "As I understand it, they are low on funds and need the cash to operate their programs."

The final agreement still marked the first time in hockey history that Canada would pit its best players against the best Europeans—the IIHF and IOC be damned. It would also be the first time Canada had ever assembled its best players on one team, for any competition—if Eagleson could deliver them.

But because Ahearne had already announced the series, before securing the NHL owners' approval, "that gave [NHL president] Clarence Campbell the jump on me," Eagleson says. "Before I could say the players were in favour, Campbell came out and said no NHL players would play on that team. So now we're behind."

Eagleson fought back. "I had enough NHL clients who would play for their country, *without* their owners' consent, to field a better team than we'd ever had before. I knew if I could get Orr to play, the others would follow suit."

But after Boston's Weston Adams publicly declared that no Bruins would play, Eagleson knew he had to convince some of the owners to back the series. So he secured support from the three Canadian NHL franchises—Montreal, Toronto, and Vancouver—then recruited Chicago's Bill Wirtz and New York Rangers chairman Bill Jennings by offering them seats on the committee. With their help Eagleson believed he could get all the NHL players Team Canada wanted, so it seemed like the contract concessions wouldn't matter once the puck dropped.

After all, just two days after they signed the contract in Prague, the Soviets lost, 3–2, to the Czechs, then tied the Swedes to finish with an underwhelming 7–1–2 record, and the silver medal, with the Czechs winning gold for the first time since 1949. If the Soviets couldn't even beat the Czechs or the Swedes anymore, what chance did they have against a team of NHL players?

Interestingly, no one in 1972 called the upcoming competition the Summit Series, just the "Canada–USSR Series." As bland as that might have been, it was at least accurate, unlike the name offered by the Government of Canada's Ministry of Foreign Affairs: "The Friendship Series," a title no one could have used that September with a straight face.

3

THE MAVERICK IN THE MIDDLE

If the series itself was an unlikely event, it only made sense that Canada would be coached by an unlikely leader.

Harry Sinden grew up in Toronto with two outdoor rinks across the street, where he spent his days. At night, "I can vividly recall lying in bed, listening to Foster Hewitt broadcast the Leafs game," he wrote, "and crying my eyes out if they lost. And I mean cry."

His dad, Harry J. Sinden Sr., "wanted me to be a hockey player. Yet he never pushed me, and I will always be grateful for that. I read and hear nowadays about parents who shove their kids into sports, and it only makes my love for my father that much greater."

When Sinden turned 16 the Montreal Canadiens invited him to their training camp, one of only five players from the entire province to be summoned. "I was very proud," he wrote. While playing for a junior team in Oshawa, Ontario, Sinden filled in for a teammate on a blind date—and met Eleanor, his future wife. "That was one time I didn't mind being a substitute."

Sinden proved to be a very good defenceman, but in the mid-'50s, that wasn't nearly good enough. Instead of today's 32 franchises with 25-man rosters, offering a total of 800 NHL jobs averaging $2.5 million (U.S.), Sinden was fighting for one of 90 jobs that paid a few thousand dollars, with Jean Béliveau leading the league at $21,000. Sinden, aged 20, had to choose between the Boston Bruins' training camp in Hershey, Pennsylvania, and a job at General Motors with a spot on the Whitby Dunlops, a top senior team. "The toughest decision of my life," he says today. "I assessed my chances of going to the NHL as less than 50 percent." He turned down the Bruins, starting a lifelong pattern: when most men would zig, he would zag.

In his book, *Hockey Showdown: The Canada-Russia Hockey Series*, Sinden wrote, "To me this was a great way to live. I was making $60 a week as an engineer [at GM] and $15 per game as a hockey player. We played a 54-game schedule in an eight-team league . . . I never considered myself an NHL player until I got up to the league and started coaching. Then I realized that perhaps I . . . could have made it."

The Whitby Dunlops, sponsored by a rubber manufacturer, played in the Ontario Hockey Association Senior A league, whose teams would win two dozen Allan Cups and represent Canada in four World Championships and four Olympics.

"This was very serious hockey," Sinden says. "Every team had two or three really good players. I know a number of them who could've made it to the NHL."

Sinden worked on the day shift for two weeks, then from 4 p.m. to midnight for two weeks, and finally from midnight until 8 a.m. for two weeks. If the Dunlops played out of town, Sinden often went straight to the factory after games.

"I look back and think it was a period of unbelievable dedication," Sinden recalls. "You'd have to be dedicated, or you'd never do this."

Sinden wasn't the Dunlops' best player, but his peers voted him captain. The Dunlops claimed the 1957 Allan Cup, which earned them a berth in the 1958 World Championship in Oslo,

Norway. Because the Soviets had already beaten the Canadians in 1954 and 1956, and Canada boycotted the 1957 Worlds after the Soviet Union invaded Hungary, the stakes were high.

Before the Dunlops left for Europe, the AHL's Cleveland Barons made Sinden a tempting offer. The Barons played in one of North America's finest facilities, the Cleveland Arena, which hosted the world's first rock and roll concert in 1952. Their first owner, Albert C. Sutphin, paid his players so handsomely that more than a few turned down the NHL to stay in Cleveland, which helps explain why future NHL Hall of Famer Johnny Bower played nine seasons for the Barons.

Sinden had been waiting for this chance for years, but he declined. "I know it sounds corny," he says, "but I wanted to regain the crown for Canada in the worst way." Once again, Sinden took the path less travelled.

In Oslo the determined Dunlops outscored their first six opponents, three of whom had already won world titles themselves, by the combined score of 78–4, an average of 13–1—one of the most impressive runs in the history of the World Championship. Before the Dunlops' final game, against the Soviets, they received a telegram from Prime Minister John Diefenbaker, signed by thousands of Canadians, urging them to win the title for Canada. This game mattered. The Soviets gave them everything they had, but the Dunlops won a good battle, 4–2.

Sinden still recalls standing on the podium between the captains from the USSR and Sweden. "That wonderful feeling," he says, getting wistful, "standing there, while they pulled the flag up and played 'O Canada.' I still get chills. You don't get many moments like that." Any regrets? He smiles. "Do you *think* I have any regrets? It wasn't just for me. The whole country cared."

Still, the Soviets made an impression on the young Sinden.

"I couldn't believe the way they played," he says. "Even the way they skated. Their strides were shorter and lighter, and they wouldn't wait for the pass, they'd just take off, going full speed, and if the pass was behind them, they wouldn't stop, they'd just pull it up with their sticks. It's only a microsecond difference, maybe, but it's a big difference. Our guys stop a split second to take the pass on their sticks. The Soviets were *gone*. We still don't do it as well as they do."

For the 1960 Olympics in Squaw Valley, Canada sent the Kitchener-Waterloo Dutchmen, but the Dutchmen asked Sinden to join and even named him captain. The Canadians intended to avenge their loss to the Soviets in the 1956 Olympics, but they overlooked the American college kids—a level of hockey nobody took seriously. U.S. goalie Jack McCartan kicked back 39 shots, and the Americans upset Canada, 2–1.

"We took a few penalties, too," Sinden says, "as Canadian teams tend to do. When we start to lose, we lose our discipline. This seems to be true of all Canadian teams. In the locker room after the game, we were very quiet. It was so shocking. *Shocking*. Honestly, losing that game [to the Americans] was the lowest point of my career. It sticks with me to this day." The silver medal was little consolation.

Twelve years later, when Sinden showed grainy black-and-white films of those 1958 World Championship games to the Summit Series players, they would not give him the response he was hoping for.

In 1962–63, Sinden won the league's MVP award as player-coach for the Kingston Frontenacs, then coached the Oklahoma City Blazers. With Gerry Cheevers, Bill Goldsworthy, Wayne Cashman, and J.P. Parisé, they beat their bitter rivals, Tulsa, for the 1966 Central League title.

"I loved Oklahoma City," Sinden says. "We led all minor-league teams in attendance with 9,000 a game. We just had a great time.

But I learned if there's one aspect of coaching you better know, it's this: you can never show any phoniness. If you give them a serious talk before the game, it has to come from your heart. You can't make it up. The players, they smell bullshit in two seconds."

Sinden also learned the limits of coaching. "Most sportswriters think a huge part of winning is the mental preparation before the game," he says. "But I know everything can be perfect, and you can still go out and flop. And other nights, the opposite. You can't be sure until you take the ice."

The Boston Bruins tapped him the following fall to take over their moribund franchise, which hadn't made the playoffs in eight years or won the Stanley Cup in 25. At 33, Sinden was the NHL's youngest coach, leading the NHL's youngest team—including an 18-year-old phenom named Bobby Orr, as smooth as he was shy.

Sinden learned to "worry less about having the players turn against you. When good players aren't playing well they turn to the coach as the problem. Ted Green once told me to fuck off in practice. I threw him off the ice. You get the impression everyone hates you, based on small things, but they're just frustrated."

Sinden's bigger problem was adjusting to NHL ownership. When the 1966–67 Bruins finished in last place for the sixth time in seven years, "This made me an easy target for the front office," and created another lesson he would remember. The next year Boston traded for the Chicago Black Hawks' Phil Esposito, a rough-skating, outspoken forward—the opposite of Orr in almost every way—who happened to have an unequalled knack for banging in goals.

"The Espo trade was obviously important," Sinden says. "The potential energy was there, but it was Orr who made the other players take off. Listen, you only had to see him practise a couple times to realize this guy is unreal. Unlike anything I'd ever seen—and I think just about anyone who saw him play would tell you that. And I think that motivated them more than anything I did.

He brought out the best in all of them. How can you not play better with him on your team?"

Esposito had already been a three-time 20-goal scorer in Chicago, but once he joined forces with Orr, then a 20-year-old defenceman entering his third season, the chemistry was immediate. Their first season together, 1967–68, marked the first of eight straight seasons Esposito led the league in assists, goals, points, or all three. When Esposito wasn't leading the league, Orr usually was. Bumper stickers around town soon proclaimed, "JESUS SAVES! *But Esposito scores on rebounds.*"

Sinden built a squad that was as tough as it was skilled, finishing third in his second season. In his fourth year, 1970, "We were the league's dominant team," Sinden says. "The only team that was comparable was the New York Rangers. They had that great line of Jean Ratelle, Rod Gilbert, and Vic Hadfield, with Brad Park on defence. But the margin was Orr."

The first of the Bruins' three playoff series proved to be the important one—a 4–2 win over the Rangers, with three of the games decided by a single goal. "That was a great series—really, *the* series." Sinden says. The Bruins then swept Chicago and St. Louis, 4–0 each, to win the Stanley Cup for the first time in 29 years. "Ending that drought—that was just a great feeling, relief, and ecstasy, all in one."

WHILE the Bruins were steamrolling through the playoffs, Sinden's contract talks were going nowhere. He was making $17,000 a year while his peers were making $25,000 to $30,000, but the Bruins refused to go any higher than $19,000. The owner also advised Sinden to spend the $2,000 raise on clothes, because he didn't like what Sinden had been wearing behind the bench.

"I would have stayed for $25,000," Sinden says. "But I couldn't even get them to $22,000. I felt like they were sending a message: 'Without Orr, you're nothing.' Heck, maybe they were right, but I didn't want to accept it."

So, just a few days after winning the Stanley Cup, Sinden left hockey altogether to join a friend's company, Stirling Homes, which made prefabricated homes in Rochester, New York—for the princely salary of $45,000 a year. The Bruins made no attempt to keep him, but Sinden received coaching offers from Toronto, St. Louis, and the New York Islanders, who would play their inaugural season in 1972–73. Sinden, characteristically, declined them all. But two years later, in the spring of 1972, the construction business was going bankrupt right when a new opportunity popped up: Team Canada needed a coach for the Summit Series.

Although Sinden hadn't coached in two years, he had three things few NHL coaches could claim: experience in international hockey, a mountain of motivation—if anyone had something to prove, it was Harry Sinden—and free time. "I humbly considered myself a leading contender for the job as coach," he wrote. "I used pure logic to make this brilliant deduction. With the series being played in September, when every pro hockey team is in training camp, who else would be available? I sensed right away this series would become the most famous in the history of hockey, and I wanted to be part of it."

Besides, it looked like light duty: coach the best players in the world for eight games against the woefully overmatched Soviets. How hard could it be?

On June 4, 1972, Sinden met Eagleson and some associates in a Toronto hotel room to interview for the position. Sinden shot Eagleson straight: he wanted the same money he was making at Stirling Homes; he didn't want any board members meddling; and he insisted on doing everything the way he wanted—a lesson he'd learned dealing with the Bruins' front office. Another NHL executive might have told Sinden to take a hike, but Eagleson appreciated Sinden's candour.

"I knew him from spending a lot of time with Orr," Eagleson says. "I thought he was a good coach. I wanted somebody who wasn't with a team, and my first thought was Harry—and I didn't have a second one."

They had only one question: Why did Sinden want to keep 35 players on the team? His answer was simple: since they couldn't find a worthy foe to prepare—who could challenge this dream team?—they needed enough players to run an intra-squad scrimmage themselves. Satisfied, Eagleson asked Sinden to leave the room so that Eagleson could discuss it with his informal committee.

"Everyone was on board with Harry," Eagleson recalls, except CAHA president and Hockey Canada board member Joe Kryczka. "He assumed everyone else would agree with him. No one did, and he was such a jerk about it that he didn't persuade anyone."

Eagleson brought Sinden back in and offered him the job, and Sinden accepted.

Sinden had always coached solo, and he liked it that way. "When I was coaching by myself," he says, "I could have a sort of play-by-play behind the bench, telling the guys what was good and what was not so good, as they were watching. Fixing it between periods? Too late. No one can see what you're talking about. The best time to teach is during a game. But you can't just bury the guys on the ice, or the guys on the bench are going to be afraid you'll say terrible things about them when *they're* on the ice. So I always had the whole bench to myself. My wife said, 'Why don't you stop walking back and forth?' 'Cause I can't!"

With Team Canada, however, Sinden made an exception to his "no assistant" policy when he asked former Montreal enforcer John Ferguson to assist the team.

"I didn't know Fergie that well," Sinden says. "But everyone had such respect for him. His heart was in every game. I'd been out of the league for two years, so the fact that Ferguson had recently retired was valuable. He had a good handle on who was who."

Ferguson told Sinden he would accept, on one condition: he would get to pick two players. Sinden agreed—and it would prove to be one of the most important decisions he would make.

4

INVENTING A TEAM

Next step: pick the players.

The trio of Sinden, Ferguson, and Eagleson convened at the Skyline Hotel near Toronto's airport in mid-June, with slightly less than two months to select and secure the players who would report to training camp on August 13.

But before they decided who they wanted on their team, it seemed like a good idea to name the team they'd be asking them to play for. To that end, they brought in some marketing friends of Eagleson's to help, pro bono. Contrary to other accounts, Sinden and Eagleson both recall that Mike Cannon came up with "Canada's Team," which was quickly converted to "Team Canada," marking the first time the name had been coined. Everyone immediately liked it, so that was quickly settled.

On the same day, designer John Lloyd created the team's iconic sweaters by cutting a silhouette of half a gigantic maple leaf out of a red jersey and attaching it to a white one, then taking the negative out of a white jersey and stitching that onto a red one. And just like that, the most famous name and sweater in Canadian hockey history were born—all within 24 hours.

It would take a little longer for Sinden, Ferguson, and Eagleson to figure out who would be wearing those sweaters. Armed with only pens, note pads, and a list of some 270 NHL players, all but a handful Canadian citizens, they worked to whittle that number down to 35 players.

The first half of their wish list came together easily, with strong consensus.

In goal: Ken Dryden, Tony Esposito, and Boston's Gerry Cheevers, who'd just won his second Stanley Cup.

On defence: Bobby Orr and New York's Brad Park and Rod Seiling.

On offence, their cup runneth over: New York's Goal-a-Game (GAG) Line of Vic Hadfield, Rod Gilbert, and Jean Ratelle; Boston's Phil Esposito, Wayne Cashman, and Derek Sanderson; Montreal's Yvan Cournoyer and Frank Mahovlich; and Chicago's Dennis and Bobby Hull.

Of these 16 players, 11 would become Hall of Famers. Not a bad start.

Then they discussed, debated, and haggled over the rest of the roster before agreeing on six more defencemen: Montreal's playmaking pair of Jacques Laperrière and J.C. Tremblay; Chicago's unglamorous but solid defensive duo of Pat Stapleton and Bill White; and Boston's Don Awrey and Dallas Smith, hard-nosed blueliners.

Filling out the forwards got a little trickier. After adding New York's Walt Tkaczuk and Detroit's Red Berenson, experienced forwards who could be trusted at both ends of the ice, Sinden often deferred to Ferguson's first-hand knowledge, since Ferguson had retired a year earlier, and Eagleson's knowledge of their personalities.

"You guys discuss the hockey talent," Eagleson recalls telling them. "I'll tell you what I think of them as young men and how they'll fit in with everybody.'"

Toronto's Paul Henderson and Ron Ellis, both strong-skating

defensive forwards, figured they were borderline candidates for Team Canada, a squad they desperately wanted to make. But when their centre, Norm Ullman, a future Hall of Famer on the back end of his career, was rumoured not to be a candidate, "Ronnie and I looked at each other and wondered if *we'd* make it," Henderson recalls. "Then we heard they wanted two-way players. Well, that's us, right?"

"Fergie and Harry agreed on [Paul] Henderson because he could fly," Eagleson recalls, "and they thought we'd need some speed against the Soviets." It didn't hurt that Henderson had just finished his best year, scoring 38 goals, and was one of Eagleson's clients.

Compared with the flashy play of the GAG Line, Esposito, and Cournoyer, Ellis played a quiet game—by design. Once Toronto called him up for good in 1964, he scored between 19 and 35 goals a year, and added about as many assists. But he did a lot more than that for his team, because he knew he had to.

"You get to the NHL and you discover pretty quickly that every team already has scorers, scorers who can score more than you can," he recalls. "So I figured out that if I planned to stay in this league, I had to become a two-way player."

Typical was Ellis's 1971–72 season, in which he played in all 78 games, with 23 goals, 24 assists, and a mere 17 minutes in penalties, while doing all the intangibles—backchecking, blocking shots, killing penalties—that don't show up on the score sheet but that smart coaches love.

But, back in the hotel room, Eagleson recalls, "I don't think Ronnie was on anyone's particular radar until Fergie spoke up: 'Harry, I played against this guy for four or five years and there isn't a better defensive right wing in the league.'"

Unbeknownst to Ellis, he had just passed the tryout.

"Then it came down to Davey Keon, Bobby Clarke, and somebody else," Eagleson recalls. "I can't remember who." Not surprisingly, Sinden favoured Keon, a future Hall of Famer who had led the Maple Leafs to their last Stanley Cup during Sinden's tenure with the Bruins, while Ferguson favoured Clarke.

FOREVER called Bobby in the NHL, everyone calls him Bob back in tiny Flin Flon, Manitoba, where his father mined copper and zinc.

"My dad was an easygoing guy," Clarke says, then grins. "My mom wasn't."

You don't have to ask whose DNA their son inherited.

Clarke grew up playing hockey, like all Flin Flon boys, and he was good at it from the start, playing a furious style that maximized his skills. But at age 12 he feared his career might be over before it started when the local doctor diagnosed a mysterious illness as diabetes.

"I didn't know a single kid or adult who had diabetes," Clarke says. "I don't think I even knew what diabetes really was."

Clarke had one question: "'Can I still play hockey?' I remember the doctor saying, 'You can still play hockey, but you might want to be a goalie. It's a little bit less hassle.' I don't know if goalies would agree with that.

"Diabetes didn't scare me. I never thought, 'Poor me, why me?' None of that ever crossed my mind." The only thing that has ever really bothered him about the disease is being described as "a diabetic hockey player. I'm not a fucking diabetic hockey player! Always hated that. I'm a hockey player who has diabetes."

His dad urged him to stay in school, "because I don't want you to have to work with your back like I do," he told his son.

But Clarke dropped out after Grade 10 to pursue his dream of playing for the Flin Flon Bombers. It was an all-or-nothing gamble: if he lost, without a high school diploma, he'd likely be in the mines with his father, working with his back. But the Bombers' coach, a man named Paddy Ginnell who'd won the team's only

Memorial Cup as a player, thought Clarke might be able to make it if the NHL wasn't scared off by his diabetes—a disease few people then knew much about.

Before the 1969 NHL draft, Ginnell drove Clarke 16 hours to the Mayo Clinic in Rochester, Minnesota. When the doctors told them there was no medical reason why Clarke couldn't play in the NHL, "Paddy said, "Can you put that in writing?" They did, and Ginnell had that letter sent to all 12 NHL teams drafting that year.

It helped—to a point. In the first round all 12 clubs passed on Clarke, but the Flyers took him in the second round, 17th overall. Even Clarke admits, "I didn't know if I was good enough to make it. I never saw myself as a special player, but I always thought I was important to the team. Lot of teams have great players—and they still lose. I was taught in junior hockey that *teams* win, and I had a responsibility to be a good teammate. All I wanted was a chance."

He made the most of it, applying an intense focus to every drill in practice. "How are you going to get better if you're just doing what they tell you?" he asks. "I told myself every day before I went on the ice, 'Today I'm going to make every fucking pass good! Don't just skate because the coach tells you to. Skate your best to get better.' I wasn't comfortable. I was scared to death."

Clarke would become the only Hall of Famer from the 1969 draft. Ferguson didn't know all this about Clarke, but he knew enough, and probably sensed the rest.

"Fergie was very pro-Clarke," Eagleson says. "He said, 'Harry, you haven't seen him play, but trust me: this guy is going to be a superstar and he's tough and we need a tough guy at centre. So we've got to take Clarke.'"

The tipping point: in 1971–72 Clarke, in his third season, tallied 81 points, while Keon, in his 12th season, totalled 48, the lowest since his rookie season.

"Harry was worried about the offence," Eagleson says, "and that persuaded him Clarke's who he needed."

Henderson, Ellis, and Clarke had all made it—but not by much.

"I'll put it this way," Eagleson says. "The three guys on Clarke's line were among the last five players to be picked."

Without realizing it, Sinden and Ferguson had just rescued Team Canada's most valuable line from the rejection bin.

WITH 29 players on their list and six to go, Sinden was willing to entertain other factors.

"When we got stalled on player 30 or 32," Sinden recalls, "one of Eagleson's clients would come into play, so they had a little advantage. On the other hand, they were all good players. He didn't suggest any misfits. And it was clear a lot of the players were going to come from the Bruins, too, which helped."

While it is undeniably true that Eagleson advocated for his clients, the ultimate impact on the team was far less than commonly believed. Of the 35 players on the first list, eight were Eagleson clients: Bobby Orr, Paul Henderson, Ron Ellis, Bill White, goalie Eddie Johnston (who would be added later), and three young players: centre Marcel Dionne and defencemen Dale Tallon and Brian Glennie. Only three of the eight would play against the Soviets. "So all this bullshit that I filled the team with my clients is just that: bullshit," Eagleson says.

With a few spots left, Sinden made good on his promise to Ferguson: he would get to pick two players. Ferguson didn't hesitate: he wanted former Montreal teammates Pete Mahovlich and defenceman Serge Savard, one of the anchors of Montreal's next dynasty. Because Savard was recovering from a broken femur, no one knew if he would play—but that was a chance Ferguson was willing to take.

Pete Mahovlich's selection surprised no one more than Pete Mahovlich. "I always wondered how I got picked, because I didn't think I should be on the roster and I was not one of Eagle's clients," Pete Mahovlich says. "Two years later Eagle told me Fergie picked me and Serge. We were both very good friends with Fergie, and he knew what we were all about, good team guys."

A few months later it would become clear that if Ferguson had done nothing else for Team Canada, picking those two players would have been enough. Ferguson also put in a good word for Vancouver's Dale Tallon, a young defenceman.

"I was living in Montreal that summer, recovering from knee surgery after my second year in the league," Tallon remembers. "A friend put together a good skate Monday nights at La Prairie, with a bunch of pros. Ferguson played there, and I had a good relationship with him. In the locker room after one of our skates the Russian series came up, and I told him I'd love to be part of that. A few weeks later I got the invitation. It was a thrill and an honour! I was a natural centreman, but I had my best year as a defenceman my rookie year in Vancouver. But I said, 'Sure, whatever role you want me to play!'"

Savard, Pete Mahovlich, and Tallon had little in common except high character, team spirit, and competitiveness—the kind of players Ferguson loved.

Finally, they added Minnesota's gritty forwards J.P. Parisé and Bill Goldsworthy, and three up-and-comers: Mickey Redmond, Gilbert Perreault, and Jocelyn Guèvremont.

"Really, we were picking two teams," Sinden recalls. The first consisted of the established All-Stars at the top of their wish list, whom the coaches planned to play during the four games in Canada. The second was comprised of the young phenoms whom Sinden expected would take over for the remaining four games in Moscow.

All these plans assumed that every player Sinden wanted would eagerly sign up for the squad, and the series would be the rout everyone in Canada expected.

5

MAKING THE CALLS

Putting together a list of players on legal pads is one thing. Getting all those names on the ice is quite another.

Sinden soon discovered that there was a third team, featuring some of the game's best players, players they wanted but who wouldn't join the team due to injury, personal or professional conflicts, or simple lack of interest.

Atop the injured list sat the best player in the world, Bobby Orr, who had undergone knee surgery just days after winning his second Stanley Cup that spring. But Orr remained optimistic that he might be able to play in Moscow, if not sooner. Sinden didn't think too hard before deciding the mere possibility of Orr playing half the games justified saving him a spot. The Soviets, to their credit, allowed Sinden to hold an extra roster spot for Orr, because they wanted to see him play, too.

What made Orr so good? Eagleson might have said it best: "Orr could do everything better than everyone."

Unbeknownst to Orr's future teammates, however, he remained a business partner on the series with Eagleson. When Hockey Canada executive vice-president Allan Scott announced to the board that he had sold the broadcast rights to MacLaren Advertising, which produced *Hockey Night in Canada*, for

$500,000, and it was a "done deal," Eagleson thought the fee was too low and demanded an open bid. The board agreed. Eagleson formed a company called Ballard Orr Enterprises and submitted a bid for a guaranteed $750,000, with all profits to be split 50-50 between Hockey Canada and the NHL players' pension fund. The latter pleased the NHL owners, since they were primarily responsible for those contributions, and it warmed them to the idea of releasing their players for the event.

Eagleson offered to withdraw the bid if MacLaren matched it. When MacLaren declined, Eagleson did what he did best: worked the phones, tapping his business contacts for more than $2 million in ad sales, then brought in CTV as Ballard Orr's broadcasting and production partners. (No one seemed bothered by Eagleson's apparent conflict of interest as a member of Hockey Canada, while bidding to acquire the broadcast rights *from* Hockey Canada.)

It was a big bet, but a good one. The four games in Canada sold out in a flash, while travel agents booked some 3,000 travel packages from Canadian fans eager to see the games in Moscow. Interest was already sky high, foretelling good ratings.

When the coaches turned their attention from Orr to the other 34 players on their list, they might have been tempted to think the heavy lifting was behind them. All they had to do now was tell the chosen few the good news: they'd been selected to represent Team Canada against the mysterious Soviet Union. Sells itself, right?

But a task that would probably have been easy, even fun, a decade earlier had become another minefield. In 1962 the NHL regular season ran 70 games. In 1972 it lasted 78, which tacked on another two weeks of play. Likewise, the playoffs now consisted of three rounds, not two, which added another two weeks. Thus, if the players Sinden wanted were to show up at Team Canada's camp on August 13, they would be losing about 10 weeks of vacation they would have had in 1962.

Further, in 1962 the NHL had only six clubs, so players were paid far less. Ten years later, the expansion of the NHL to 16 teams and the creation of 12 World Hockey Association (WHA) franchises that would start play in 1972 meant almost five times more teams were bidding to increase salaries, options, and expectations. As the leagues spread across North America, so did the players. The popularity of hockey schools, which many players used to augment their salaries, grew accordingly. Some of these new opportunities would have to be sacrificed if a player reported a month before most NHL training camps would start.

And what did Team Canada have to offer? Not a cent for playing eight games against the Soviets, and a mere $500 a game for six exhibitions: three public intrasquad scrimmages in training camp, two games against the Swedish national team, and a final exhibition against the Czechs on the way home. That added up to $3,000, plus a $17 per diem and a free trip to Europe.

So Sinden had to ask NHL All-Stars, including 16 future Hall of Famers, to give up increasingly valuable vacation time in exchange for almost nothing. The rewards would be intangible: the honour of being selected, the thrill of playing with the best, and the experience of representing Canada. As they say, some missions are for God and country. Who would answer the call? Sinden, Ferguson, Eagleson, and Eagleson's assistant, Bob Haggart, decided to phone the players and find out.

"The players were all professional," Sinden recalls, "but some of them weren't sure what I was talking about, who we were playing, and when it was all going to happen." Sinden decided he had to promise the players that everybody who came to camp would make the team and play in at least one game. "Well, I couldn't very well ask the best players in the world to give up a good chunk of their summers and then cut them or not play them. That would be humiliating. And I'm not sure how many would have shown up!"

Since the series was being discussed publicly as just a bunch of glorified exhibitions against an inferior opponent, it seemed entirely plausible to everyone, even with 35 players on the roster, that they would all get in some games. Sinden and the others asked only one thing in return: do not tell anyone that you've been selected until the roster was announced at a press conference to be held after they returned from their meetings in Moscow three weeks later, in early July. They didn't want to confront the NHL owners until it was absolutely necessary.

They needed a good sales pitch and, occasionally, a bit of muscle.

"And here's where Eagleson really helped," Sinden says. "He followed up a lot of my calls and helped convince them they should do this. He had relationships with almost all of the guys, and some of them were clients of his, players he'd gotten good contracts. He was also a good organizer, and he was *relentless*. I don't think I've met too many people with more energy than Al. He worked day and night and never stopped—a windmill. And you needed that, not just to get some of the more reluctant guys signed up, but to handle serious conversations with Hockey Canada, and sending people to Moscow in July to set the whole thing up, and getting the TV people squared away. Al worked his ass off."

The series remains the high point of Eagleson's career—indicated by the fact that his email address, phone number, and licence plate all end in 1972. "How much do I remember about 1972?" he asks. "It'd be a hell of a lot easier if you asked me what I've forgotten. I lived it! This was my 24-hour-a-day job from the first of April until the end of September. But [Sinden and Ferguson] worked their asses off, too. I spent more time with them than I ever have with anyone, before or since. From dawn to dusk and then some, we did everything together, and for months."

"Harry was the coach," Rangers defenceman Rod Seiling says. "There wasn't any question about that. But we always had the sense it was Eagleson's show. He was always front and centre. He was the one who got us out to the camp in August."

But some were easier to convince than others. Walt Tkaczuk told Sinden he didn't want to leave his hockey school, so he declined. Bobby Orr's defensive partner, Dallas Smith, had just finished his second of four straight All-Star seasons while winning his second Stanley Cup. You'd think he'd be a shoo-in, but as Savard recalls, "He wouldn't come because he wanted to work on his farm out west." Likewise, Montreal's Hall of Fame defenceman Jacques Laperrière turned Sinden down because, he said, his wife was expecting a baby. Jean Ratelle's, Guy Lapointe's, and Brad Park's were, too, but all three signed up. "Lappie was always '*non*' before '*oui*,'" Savard says. "What a great rendezvous Lappie missed!"

Park grew up in Scarborough, now part of Toronto. He and his wife, Gerry, were staying with his parents when the kitchen phone rang. Park, just 24, was excited to get a free trip to Moscow, which seemed like the dark side of the moon in 1972. They hoped their first baby would arrive on time in early August, but they decided the opportunity was too rare to pass up, no matter the potential complications.

Most were flattered by the invitation. When Sinden called Dennis and Bobby Hull, they were working at their hockey school in Chicago, and both said yes. Done.

"I was on my farm in Waterloo [Ontario]," Seiling recalls. "I had just come in the house when my wife says, 'Harry Sinden is on the phone.' Now, I knew I wasn't getting traded, so I had no idea what he was calling for. When he said I'd been picked to play for Team Canada, I was honoured. I don't know if I was excited, because we hadn't given much thought to the Soviets. I don't think any of us had any sense of the challenge ahead of us. But any time you put on the Canadian uniform, it's special—and I already knew how that felt from the Olympics.

"When you stand on the blue line and they play the national anthem, it gives you a feeling of pride that wells up inside you. It's a privilege. You never forget it. Not many people get a chance to represent their country. Well, this was all that, but on a much bigger stage. Harry didn't have to ask me twice. I was going."

Ron Ellis followed suit. "We were getting a chance to represent our country," he says. "Back then, pro players couldn't be in the Olympics or the World Championship. A few of the guys had done it before they turned pro, but for most of us, this was our first chance—and, we assumed, our last. Plus, the way this was set up, we were representing the origin of the game. There was a point to it."

Bob Clarke and his wife, Sandy, were back at his parents' home in Flin Flon, where their first son, Wade, had just been born in June. When Eagleson called to invite him to play on Team Canada against the Soviets, Clarke recalls, "I think I only had two questions: 'When do you want me?' and 'Where do you want me?' Getting chosen for that, it was such an honour."

"It was a novelty for all of us," Rod Gilbert recalled. "A novelty to play the Russians, and to play with all the best players."

"The novelty was less about playing the Russians," Park adds, "because what did we know about them? It was about playing *together.* We'd never done that."

Park's teammates echo his observation: the appeal was playing *with* the best, in something more meaningful than an All-Star Game.

"The All-Star Game was a great honour," Yvan Cournoyer explains. "But it's not the same. Here, we were playing for something big. We were playing for *Canada.*"

They figured the real competition wouldn't be the Soviets but the training camp beforehand, when the coaches would determine the lineup for September 2.

"You never had the top players playing for their country before," Savard says. "So you wanted to be part of that."

Savard wanted to be part of it very badly, but thanks to two serious leg injuries, he didn't think he'd be able to. But then, he'd beaten the odds before. Savard grew up in a tiny town called Landrienne, Quebec, almost 600 kilometres (360 miles) northwest of Montreal, where his father served as mayor. Somehow the Canadiens found the big 15-year-old and invited him to their camp.

"Never been to Montreal," he says. "I would listen to the Canadiens games on the radio, because we didn't get TV in my town until 1957, and imagine what it was like. Such a big city! For me, Montreal was like going to heaven."

As a mere 21-year-old in 1967–68, he had earned a regular spot on the Canadiens blue line en route to his first Stanley Cup. The next year he became the first defenceman in NHL history to win the Conn Smythe Trophy as playoff MVP, winning his second Cup along the way. But in his third season, 1969–70, he was covering New York's Vic Hadfield when he crashed into his own net and shattered his left leg in five different places, requiring three surgeries in one week.

"Got two pins in my leg," Savard says. "I asked my doctor, 'Is my leg stronger now than before?' He said, 'Actually, yes—except between the two screws. It can crack between them.'" The next season, in January of 1971, "that's exactly what happens: it cracked between the two screws. So I have to get a bone graft from my hip bone to my femur, and I missed a full year. I never really got injured badly after that. But I was 26 by then, so I was not a puppy."

Because Savard had returned for only the last 26 games of the 1971–72 season, most assumed he would need to rest and rehabilitate before the next season.

"I was starting to feel pretty good," Savard recalls, "but after you miss a full year, you're not going to be the first choice for a series like that. So when Fergie asked me, 'Why don't you come down to camp?' I thought I'd just work on recovering, getting back in shape. Probably the only reason I went to camp was because of Fergie, my friend. I had no idea what was ahead."

Perhaps the hardest nut to crack—and the most important, in hindsight—was Sinden's former star centre, Phil Esposito. Despite the fact that Sinden had coached Esposito for only three years, they'd won their first Cup together and remained good friends. But when Sinden called him, Esposito gave him a flat no. Sinden called again. No.

Unlike the Rangers, Canadiens, and Maple Leafs, who saw Esposito as a one-dimensional player with little more to offer than garbage goals, Sinden knew how much Esposito could contribute , so he would not take no for an answer.

"I turned Harry down three times," Esposito recalls. "It wasn't about Harry. I didn't like Eagleson—or trust him. When I was the NHLPA president, he told me to shut up. I told him, 'Don't ever do that to me again.' Then, at another meeting in the Bahamas, he did it again, and I got up and left. Parkie despised him, too. So when Harry called, I said, 'I'm not interested.'"

It didn't help that Phil and Tony were making good money running a hockey camp in their hometown of Sault Ste. Marie, Ontario. "I'd scored 100 points, we'd just won our second Cup, I'm making $100,000 a year, and my brother and I have got a hockey camp. What do I need to play in Moscow for?

"I didn't think playing on this team [against the Soviets] would prove anything I hadn't already proved," he says. "And hey, I wanted some time off, dammit! So I turned him down. Then Bobby [Orr] calls me and says, 'Phil, I can't play. We really need you and your brother—*really* need you.'

"I didn't know Bobby was part of the TV deal with Eagleson and all that, but I had to be very careful because Bobby Orr was on my team and my friend. We weren't as close as we should have been. I was married, he wasn't. But I was the perfect guy for him, because he bolted out the door after each game to avoid the press, while I'd sit and talk with the reporters for hours. That covered for him.

"So when Bobby asked me and Tony to play, I had to call Harry back and tell him we'd play. When I told Tony, he was so mad at me! 'Why'd you do this?! Why are we going? Who are we playing?' I said, 'We're playing the Russians—that's all I know! How good can they be? Cakewalk!'

"Ha! 'Cakewalk!'"

If some can't remember getting the call, others will never forget it.

In the spring of 1971, a young goalie named Ken Dryden made his NHL debut for the Montreal Canadiens with just nine games left in a disappointing regular season. But after he won six straight, letting in only 11 goals, the Canadiens put him in net for the playoffs, where he won 12 of their 20 playoff games, including a Game Seven against Boston's offensive powerhouse and another Game Seven in Chicago for the Stanley Cup. Dryden became the only player in NHL history to win the Conn Smythe Trophy as the playoff MVP, then win the Calder Trophy as rookie of the year the *following* season, 1971–72. Still, with only one full season of NHL experience, Dryden was not certain he'd be getting the call from Sinden.

"I knew the series had been announced, and the calls to players were being made," Dryden recalls. "But you don't focus on that because you don't want to be crushed if you don't get the call. I'm trying *not* to think about it, so it was great to be in Vienna with my wife in early July. The call comes into our hotel straight from Harry. 'We want you on the team.' And I say, 'That's terrific.' It was an honour, and I figured it had to be more fun than Montreal's training camp."

In Dryden's book *Face-Off at the Summit*, he wrote, "Like about 22 million other Canadians, I wanted to play the Russians . . . I can understand the mood of the Canadian people, because I am Canadian, too. We are all frustrated. All of us. Hockey is an intimate part of our life in this country, and now the Russians are coming to challenge it. They are challenging Canada's right to be the best at something. You may be the biggest hockey fan in Boston or New York or Chicago or Los Angeles, but I'm certain that you don't understand this. You must be a Canadian."

ONCE Sinden and his assistants had finished rounding up 35 players, they flew to Moscow to hammer out the series' remaining details with the Soviet hockey officials, after which they planned to introduce the team to the public on July 12.

A month after taking the post, Sinden had already grown weary of the meddling from Hockey Canada's Joe Kryczka and other officials, who had broken their promise to leave him alone. To insulate himself, Sinden set up an informal group they called Team Five to run things—a tight circle consisting of himself, Ferguson, Eagleson, and two Eagleson employees, Bob Haggart and Mike Cannon.

In mid-July, a month after Sinden took the post and a month before Team Canada's training camp, Team Five flew to Moscow—over the objections of Hockey Canada's leaders, who warned Sinden that the Soviets wouldn't even talk to them. But Sinden believed their objections were a cover for their real motives. "The Hockey Canada people were afraid we'd screw up the series with the Russians," he wrote, "and cost them a lot of money."

Given this backdrop, when Team Five arrived in Moscow they were surprised to see the entire Soviet contingent, including Coach Bobrov, waiting at the airport. Right off, they said, "All we'll need is 10 minutes to straighten out these matters."

"If that's the way you feel," Sinden replied, "it won't even take five."

The Soviets played the role of grateful protégés perfectly, telling the Canadians, "We're so happy to have this series because we were getting bored by the lack of competition. This will renew our interest in the game." They seemed to view the series merely as an experiment to see how much they still had to learn.

"The official meeting was very rewarding," Sinden wrote. "They gave us everything we wanted, except a change in the refereeing." This second Canadian contingent gave the issue no more thought than the first had in Prague months earlier. "When the business was out of the way, the Russians decided it was time for some toasts. Out came the vodka—Kristal vodka . . . We learned that the custom is for each man to toast everyone else. The Russians would toast one of our players . . . or our officials . . . or Canada. We'd have to do the same thing for them.

"'Bobby Orr.' Zip! Over the gums. No ice. No mix. No nothing. Straight vodka. I'll say this about Kristal—after a few it doesn't seem all that bad. Our embassy officials and our interpreter said they had never seen the Russians so open and friendly about anything."

The Soviets were setting their trap so well, the Canadians were the last to know they were walking right into it.

"Fergie and Bobby Haggart were the first to go," Sinden wrote of their celebratory drinking session. "They both slept for 16 straight hours."

The honeymoon was over, but the hangover was on its way.

TEAM Canada couldn't do much about Bobby Orr's knee, but the next batch of scratches was strictly self-inflicted, the result of the NHL's hubris and greed.

Amazingly, every player Sinden and his assistants had called to join the team had kept his promise to keep his mouth shut—until Bobby Hull went to Halifax for a golf outing in early July for *Hockey Night in Canada* announcer Danny Gallivan. When Hull casually mentioned to a reporter that he'd been named to Team Canada, the story went national. Hull, who had scored 50 goals for the fifth time that year for the Chicago Black Hawks, had just signed an unheard-of 10-year, $1.75 million contract with the WHA's Winnipeg Jets, including a whopping million-dollar signing bonus.

Hull's unprecedented deal, and the attention it brought to the nascent 12-team league, hit the stodgy, stable NHL like an earthquake, threatening to bring the NHL's half-century monopoly tumbling down. The last thing most NHL owners wanted to do was showcase players who might end up jumping to the upstart league. So when Hull let it slip that he'd been named to Team Canada, he gave NHL president Clarence Campbell an opening. While the NHL didn't control the Summit Series, its team owners could block the players under contract from playing in it, which gave the owners more than enough power to make trouble.

Because Sinden, Ferguson, and Eagleson were still in Moscow, "That allowed Campbell to get the jump on us," Eagleson says. "He didn't waste it."

Campbell rushed to announce that "if a single WHA player joins Team Canada, the NHL will bar all its players from competing in the series."

To keep Team Canada "traitor-free," the owners insisted that all Team Canada players had to be signed by an NHL team by August 13, the day Team Canada's training camp would convene in Toronto. In other words, whoever wanted to play in the WHA would not be playing for Team Canada.

"He had us, and he knew it," Eagleson says. "But I still believe if Bobby [Hull] had kept quiet until we could hold our press conference, we could have had Bobby and everyone else there in Team Canada sweaters, and the country would have loved it. It would have been a whole lot harder for Campbell to pull Bobby out once everyone sees that. The public would've crucified Campbell. But there it was, so we were screwed."

Campbell's edict was petty, provincial, and selfish, but when you consider that 13 of the NHL's soon-to-be-16 franchises were located in the United States, where few knew anything about the pending Soviet series, the owners had strong incentive to put their profits ahead of their patriotism. Insurance for the Team Canada players was going to be exorbitant as it was, and it wasn't clear if the insurance companies would protect the athletes if non-NHL players participated.

Hull was banned from Team Canada. Three more players on Sinden's list—Boston stars Derek Sanderson and goalie Gerry Cheevers, and Montreal's seven-time All-Star defenceman J.C. Tremblay, fresh off his two best seasons—would be dropped from Team Canada as soon as they signed their WHA deals. Sinden almost lost a fifth player when Dennis Hull protested his brother being blackballed.

"The owners of the NHL didn't want us mingling with *those deserters*," Dennis Hull recalls. "So when Bobby was dropped, I told Harry I wasn't coming. But when I told Bobby, he said, 'Don't worry about me. You go and represent the family.' So I called Harry back within an hour and said I'd be happy to go if he still had a spot. Harry, God bless 'im, said, 'Sure, come on back.'"

No one knew it then, but on these quick decisions Team Canada's fate would ride.

The series had already captured the imagination of Canadians, so Campbell's decision to block four top players outraged hockey fans north of the border eager to see all of Canada's best players crush the Soviets once and for all. Even Toronto Maple Leafs owner Harold Ballard, the irascible, unpredictable, avowed enemy of the WHA, argued the series was the "unofficial World Series of hockey and we want to win," adding, "I don't give a damn if Hull signed with a team in China. He's a Canadian and should be on the Canadian team."

If Campbell thought the issue would soon fade, he was woefully mistaken. Millions of Canadians protested the NHL owners' decision to ban the WHA players through marches, newspaper ads, telegrams to politicians, and a billboard reading, “To Russia with Hull,” a riff on a popular James Bond movie title.

Since Prime Minister Pierre Trudeau had already spent a fair amount of diplomatic capital setting up the series and was about to call a general election, he couldn’t ignore the escalating issue, either. In a last-gasp attempt to unravel the matter, he summoned Hockey Canada officials to his office, but they had their orders, too, and hadn’t come to negotiate.

As Roy MacSkimming writes, the day after the failed meeting, Trudeau, “suddenly possessed by a passion for hockey previously hidden from the voters,” sent telegrams to the NHL, the NHLPA, and Hockey Canada. “You are aware of the intense concern which I share with millions of Canadians in all parts of our country, that Canada should be represented by its best hockey players, including Bobby Hull and all those named by Team Canada, in the forthcoming series with the Soviet Union. On behalf of these Canadians, I urge Hockey Canada, the NHL and the NHL Players’ Association to take whatever steps may be necessary to make this possible . . . I would ask you to keep the best interests of Canada in mind and to make sure that they are fully respected and served.”

Despite weeks of public pressure from the top on down, the NHL owners weren’t budging. On August 2, Hockey Canada issued its final statement on the matter: “No player who defected to the WHA from the National Hockey League will play for Team Canada.”

Sinden had nowhere to turn. He hated to lose those players, but he knew it was either that or risk losing the NHL players, too—and with them, the entire series. But the critics, fans, and players picked up the issue and never let it go.

“Team Canada?” Pete Mahovlich asks today. “No, Team NHL.”

Phil Esposito agrees. “We should’ve never been called Team Canada, because we weren’t. How can you call it that when they kept four or five of Canada's best players off the team? When I brought that up in an early team meeting, 'Why not Team NHL?' I was told to shut up."

Even Tarasov said, "Their best players are Bobby Hull and Bobby Orr . . . Hull against us would be worth one or two goals a game."

"I was just a kid," Gretzky says. "I didn't know anything about the NHL's conflicts with the WHA, but it didn't make any sense to me that Bobby Hull couldn't play. Honestly, it still doesn't. And at the other end, Bobby Orr was young! Just 24. He would have played 30 minutes a night! He's still—*still*—the greatest defenceman who ever played."

But few thought blackballing the WHA players would harm Team Canada's chances. After all, why would the *Titanic* need more lifeboats? It was unsinkable.

By early August the original list of 35 players had been reduced by eight, almost a quarter of the total. Sinden replaced Bobby Hull with Buffalo's Rick Martin, Sanderson with the venerable Stan Mikita, Cheevers with his Boston backup, Eddie Johnston, and Tremblay with Montreal teammate Guy Lapointe.

But they wouldn't know how much the team had lost or gained in the bargain until the games started.

6

TEAM OF RIVALS

Team Canada might have boasted the greatest collection of hockey talent ever assembled, but that still didn't make it a *team*.

The reason is simple: All-Star hockey teams have none of the chemistry and c ohesion required of championship teams. Unlike baseball, whose All-Star Game functions about the same as a World Series game, hockey puts its players in constant motion, requiring the highest levels of teamwork to achieve greatness.

Consider the NHL All-Star Games played between 1947 and 1968, which usually pitted the defending Stanley Cup champions against an All-Star team. In the 19 contests played between the Stanley Cup champions and the best of the rest, the All-Stars won nine and the defending champion seven, with three ties—about even. But the defending champions outscored the All-Stars, 54–47. How could the best players from *five* NHL teams not out-score one team? The All-Stars had more talent, but they weren't a team. And that was the hidden challenge facing Team Canada. Would the team function like a unified Stanley Cup team or like a scattered All-Star squad?

Team Canada's chemistry problems went deeper than that. These 35 players actually hated each other—and they had been systematically trained to do so. Because the NHL would not adopt free agency until 1976, of Team Canada's 35 players, only eight—less than a quarter—had played more than a few games for more than one NHL team. Further, because all but two of the 28 who would play in the series had been drafted by an Original Six NHL team when they were still in their teens, the vast majority knew almost nothing but one organization for their entire playing careers. The fiercest hockey rivalries weren't between nations, but NHL franchises.

When teams still travelled by train, Ted Lindsay once told me, the Red Wings would play in Montreal, then both teams would take the same train back to Detroit for the rematch. On the return trip, the Red Wings wouldn't dare walk through the Canadiens' team car to get to the dining car; they'd wait for the train to stop at the next station, then get out and walk around the Canadiens' car to the dining car. Even in the late 1960s, Berenson says, "You might walk through the opposing team's car, but you didn't say a word, and they didn't, either. You could hear a pin drop."

One night early in Savard's career, after a game in Chicago, he and some young Montreal teammates went out to a bar. They happened to run into some Black Hawks players and started drinking and laughing together. But their fun ended abruptly when tough guy John Ferguson grabbed Savard's elbow and said, "These aren't your friends. They're the enemy. Get moving." Ferguson was not making a suggestion. Savard and company did as instructed and retained the lesson: your friends wear the same sweater you wear.

Brad Park recalled a similar scenario a few months before Team Canada was announced. After the Rangers played a game in Boston, Park invited a new player, Gene Carr, out for a beer. Park took Carr to Brandy's, near Brighton.

"As we walk in I order a beer, and Gene says he's going to the bathroom," Park recalls. "When he comes back he says, 'You'll never guess who's in the back: Bobby Orr and Johnny McKenzie! Let's go meet 'em.'"

"No," Park said, putting his coat on.

"What are you doing?" Carr asked.

"I'm leaving."

Park paid his tab, grabbed his coat, and headed out the door. Carr stayed, presumably to drink with the Bruins in the back.

"The next day," Park says, "I chewed his ass out like you couldn't believe. Pallin' around with opponents—and especially our biggest rival—it just wasn't done. Look, they might have been good guys. We didn't know. We didn't *want* to know. It'd just mess you up! Even during the summers, when guys came back home, you didn't hang out with each other at the lake or the golf course."

Such cold conduct wasn't merely a custom.

"Campbell put in a non-fraternization rule," Sinden says. "You couldn't even play in a foursome on the golf course with your opponents. Campbell thought that was part of the appeal of the sport, the bitter rivalries. That's what brought the fans in. That might sound crazy today, but he might have been right. And I've gotta tell you, Fergie was the worst! Or the best, depending on your view. He once walked out of a golf tournament the second he saw players from other teams there."

Original Six opponents could avoid each other in trains, in bars, and on golf courses, but they couldn't at the annual All-Star Game—though they did their best.

"In the locker room, you'd have five Rangers together in that corner over here," Park recalls, "then five Canadiens over there and five Bruins over there. And we wouldn't even talk to each other. We'd just nod at each other, and that was it."

Minutes later they would take this cold-shoulder approach onto the ice. In the 1972 All-Star Game, held in Minnesota, the heavily favoured East squad, featuring five of the Original Six teams, trailed 2–1 late in the second period. Park snapped a breakaway pass to Boston's Johnny McKenzie, who then beat Minnesota's Gump Worsley to tie the game, 2–2. It was a pretty pass on an important goal, but as Park recalls, "I didn't congratulate him, and he didn't say thank you, not even a hand gesture. And I wouldn't have expected him to!"

What little they did know about each other usually didn't help.

"You think I enjoyed playing against Bobby Clarke?" Park's best friend, Rod Gilbert, asked. "He put me out of the '71 season with a knee-on-knee hit."

"There was no love lost between any of us," Park concludes.

The Canadiens say the same things the Rangers do.

"I didn't like Phil," Cournoyer says, referring to Esposito. "But it was not personal. They were rivals. They didn't like us, either!"

"I never liked Phil," Savard adds. "I never liked any of the Bruins, but especially Phil because he was arrogant and just scored goals in front of the net. Nothing else. They were the most hated team in the league—until the Flyers!"

Cournoyer and Savard both laugh.

"I didn't like Bobby [Clarke], either!" Cournoyer says. "But it was the same as Phil. It wasn't personal."

Park explains, "It was just understood back then that we didn't like each other. We weren't friends. But really, we didn't know each other."

No one on Team Canada thought that would matter.

7

THE TOUGHEST CAMP EVER— AND NOT NEARLY TOUGH ENOUGH

On Sunday, August 13, 1972, the 35 charter members of the newly minted Team Canada reported to Toronto's luxurious 33-storey Sutton Place Hotel. Finished just five years earlier, it had quickly established itself as Toronto's place to stay for the rich, famous, and powerful. Years later it would serve as the epicentre of the Toronto International Film Festival, with the likes of Christopher Plummer, Paul Newman, and Sophia Loren camping out there.

"Sutton Place's guest list read like a who's who of the time," the *Toronto Star* reported. "It had gleaming marble floors, crystal chandeliers throughout, a dining room with a piano, surrounded with fresh azalea flowers year-round and a ballroom where countless parties were held. It even had a butler, something unique at the time . . . [and was] once dubbed one of the best in the world by the TV series *Lifestyles of the Rich and Famous*."

"Teams didn't stay at the Ritz in those days," Seiling says. "So the Sutton Place was a nicer hotel than we'd usually get."

It was certainly nicer than the Soviets' accommodations: an army barracks called Arkhangelskoye, just outside Moscow, where they lived and trained 11 months out of the year. Their rooms were as small as college dorm rooms, but not as nice. They worked out four times a day, every day, then killed the rest of their time reading, playing chess, or talking, talking, talking with the same 20 teammates they knew better than their wives, with whom they might stay a dozen nights a year. Everything they needed had to come through their coach, who controlled their access to hard currency, visas, cars, apartments, even daycare for their children.

The compound was surrounded by a 12-foot-high (3.5-metre) fence, with a single gate that soldiers patrolled 24 hours a day. Over the years a number of players tried to escape, but they were always caught and punished severely. They were the best players in Europe, but at home they were treated like prisoners.

"No, worse than prisoners," Soviet legend Slava Fetisov once said, grinning. "Sometimes prisoners get out. This was total control. When you're 18, you're so ambitious, you don't care about much else, just hockey. You live in barracks all year, it's okay. But later, you see life is too short to be a robot."

By living and working together 24 hours a day for 11 months, however, they bonded better and trained harder than the Canadians—and it wasn't close. When the Canadians arrived in Toronto on August 13, they didn't know the Soviets had been preparing specifically for them since July 5.

Because Savard wasn't initially named to the team, since he was recovering from his leg injury, his appearance in the hotel lobby surprised some.

"The first guy I see is Red Fisher," Savard recalls, referring to the legendary Montreal columnist. "He asks me, 'What are you doing here?' I say, 'You'll find out.'" He would.

The players left their farms, their hockey camps, their golf courses, their lakes, their homes, and their families. They came by planes, trains, and automobiles. A few showed up in decent shape, most notably Pat Stapleton, who'd been working on his farm in Strathroy, Ontario; Paul Henderson, who knew he would need an edge just to make the lineup; and Bob Clarke, who had been running on the roads of Flin Flon, which he'd been doing for years. When Clarke was still playing juniors, Teddy Hampson, who would play almost 1,000 games in the NHL and WHA, returned to Flin Flon and ran every day, when that was still considered strange.

"Once I'd seen Teddy doing it, I just picked it up," Clarke says. "When I got to camp I wasn't in hockey shape, but my legs were strong and I had youth on my side." Because of his diabetes, "I watched what I ate, always eating the right amount of breakfast, lunch, and dinner."

But most did not. Phil Esposito, who had battled the scale since he was an 18-year-old, recalls showing up for camp 15 pounds overweight.

"Man, I never trained," he admits. "The only one fatter than me was Pete [Mahovlich]. Both of us couldn't fit through the door at the same time."

"You just finished the playoffs, it's the middle of your holidays, and you're having a rest," Pete Mahovlich explains. "No, I didn't train."

"You have to understand," Pete's brother, Frank, adds, "there were no conditioning programs—*none*—until the '72 series. That's when all that started. Back then guys had farms and summer jobs."

"I was back in Montreal for the summer," Jean Ratelle recounts. "In those days you *couldn't* work out. You've got to work a job in the off-season. I was working at a golf course in Ville de Brossard, outside Montreal, in the pro shop. If I wanted to work out, I'd have to go to the YMCA in Montreal. After work it could take an hour to get there. I wouldn't get home until eight, then you don't have time to live! Training with weights? Forget it. We didn't have any weights!

"I knew I was going to get the call [to play on Team Canada], but I didn't know how much I'd be playing." So, in late July, with about three weeks before they had to report, Ratelle had started jogging a mile a day, "and I hated jogging! You hate to give away your summer after a long playoff in those days. My mindset was I'm going to go work as hard as I can and try to help the team. And I didn't think about it too much more than that."

"Look, there wasn't much ice around even if you wanted to skate," Seiling says. "I don't think many of us thought too much about it. In the NHL we had a 20-game exhibition preseason, all over North America. It was ludicrous! We'd play up and down the East Coast, then Saskatoon, Winnipeg, you name it—all these towns with no NHL teams. And that was just to get to the opener. So getting into shape was no issue, normally. You had a whole season."

"There's a certain rhythm to a season," Ken Dryden says, "a certain wind-down time after the playoffs, when you go to the golf course. Then a few weeks pass, then a month, and then you start becoming aware the season is coming again. So you start playing more golf, maybe more tennis, gradually becoming more physical. You start eating less and drinking less. You let yourself get to eight pounds over your playing weight, and you know you better get it down to six, then to four and three. You're not trying to get in game shape—not yet—you're simply trying to get everything within *range*, close enough that the next steps will get you there: the camp, the regular season, then you'll be ready for the playoffs. That was always the focus: to peak for the playoffs.

"It's kind of a gentle slope. It probably started with baseball spring training, years ago. You don't spend two months in Florida because you're already in shape. There would be no point. Same thing with an NHL training camp. You don't *arrive* in shape. The camp is supposed to *get* you in shape. So when people say this—that we were not in shape at camp—it's not incorrect. But that's what 'spring training' is for. So each day you dive in, and it goes up and down. The next day you feel aches and pains, but you know you're going to get into the rhythm of it.

"In a typical NHL training camp, after a week or 10 days you're finally playing exhibition games, but the other guys are all in equally bad shape, but slowly getting into better shape. That was how it normally went.

"But not this time. This wasn't normal."

TO this day, the players have a range of opinions on just how serious Team Canada's training camp at the old Maple Leaf Gardens actually was, but everyone agrees it was more rigorous than any NHL camp. After a 90-minute practice in the morning, they put their wet equipment back on in the afternoon for 60 minutes more, and kept it up from August 14 to September 1, the day before the series started.

"Let me just say this," Esposito says, smiling. "It was a lot more than I would have liked!"

Harry Sinden and Ken Dryden both came to camp with tape recorders to document their daily thoughts, then turned their tapes into essential books on the series. Sinden produced *Showdown*, while Dryden wrote *Face-Off at the Summit* with Mark Mulvoy, who covered the series for *Sports Illustrated*. From the camp's first days, Dryden reported, "We are training with an obvious air of enthusiasm which is not often found at most [NHL] training camps."

"When some guys say we were not working hard, I disagree," Serge Savard says today. "It was a tough, tough, *tough* training camp. It was 100 degrees [Fahrenheit—about 38 degrees Celsius] in the building all the time, and we skated twice a day for almost three weeks. When we were done I was in quite good shape, actually, because training camp was so hard."

"We worked hard, I'm telling you, and it was hot in Toronto," Sinden concurs. "There was no air conditioning in that building. The ice was lousy, which makes everything harder. It was a good, really hard camp—harder than the camps I ran for the Bruins. The big motivating thing for the players at camp wasn't the Soviets, but getting in the lineup. Absolutely."

But Team Canada's training camp was still missing something essential: a greater purpose. The players simply didn't take the Soviets seriously.

"At camp, we worked," Savard adds, "but no one was worried. Some of the guys left training camp a few times to go back to their hockey schools."

"Like Serge said, it was a hard training camp," Cournoyer says, "but mentally it was not hard, because we did not believe the series would be challenging. It's fun. What the hell? We take a day off here, a day off there. You are not focused like you need to be, and you can't really get ready mentally for a big series that way."

Cournoyer grew up in Drummondville, Quebec, an hour from Montreal. "When we got TV in our town for the first time," Cournoyer recalls, "I went to the TV store to watch the Canadiens through the window. Amazing!"

Of the 30 "notable people" on Drummondville's Wikipedia page, half are hockey players, including Yvon Lambert, Marcel Dionne, and Cournoyer, nicknamed "Roadrunner" for his amazing speed. When he was 18 he had to get his pants specially tailored due to his massive thighs, often described as "tree trunks."

The Canadiens picked him up in 1963, but coach Toe Blake didn't trust him enough in the defensive end to give him a regular shift. When Claude Ruel took over in 1968, Cournoyer became a full-time player and scored a career-best 43 goals. By 1972 Cournoyer had a reputation as an offensive-minded speedster, but those labels sold him short. He had worked hard to become a decent defensive player, and his charming personality belied his intense competitive spirit. Thinking back on his 10 Stanley Cups, he admits, "I don't know them all. But I know the only one I lost: '67 to the Maple Leafs. Can never forget that!" When a friend admitted he was afraid of getting hit, Cournoyer confessed, "I was always afraid, too—but not of getting hit. I was always afraid to lose! Maybe that's why I won so much," he adds with a grin.

Cournoyer knew that's what Team Canada lacked: a healthy fear of losing.

Dennis Hull recalls standing alongside the boards during one drill with the six other left wingers, just chatting until it was their turn. "At one point Vic Hadfield turned to Frank Mahovlich and says, 'I heard you're a painter.'

"'Yeah, I am.'

"'Great,' Vic says. 'Dennis wants you to paint his barn.'

"Frank says, 'I'm not that kind of a painter!' But it was too late. We're all laughing. Another time in the shower, I feel something funny and look down to see Vic Hadfield is pissing on my leg. No, really! I guess he did it to everyone."

None of these locker room pranks were sinister, but they set a certain tone.

"We knew some guys turned [the team] down, which told us something about this series," Bob Clarke says today. "Would anybody turn down a shot at the Stanley Cup Finals? And some of the guys who did show up bitched about losing their vacations, and took practices easy. The attitude was 'Let's just get through it, get this over with, and go get a few beers.' It wasn't a *personal* arrogance—but as a group we were. I can't recall anyone making any particular statement, but the arrogance was just around, in the atmosphere. I think everyone thought it was going to be a cakewalk." At that, Clarke looks up, smiling. "Didn't work out quite that way."

Almost everyone seemed to be telling them, one way or another, that the Soviets could never challenge them, and no one was telling them otherwise.

"Harry told everyone in camp, 'You're going to play in the games,'" Savard recalls. "Well, maybe that was necessary, but once you say that, who thinks the Russians will be any good? When you make decisions to keep everyone happy, instead of what's best for the team, who thinks *Harry* thinks this will be tough?"

Their focus wasn't sharpened by staying in one of the most glamorous hotels in the world, filled with attractive admirers—a situation rife with temptations.

Brad Park was a reliable observer of the fun his teammates were having. Because his wife, Gerry, was already overdue with their first child—the players had set up a betting pool to guess the date—the Parks stayed in Scarborough.

"All through training camp, I commuted in and out for practice," he recalls. "When we were done skating for the day, I'd have dinner and a couple beers with the guys, then go home and come in the next morning, sober as a judge. Man, I'd see more guys hungover like you couldn't believe! From the looks of it, the guys must've had a lively time in my absence. I almost wanted to put some of the guys in a shower to get them ready for practice. We weren't thinking about conditioning. We thought we *were* conditioning! If I knew then what I know now, I would've trained harder."

"There was no dedication," Park's best friend, Rod Gilbert, added. "Everyone was so sure that we were superior that we didn't give the Russians any thought. Nobody knew anything. I just got a huge contract, guaranteed three more years. And we're not getting any money for this. So why not go out?"

No one was nervous about the Soviets, but they were a bit uneasy about each other. "We were put in a situation that no one had ever been in before," Park says, "and that was before the puck dropped."

Given the bitter rivalries, Sinden wondered how that would translate to the rink. "But there were no problems in practice," he says. "They weren't friends, but they were professional." But off the ice, they reverted to form.

"Really, we had no team spirit," Pete Mahovlich says. "Everyone was just going out with their own guys."

Instead of breaking down the barriers, camp reinforced them.

"The best team ever assembled?" Pat Stapleton asked rhetorically. "Well, we would have been, if we had been a *team*. But we were not—not at first."

If the series had gone the way everyone expected it to, the Canadians probably would have been lauded for working hard while everyone else was playing golf. But they didn't prepare as hard as the Soviets had, and therefore, not as seriously as they should have. But only the Soviets knew that then.

WHATEVER the players were doing off the ice each night was eclipsed by the unprecedented amount of talent they saw on the ice each morning.

Without Bobby Orr, Brad Park stood alone as the team's top defenceman, as expected. But everyone seemed surprised by how much Detroit's Gary Bergman raised his game when Sinden paired him with Park. Chicago's Pat Stapleton and his partner, Bill White, delivered on their promise: a professional pair of sturdy, stay-at-home defencemen with good puck skills. But the camp's best duo looked to be New York's Rod Seiling, an honest, experienced defensive defenceman, and Boston's Don Awrey, a great shot blocker and penalty killer, who worked wonderfully with Seiling.

Montreal's Guy Lapointe, whom the coaches picked up when Jacques Laperrière turned them down, was sure to get some playing time, but with Savard's status uncertain, it was not clear how Sinden would use him.

The forwards carried more star power, starting with New York's Jean Ratelle, Vic Hadfield, and Rod Gilbert, the famed

Goal-a-Game Line. The previous season, the trio had finished third, fourth, and fifth, respectively, in total points, trailing only Phil Esposito and Bobby Orr—despite Ratelle playing just 63 games. Together the GAG Line tallied 139 total goals, or almost *two goals* a game, an NHL record. Playing them whenever the team needed a goal looked like Sinden's easiest decision.

Hiding at the bottom of the long list of forwards were Paul Henderson and Ron Ellis, with Bob Clarke at centre. Even though Henderson was coming off a career-high 38 goals, "making the team was not a given," he says. "And dressing for the first game in Montreal was *definitely* not a given—not even likely." They might not have made the team were it not for Ferguson's fierce advocacy of all three.

"Right away you saw that Bobby Clarke was just a younger Norm Ullman," Henderson says, "a great playmaker, just as determined and maybe a little more aggressive. The chemistry on a line, honestly, it's a mystery. Maybe we'll know in a hundred years why our line worked so well. A lot of other guys on the team just didn't seem to find the right combinations. But with Clarkie, we didn't have to make any adjustments. It all clicked from the first day."

Although Clarke watched his diet carefully, "being part of a hockey team, you need to get a beer sometimes, and I could do that if I wasn't stupid about it." After their first practice together, that's exactly what they did. Because Henderson's father had died in 1968, he confided in Ellis and Clarke that he really wanted his mom to see him play in Toronto, site of Game Two. He challenged his linemates: "Why don't we work our asses off and show these guys we can play?"

"We weren't kidding ourselves," Clarke says. "We knew we were the last line on the team. Hell, we had Ratelle and Espo and Cournoyer out there! No shame in that. So we sort of made an agreement: we're going to outwork everyone."

"We knew we were underdogs," Henderson continues. "We desperately wanted to show we could play, and we came to the rink on fire to prove it every day. When Harry had us do end-to-enders, some guys would go to the far blue line and come back, but we'd hammer the glass at the far end and come back hard.

"As a rule, the bigger star you were, the less you listened. Sinden wasn't even in the NHL anymore, so some guys might have tuned him out at first. Well, not us. We listened! We figured we might be the shutdown line—the defensive specialists, the grind line—but we didn't care. We made it clear we would do anything to play."

As with so many aspects of Team Canada, leadership had been taken for granted. And why not? Of Team Canada's 26 skaters who would get into a game against the Soviets, 18 of them, or 70 percent, would wear a *C* or an *A* on their NHL sweaters before their careers were over.

Instead of naming one captain, Sinden decided to name four alternate captains: Stan Mikita, Frank Mahovlich, Jean Ratelle—all experienced, highly regarded leaders—and Phil Esposito, who had served as an alternate captain for Sinden in Boston. But the question of who would actually lead this team would be settled early, often, and emphatically.

"In our first team meeting in Toronto, I stood up and said, 'Where's the money going?'" Phil Esposito recalls. "Eagleson says, 'Don't worry about that.' I say, 'Tell us.' He says, 'I don't want to talk about that.' I say, 'You're gonna have to.' So he finally says, 'It's going to the pension.'"

Esposito's teammates had another pressing question, and he figured he might as well be the guy to ask it: Would the team pay for their wives to join them overseas? Once again, Esposito put Eagleson on the spot, and the players heard what they wanted to hear: their wives would join their husbands, all expenses paid.

Esposito's status on the team couldn't be questioned, which helped.

"That season, Phil was the best forward in all of hockey, plain and simple," Henderson says, and it's hard to argue otherwise. In 1971–72, Esposito led the league with 66 goals, second most in league history behind only the 76 he'd scored the year before, and far ahead of Vic Hadfield and Bobby Hull, who had 50 each. Esposito finished second with 67 assists, behind Bobby Orr's 80—many of which Orr earned off Esposito's goals—for a total of 133 points. That ranked third highest in NHL history, behind his own record of 152 and Orr's 139, both set the previous year, 1970–71. In the early '70s Esposito wasn't merely setting records, but torching the record book in the same mind-blowing fashion Wayne Gretzky would a decade later.

"Phil was the best slot guy there ever was," Henderson adds. "Trying to move him was like running into a bag of cement. If Phil was in front of the net, the goalie had to make a great save. And Orr and him together? What a joke that was! How could you stop them? Hated playing against those guys. Think everyone did."

"I'd already won the scoring championships," Esposito says. "MVP awards, the Lester B. Pearson Award [since renamed the Ted Lindsay Award, given to the players' choice as MVP]. If I opened my mouth, what the fuck could they do with me—send me home? Fire me? No, I'm gonna say what I think."

Other players had enough stature to speak freely, but only Esposito repeatedly used his megaphone to stand up for his teammates.

"Phil is a one-of-a-kind personality," Henderson says. "He just *exudes* leadership. Didn't matter what we were doing, he was at the centre of it. We had four captains. But Phil was the absolute leader."

"No question," Ron Ellis agrees. "Phil was the leader from day one."

═

TEAM Canada had another, less visible leader: assistant coach John Ferguson, Montreal's recently retired enforcer. In addition to bringing in consummate team players like Serge Savard, Pete Mahovlich, Ron Ellis, Bobby Clarke, and Dale Tallon, he knew how to push the right buttons. Everyone seemed to like and respect Ferguson, even if they feared him on some level.

Born in Vancouver in 1938, Ferguson lost his father when he was nine and was raised by his mother. Lacrosse, horses, and hockey were his outlets. When he served as the stick boy for the Western Hockey League's Canucks and saw their most talented players get pushed around, he recognized the importance of a good enforcer. He realized becoming one could be his ticket out.

In 1963 Montreal called the 25-year-old Ferguson up to protect the great Jean Béliveau. Ferguson promised himself he would be "the meanest, rottenest, most miserable cuss ever to play in the NHL." Just 12 seconds into his NHL career, he got in a fight with Boston's notorious Ted Green—and beat him up. He also made himself into a good enough player to justify playing alongside Béliveau, leading the league in rookie scoring. Ferguson played his best when it mattered most, scoring 20 goals and 18 assists in 85 career playoff games.

He knew his job wasn't scoring goals but making sure opponents didn't prevent Béliveau from scoring goals. Béliveau wrote in his autobiography that Ferguson had been "the most formidable player of the decade and possibly in the Canadiens' history. His greatest contribution was his spirit... his intensity consumed him, his blood boiling when that of others simply simmered."

But with a well-earned reputation as a fighter, and no experience coaching, Ferguson's appointment to assistant coach raised some eyebrows.

On August 13, the day Team Canada arrived at the Sutton Place, Ken Dryden wrote that hiring Ferguson was "not the right approach. As our players will find out, the Russians are extremely strong and tend to disdain rough, vicious play, although they are more than capable of playing that way. We would only end up in the penalty box, and one of the strongest aspects of the Russian game is the power play."

Five days later Dryden wrote, "I owe John Ferguson an apology. I think I've misunderstood how Fergie used to play. He had an overwhelming drive to win and it manifested itself in an aggressive approach to the game . . . His inclusion is an attempt to instill this drive to win in our players, though not necessarily through Fergie's playing style. The more I think about it, the more I understand how he can help us."

As cerebral as Dryden surely is, he didn't take Rogie Vachon's job right before the 1971 playoffs because he lacked confidence, ambition, or fighting spirit. Although Dryden's engine ran quieter than most, it ran just as fast. Dryden would never subscribe to a win-at-all-costs mentality, but he surely wanted to win, he knew it would be harder to beat the Soviets than his teammates thought, and he could see how Ferguson could help them. Ferguson was also such a good guy, and a prankster, that he could break barriers better than anyone else in the locker room.

"Fergie was the toughest guy I've known on the ice," Savard says, "and the sweetest guy off it. A generous, generous guy. He was a poodle! I just loved him."

"In those days you didn't have seven assistants," Clarke adds. "So John had a lot of influence. Harry listened to him, and we listened to him. I was just 23, so when I saw John Ferguson coming down the hallway my first thought was 'I hope he's not mad at me!' He never was, but he commanded that kind of respect.

"He was successful because it was always the *team* with John. Nice person, good person, but that's what he brought to us: the team focus.

"And Fergie had *strength*. We would need that."

8

SCRIMMAGES AND SCOUTS

Brad Park had just completed his best season to date, with 73 points and his third straight runner-up finish behind Orr for the Norris Trophy, awarded to the league's best defenceman. If Orr couldn't play, the team could depend on Park—but only if he stayed healthy.

During the camp's first week, Park recalls, "Dennis Hull winds up for a big slapper at the blue line. I'm thinking, 'No way I'm blocking this shot. This is training camp!'"

Park had good reason not to. Dennis, five years younger than brother Bobby, played in Bobby's shadow his entire career, but many thought Dennis had the harder slapshot—which was saying something.

"Bobby could shoot the puck through a car wash and it wouldn't get wet," Dennis likes to joke. "I could shoot it harder, but I couldn't hit the car wash!"

So when Park saw Dennis wind up, he wisely moved out of the way.

"But as he winds up," Park recalls, "Cournoyer backchecks for some goddamn reason and it hits his stick. I turn my head to the right and the puck hits my left cheek. And I was lucky: it hits me flat, so it doesn't cut me."

"I would have apologized," Dennis Hull says, "but he was out cold!"

"In the paper, there's a picture of two guys carrying me off the ice," Park recalls. "It's 9 a.m., and I'm going to the hospital. At 10:30 that night, all of a sudden, I'm up! I'm not even groggy, so the next morning, I check myself out and get to the rink, but I'm in a fog all day." In the days before concussion protocols, most athletes got back in the game as soon as they could see straight. "I didn't go back to the rink because I was afraid of not making the team. It was out of dedication to my wife! I had to get my car at the rink to go see her. She was supposed to have the baby August 10, so I'm on pins and needles every day during camp."

"I apologized the next day," Hull recalls. "I told him I wouldn't do it again. He said, 'Me neither!'"

═

"ALL training camps are boring, but ours was worse," Sinden told *Sports Illustrated* at the time. "Let's face it: you get in shape because of real game competition."

If they couldn't have a real game until the Soviets showed up on September 2, Sinden could give them the next best thing: a scrimmage with referees, a scoreboard, and a decent crowd. In the team's first intrasquad scrimmage on August 22, Sinden's white team beat Ferguson's red squad, 8–5. Berenson scored twice, and Ellis and Clarke each added one for the white team, while Phil Esposito scored two for Ferguson's side. Played before 5,600 fans in 30 degree Celsius (86 Fahrenheit) heat, the game featured more scoring than hitting.

"Like all early season exhibitions," wrote Dryden, "the offence predominated, and in the end, fatigue was the winner." After letting in six goals, he had a long way to go, and he knew it.

Four days later, on Saturday, August 26, sitting in his hotel room a few hours before Team Canada's second intrasquad scrimmage, Dryden watched the opening ceremonies of the Munich Olympics. West Germany was eager to show the world how much it had changed since the 1936 Berlin Olympics. Organizers kept security and other militaristic elements to a minimum, while hosting the most open and friendly Olympics ever. They went so far as to name it "*Die heiteren Spiele*," or "the Cheerful Games." Watching the pageantry unfold reminded Dryden that Team Canada would be hosting its own opening ceremonies in exactly one week.

"I could feel the nervousness down to my legs," he wrote. "I shivered for a few seconds. My heart seemed to be beating faster. Pressure had hit me."

During Team Canada's second full scrimmage that night, played in front of some 7,500 fans in Maple Leaf Gardens, Dryden played the full 60 minutes and gave up all four goals for Ferguson's red team—three from Ratelle and one from Henderson—while Tony Esposito and Eddie Johnston split time for the white team, each giving up one goal to win, 4–2. It was far from Dryden's best, but much better than his first scrimmage. If he could maintain that positive trajectory, he believed he would be ready to face the Soviets one week later.

The coaches weren't worried about Dryden and were pleasantly surprised by the success of Clarke's line. "Our assets fit, and we clicked right off," Clarke says. "I was a puck chaser. I could forecheck, battle for loose pucks. Paul could fly and shoot, and he had the best scoring ability of the three of us, by far. Ronnie was a great defensive forward, something people overlook too often. He was always in a responsible position, so we didn't give up many chances. We played a style that could help almost any team: hard-working, backchecking, defensive-minded, but aggressive, and if I could get the puck to Paul in front, we could do a little damage."

Three days later, on Tuesday, August 29, the players received the scouting report on the Soviets a few hours before playing their third and final scrimmage. The report came from Toronto Maple Leafs coach John McLellan and Toronto's chief scout, Bob Davidson, who watched two games in Moscow, including an exhibition between the Soviet national team and its top Red Army squad. But they didn't get far, they didn't stay long, and they didn't get much, and what they did get probably hurt more than it helped.

They returned with the welcome news that the critics of international hockey had been right all along: Team Canada was leaps and bounds ahead of the Soviets, who had only one or two players who could make the roster of one of the NHL's 16 teams, and none who could play for Team Canada. They were particularly unimpressed with the Soviets' 20-year-old goalie, Vladislav Tretiak, who had been brutal in the one game they saw him play, letting in eight goals against the national team. McLellan and Davidson concluded that in every game Tretiak played, Team Canada would enjoy "a five- or six-goal advantage."

Scouting a goalie for one game is never a good idea. Almost any netminder can get hot or go cold for a single game, but the report was especially misleading in Tretiak's case. The scouts didn't know that Tretiak had spent the previous night at his bachelor party and would be getting married the following morning.

Tretiak hadn't performed well at the World Championship that April, either, when the Czech national team revealed his weakness. According to Mark Mulvoy's first dispatch in *Sports Illustrated*, which ran after Game Four, there had been rumours that the Soviets' new coach, Bobrov, "was going to option Tretiak to Siberia. 'He had a terrible glove hand,' said [Vladimír Kostka], the Czech coach. 'I don't know how he did it, but he must have learned to use his glove hand during the summer.'

"That he did," Mulvoy continued. "After every workout this summer Bobrov and his assistant, Boris Kulagin, kept Tretiak on the ice for at least another hour and forced him to face the firing squad, a shooting machine that fires a puck every four seconds at speeds up to 100 mph [160 km/h]. Tretiak now owns the fastest glove hand in the USSR. 'He certainly is not the same goalie we used to plan our game around,' said Kjell Svensson, Sweden's coach."

But what Mulvoy, Kostka, and Svensson found out before the series started, Team Canada's scouts didn't.

"The problem we had," Dennis Hull cracks, "is that our scouts were from the Leafs!" They were in the midst of a 30-year run in which they never finished higher than third in their division. "And they think they know how to judge a player?"

"Geez," Esposito concurs, "no wonder the Maple Leafs always end up in last place!"

In fairness to the scouts, Canadian coaches and players had been stubbornly insular from the time they invented the sport, making them too receptive to unfavourable assessments of their opponents. During the 1960s the NHL featured exactly one European player, a Swede named Ulf Sterner who played four games for the Rangers, and one American, Tommy Williams, a solid forward for the Red Wings. The 1972 All-Star Game featured 38 players, every single one Canadian. Unlike today, when each country's best players join their respective national teams when they're 16 years old and play against the world's top players their age for years, only six members of Team Canada had ever played against the Soviets: Sinden, Berenson, Seiling, Savard, Brian Glennie, and Dryden. But it was no accident that those six people were the least likely to dismiss the Soviets as imposters.

When Dryden heard the scathing scouting report of the Soviets, he wrote, "I'm not convinced. By North American standards, which McLellan and Davidson are used to, the Russians pass too much, don't shoot enough, and are too small. By European standards, though, these are not weaknesses. Who is right?"

"I knew going in that they weren't going to be the pushovers that everyone expected them to be," says Rod Seiling, who had played against them in the 1964 Olympics. "I'd seen how well they played as a unit, how disciplined they were, and I knew that they were going to be in great shape. I never predicted how many games they would win, but I knew these games would be tough battles. And I also knew they weren't choirboys, either. The hacking, the kicking, the spitting, all that stuff, I'd experienced many times in previous games."

But Seiling's teammates gave little thought to the Soviets, and most couldn't name a single Soviet skater. They knew even less about how much the Soviets knew about them. The Soviets had been keeping tabs on the Canadians from the day Tarasov started his clinic at the children's park in 1946. He had studied Canadian hockey carefully, so that he could create a system to counter it. For the upcoming series, the Soviets scouted the Canadians better than any opponent they had faced.

According to MacSkimming's *Cold War*, the Soviets had broken down film from the 1971 and 1972 Stanley Cup playoffs to study most of Team Canada's best players performing at their best. To leave no stone unturned, the Soviets sent the national team's assistant coach, Boris Kulagin, and former assistant coach Arkady Chernyshev, a Tarasov protégé, to attend every Team Canada practice and scrimmage. They were making no secret of it, and the Canadians didn't seem to care.

Well, most of them didn't. Dryden noted that Chernyshev was jovial, but Kulagin "never cracked a smile." Whenever Dryden gave up a goal in practice, he'd look up into the stands to see if they were taking notes—and they always were.

"If, say, Frank Mahovlich takes 1.96538 seconds to go from blue line to blue line," Dryden wrote, "I'm sure the Russians know it by now."

"They had their two coaches sitting up in the stands watching everything we did during the past two weeks," Sinden wrote, "taking enough notes to fill an encyclopedia."

But to avoid rousting the slumbering Canadians, Soviet officials kept up their shtick as humble hockey enthusiasts seeking an educational experience. The Soviet scouts went so far as to ask Bobby Orr, sitting in the stands, to sign a stack of autographs, as though they were mere starry-eyed fans.

"It was not being framed as a big competition," Ron Ellis remembers. "At least, not in Canada. It was being primed as an international friendly, and the Russians were coming to learn how the game is played at the highest level. I felt like they're going to be embarrassed, right? But I think they thought they were ready. Hell, they were already practising on Montreal time when they were in *Moscow*. I love that. So, no, they weren't coming over here to learn, no matter what they said. They were coming over here to beat us. But none of us had any idea about that."

"When I think back on that camp," Pat Stapleton said, "I can see what I couldn't see then: we'd been suckered—and we bought it, hook, line, and sinker."

On Tuesday, August 29, the same day Bobby Orr's doctors cleared him to play in the series, Team Canada played its third full scrimmage, the final dry run before the opener against the Soviets four days later.

The Canadians looked like they were putting their game together, individually and collectively. Sinden's white squad beat Ferguson's red team for the third straight game, this time 6–2, but goaltenders Tony Esposito and Dryden had regained their form, with Dryden throwing a shutout during his time in net. The defence seemed solid throughout, led by the New York–Boston pairing of Rod Seiling and Don Awrey. The GAG Line struggled once again, but Clarke scored one and Henderson two.

"Once you get a little confidence," Henderson recalls, "it's pretty easy to keep it going. You feed off each other. If nobody was looking at us as anything special—and look, with so many Hall of Famers, I'll concede that we weren't standouts—we knew how determined we were, and it was starting to show."

"Why wouldn't it work?" Clarke asks. "We were three pretty good players who worked our asses off, and a lot of other guys didn't. They just assumed they were going to play. We didn't assume anything. We couldn't afford to. We just wanted a chance to prove we could play. That's different."

They believed they had made their case. "We'd made it a point to force Harry's hand," Henderson says, "so he couldn't say no. And that's what we did."

AT 9 p.m. the next night, Wednesday, August 30, Aeroflot's Flight 301 delivered the Soviet players, coaches, and staffers to Montreal. The next morning they ran through a 90-minute skate without a single player taking a break—a workout, MacSkimming wrote, that "would put most Canadian workouts to shame."

At 8 p.m. that night they did it all again for 60 minutes. When someone asked a team translator if the players were wiped out after the travel and practices, he explained that they had already been living on Montreal time for two weeks. No adjustments were necessary. That came as news to the Canadians. But the translator left out an important detail: the Soviets had begun training for this series not two weeks earlier, like the Canadians had, but two *months*.

The scouting reports the Soviets had been collecting on the Canadians didn't elicit awe or laughter from their players, just a healthy respect—exactly the attitude a competitor needs before a big contest.

"As captain, my job was to inspire my teammates both on the ice and off," defenceman Viktor Kuzkin said. "But in this series that wasn't necessary. Everyone understood we were playing the most important tournament of our lives."

Everyone on the Soviet team, at least.

On Thursday, August 31, Team Canada's last night in Toronto,

Ferguson told Sinden, "It's as good as any training camp I was ever at with Montreal," music to Sinden's ears. But, Sinden wrote, "the psychological preparation has me worried. These guys are used to playing for money . . . Will they give their best now because Canadians want them to beat the hell out of the Russians? I don't know."

Sinden felt the time was right to shift from physical to mental preparation. "Tonight was my first shot at psyching the team," he wrote. Sinden wanted to show the world's top professionals how it felt to play for your country, "that peculiar kind of exhilaration you experience when you're a world champion," he wrote. "I wanted them to relive with me on film those beautiful moments when I stood on top of the world . . . the goosebumps popping out all over me as I stood on the victory block . . . as our flag went up slowly and they played 'O Canada' . . . Money can't buy it. Not even Stanley Cup money."

For Sinden, that day was March 9, 1958, after the Whitby Dunlops had vanquished the Soviets, 4–2, and he mounted the podium to accept the gold medal.

"I was 26 when we won in Oslo, and so proud," he wrote. "All Canada had wanted us to hang one on the Russians that day and we did. In 1972 the nation wants it again and it's my job to make sure this team is ready to do it."

So Sinden showed them film from the 1958 World Championship.

"Whenever I had something good to say about international hockey," he recalls, "they rolled their eyes. They never believed me. So I wanted the film to convince them the Soviets could play, and show them what it felt like to play for your country. Well, it didn't go as planned. Really, it backfired pretty badly."

It didn't help that the 1958 finals had been played outdoors in minus-11 Celsius (12 Fahrenheit) weather, the black-and-white film was grainy, and everything looked more than 14 years old.

"They were laughing," Sinden recalls. "In Oslo we wore silly hats to keep warm, and the [Team Canada] players could see me on the ice—and all that got them laughing some more. It didn't make the impression I was hoping for!"

When Sinden appeared on screen, Esposito cracked, "Who's that little kid with the hat?"

"I remember one Russian guy," Dennis Hull says, "who looked like Charlie Chaplin out there."

That happened to be Boris Mikhailov. While Hull's comment got more laughs, the Canadians would have a different impression of Mikhailov a few days later.

Recognizing his mistake, Sinden replaced that film with more recent footage of the Soviets—but this only made matters worse. The first film showed the 1969 World Championship, in which the Soviets beat the last amateur team Canada sent—hardly Team Canada–calibre. The next, from the 1972 World Championship played just four months earlier, showed the Soviets losing to Czechoslovakia. When the Team Canada players weren't making sport of the Soviets, they were picking them apart for every little thing from their shots to their sticks.

Sinden had hoped to bring out their pride and patriotism, but they went away more convinced than ever that no one outside the NHL played serious hockey. Sinden cut the film session short "before we got too full of ourselves," he says.

Too late. Alan Eagleson said it publicly: "We will win eight games to nothing."

Even cooler heads like the Montreal Canadiens' new coach, Scotty Bowman, agreed. "Anything can happen in a hockey game or series," he said. "But we have the better players and should win all eight games."

Dryden recognized the situation for what it was. "We Canadians find ourselves on a one-way street," he wrote at the time. "We must score an overwhelming 8–0 victory. Anything less will be a shattering defeat."

"Harry was constantly warning us that the Russians were better than we thought," Stapleton said. "'They're getting ready for us! They're not coming over here to fail!' and all that. But he was getting drowned out by everything else—the scouts, the film, the media telling us we had it in the bag. So we're hearing all this on one side, and Harry's playing Chicken Little on the other. Who would *you* believe?"

In 48 hours they would find out for themselves.

9

THE RUSSIANS ARE HERE

Wearing their black Team Canada blazers, with a maple leaf patch on the pocket and TEAM CANADA EQUIPE stitched over it, the players boarded two planes—a precaution the owners requested—for the short flight from Toronto to Montreal on Friday, September 1.

A few hours later in Montreal, the Canadians practised first, with the Soviets watching from the stands. "The [Canadian] players were just like little kids showing off for their parents," Sinden wrote. They fired slapshot after slapshot at the goalies, off the boards, and against the glass. Watching this, Soviet defenceman Alexander Gusev confessed, "I thought I had one of the hardest slapshots in the world. When I arrived in Montreal, I discovered that almost every Canadian's shot was at least as hard as mine."

When it was the Soviets' turn, the curious Canadians stuck around to watch. The fact that the normally super-secretive Soviets did nothing to prevent them from doing so should have been a tipoff: they were about to put on a different kind of show, and it worked. The Soviet practice fed the Canadians' overconfidence.

"My first thought: 'Their equipment is horseshit!'" Park recalls. "They were using the same skates and sticks I used in the

’50s. *These* guys are supposed to give us a run? I don’t think so.”

In his column titled “Fearless Forecast: We’re Ready and We’ll Win,” Ted Blackman of the *Montreal Gazette* predicted an eight-game sweep for Canada. “On the other side of the Forum,” he wrote of the Soviets’ practice, “Phil Chiarella, the skate man, was baffled. He had noted the inferior quality and horrible condition of the Russians’ footgear—odd-coloured laces, some of them knotted, the ankle supports so weak from wear they offered little support. ‘You get better stuff at a garage sale in Flin Flon.’”

Sinden knew better. “The Russians were unimpressive, but they never look good in practice by our standards,” he wrote. “Our guys just couldn’t seem to understand this. After we watched their practice our players were very critical . . . I tried to stifle those comments. I told the players, ‘Listen, those guys aren’t as bad as they looked.’” Sinden’s warnings fell on deaf ears.

Bobby Orr sat with his teammates to watch the Soviets. “They seem to be shooting off their rear foot,” he told Mark Mulvoy, while watching them toss easy shots at Tretiak from 25 feet (7.5 metres). “Imagine if Dennis Hull were out there! The poor goalie wouldn’t have a chance.”

September 1, 1972, marked the last day the Canadians mocked the Soviets.

AFTER 18 days of training camp, Sinden and Ferguson had to pick 17 skaters to dress for the first game.

Sinden had agreed with the Russians to stick with the NHL limit of 19 players. With two spots reserved for goalies, that meant they could either pick three pairs of defencemen plus 11 forwards, to fill three lines with two extras, or dress 12 forwards to fill four full lines, with five defencemen—two pairs and an extra. Sinden and Ferguson decided to go with four full forward lines and five defencemen.

A few days earlier, in Toronto, they had concluded the team was strongest at forward, so they decided to load up the front lines and attack to get the Soviets on their heels. Whenever they couldn't choose between two players, they'd pick the better offensive player. But Sinden admits today that they had another consideration: having promised 35 players they would all get into at least one of the eight games, "We were trying to work in some more forwards, because we knew it would be harder to get that many forwards into the lineup."

The first dozen spots were easy, just as they had been two months earlier when Sinden and Ferguson were compiling their wish list for the team. They started with Phil Esposito, Yvan Cournoyer, and Frank Mahovlich, a line Sinden thought "should be dynamite," and the Rangers' Goal-a-Game Line: Rod Gilbert, Jean Ratelle and Vic Hadfield. Although the GAG Line had had only "a pretty good camp" in Sinden's estimation, it was still "one of the best offensive lines in the history of the NHL."

For the third set, Sinden wrote, he picked "the best line in training camp": Clarke, Henderson, and Ellis. The coaches picked their fourth line on the same basis, favouring offensive players who had displayed good chemistry in camp: Detroit's Red Berenson and Mickey Redmond with Montreal's Peter Mahovlich.

Because Sinden's international experience told him his players would likely take more penalties than the Soviets, he made sure six of his forwards were "terrific penalty killers": Esposito, Berenson, Ellis, Clarke, and the Mahovlich brothers.

On defence the coaches filled their remaining five spots with Rod Seiling and Don Awrey, "the best pair in training," Sinden wrote; Brad Park and Gary Bergman; and the fifth wheel, Guy Lapointe, picked partly because the game was in Montreal.

"Goaltending also caused some soul-searching," Sinden wrote. Tony Esposito won the NHL's rookie of the year award in 1970 after notching 15 shutouts—a rookie record that still stands—and finished second in Hart Trophy (MVP) voting. The next year,

1970–71, he led Chicago to the seventh game of the Stanley Cup Final before falling to Montreal and their newfound netminder, a kid named Ken Dryden. The year after that, 1971–72, Tony posted the NHL's lowest goals-against average with a sterling 1.77. Résumés didn't get any better than his.

Sinden believed Tony Esposito had "a very, very slight edge over Ken Dryden. It's been so close, though, that you can't say Tony should definitely be the starter . . . Dryden is our pick to start. Like Lapointe, we feel that coming back to Montreal will really pick Kenny up. But, if the worst happens, we can come back with Tony in Toronto Monday night. Really, we're splitting the first two games, and coming back in the third with the guy who does the best job."

After practice, Sinden gathered the players at centre ice and told them he'd pinned the roster on a bulletin board in the locker room. He explained his logic and repeated his assurance that everyone would get into at least one game. Still, he wrote, "How do you tell an All-Star, 'I'm sorry, but I'm going with so-and-so instead of you?' For many of them, it's undoubtedly going to be the first time in their hockey lives they hear they aren't good enough. Will they take this in stride? I don't know."

That list of 16 players who would watch from the stands included veteran forwards Dennis Hull, J.P. Parisé, Wayne Cashman, and Bill Goldsworthy, and the "kids," Gilbert Perreault, Rick Martin, and Marcel Dionne, all top draft picks from Quebec who would have loved to show off for the home crowd. Even alternate captain Stan Mikita would be sitting that night.

On defence, with Orr still not ready to play despite his doctors' initial clearance, Sinden scratched Chicago's top pair of Bill White and Pat Stapleton, and youngsters Brian Glennie, Jocelyn Guèvremont, and Dale Tallon. Hardest of all would be Savard, "the fine Montreal defenceman," Sinden wrote. "Serge wanted to play [in Montreal] in the worst way, and had worked very hard for the honour. In fairness, though, I didn't think he really came on strong until the last three or four days."

On all these tough decisions, Sinden followed a simple principle: "We would dress the players who earned it in training camp."

In other words, Sinden did not play favourites, rely on reputation, or let politics get in the way, nor did he allow the process to be influenced by NHL coaches, players, or clubs he happened to like. By running a strict meritocracy, he ensured that those who had worked hardest and played best in camp got to start. This might seem simple, even obvious, but it's a safe bet most of the coaches these players had known failed to follow this basic philosophy. It's rarely adhered to in sports, school, or work because it requires a leader unafraid to anger the entitled. This approach created Sinden's biggest headaches, but it also gave his team its best chance. That's how Clarke's line rose from relative obscurity to third, and the homegrown hotshots, Perreault and Martin, found themselves in street clothes.

"If two guys weren't going to play here," Sinden wrote, pulling no punches, "it was those two. Of the 35 players, Perreault and Martin were the only ones who let down on us in training camp. Neither was playing that well, and after we finished our intrasquad games I could sense that they didn't think they were going to make it. The last week or so, they just didn't put out in practice the way they had the first couple of weeks, or the way the other guys had right along."

"All things considered," Dryden wrote, "I don't think there were any surprises."

When they returned to the locker room, Berenson told Sinden and Ferguson "to get lost for a minute," Dryden wrote. "Look," Berenson said, "we have 35 outstanding hockey players here right now but only 19 will be dressing tomorrow night. It's no disgrace not to be playing. Let's not be disillusioned. Someone had to make the choices—and it was a thankless, impossible job. Let's not be disappointed. Let's not blast the coaches. This is a team of 35 men. Let's keep it that way."

Nonetheless, after seeing the list a few heads dropped, and Perreault and Martin "felt a little sorry for themselves," Sinden said. But he didn't flinch.

Rod Seiling, who would be getting plenty of playing time the next night, raised a different concern. "When I saw the lineup, I went to Harry and asked him to dress six defencemen," he recalls, "but Harry didn't agree."

Team Canada would dress five defencemen. The Soviets would dress seven.

ANY Canadian player who woke up in his Montreal hotel room Saturday morning, about 12 hours before game time, and harboured the slightest doubt of the outcome needed only dispel it by picking up a newspaper or turning on a TV. If the members of Team Canada could be fairly accused of ignorance and arrogance before the opening faceoff, they kept their opinions to themselves. Not so the journalists, who made a case bordering on propaganda for the unquestioned superiority of Canadian hockey.

On August 19, under the headline "Canada's Battle Cry: 'Eight Straight,'" *New York Times* columnist Dave Anderson wrote that for two decades, the Russians "have attempted to counterfeit NHL hockey in the Olympic and world amateur tournaments. Now the Russians believe that their forged copy is equal to the original. It's a delusion."

But as Tarasov famously said, "To copy is always to be second best." He had sought to do the opposite: to create a truly original style, counter to the Canadians'.

Anderson's colleagues didn't fare much better, and for the same reason: most knew very little about Soviet hockey. On August 29, *Globe and Mail* columnist Dick Beddoes wrote, "If the Russians win one game, I will eat this column shredded at high noon in a bowl of borscht on the front steps of the Russian embassy. Note to Editor [Jim] Vipond: Just in case, keep the sour cream handy."

On September 2, the morning of the first game, Red Fisher was more direct: "I don't think Team Canada will lose a game."

When the columnists did give grudging nods to the Soviets, usually for their conditioning and passing, the compliments had a half-hearted feel to them. They often peppered their pieces with references to soulless robots, whom they jokingly called "Igor" and "the Russkies." They invariably followed these brief concessions with full-throated praise for the Canadians' superior talent.

Some of this borrowed wisdom came from Team Canada's scouts, John McLellan and Bob Davidson, who were especially tough on the goalie, Tretiak.

"Informed of this appraisal," Mulvoy added, "the 20-year-old Tretiak laughed. 'That night was not one of my best, true. But you must understand that I was getting married the next day and, oh, my mind was away from the hockey game."

The scouts also blew one of the fundamental principles of scouting: overestimating an opponent rarely creates problems; underestimating one almost always does. In their defence, even Sinden—generally the most respectful of the Soviets' skills and the most concerned about Canadian overconfidence—somehow let it slip to Reyn Davis of the *Winnipeg Free Press* that "he could whip the Russians with the 16 players he will have to sit out."

Overconfidence was a virus, and they'd all caught it.

Virtually drowned out by the chest-thumping were a few voices in the wilderness who warned of trouble ahead. The *Montreal Star*'s John Robertson had travelled to Moscow a few years earlier to watch the Soviets play. He bravely insisted his colleagues were way off and picked the Soviets to win the series, six games to two, including all four in Moscow. He even offered a counter to Beddoes's wager: "If Canada wins four games I'll eat this column with Russian dressing at centre ice in the Forum on any day Sam Pollock would care to name."

On the eve of the opening ceremonies, the *Montreal Gazette* published the predictions of nine respected prognosticators, including Hall of Fame goalie Jacques Plante and the biggest voices in U.S. and Canadian sports journalism. The panelists' picks added up to 66–5–1 for Canada, or better than a 7–1 average, with the *Boston Globe* concluding, "Eight-nothing Canada, and that's the score of the first game."

Eagleson added, "Anything other than an unblemished sweep of the Russians would bring shame down on the heads of the players and the national pride."

But buried in the pile of prognostications was probably the most accurate assessment of what had already occurred before the puck had been dropped. Simply by setting up the series itself, and on the Soviets' terms, John Robertson declared, "We have taken one hundred years of hockey heritage and shoved it into the centre of the table and staked it on the outcome of an eight-game series in which we sat back and allowed the deck to be stacked against us."

Whatever happened next, every word of that paragraph was true.

10

QUIET CONFIDENCE

Ken Dryden's father, Murray, was a salesman who settled in Etobicoke, a Toronto suburb. Ken's brother, Dave, six years his senior, built a great backyard rink on asphalt, where the neighbourhood kids gathered to skate in the winter and play ball hockey in the summer. Whenever Dave's friends complained about including his brother, Dave would tell them, "If Kenny doesn't play, you don't play."

Competing with kids six years older taught Ken that, if he was going to play far above his age group, he needed to possess more confidence than his peers. He developed this muscle at a young age by playing baseball, winning an Etobicoke city championship in basketball, and giving speeches to his classmates in Grade 7.

"We had all been in new situations before," Dryden says today, "and the question was: Could we recognize that, and trust that?"

Dave Dryden managed to get to the NHL as a backup during the final years of the Original Six—one of only 12 goalies to make an NHL roster. Ken eschewed junior hockey to play for Cornell University, winning the NCAA title his sophomore year, 1966–67, and losing only four games over his last two seasons.

A few days after his last college game, Dryden joined the

Canadian national team. In the 1969 World Championship, Canada won four and lost six, finishing far from the medal stand. The Soviets won their seventh straight World Championship, led by Boris Mikhailov, Valeri Kharlamov, Vladimir Petrov, Alexander Maltsev, and Alexander Yakushev—players Dryden would see again.

A year later the Canadiens signed Dryden to play for the Montreal Voyageurs, their top minor-league affiliate. In September of 1970, during the Canadiens' training camp in Halifax, they put Dryden in net for an exhibition game against the Chicago Black Hawks, who had finished the previous regular season atop the league.

"They've got Bobby Hull and Stan Mikita," Dryden recalls, "and oh my God, things I've never seen before: more speed, more talent, more everything. The pressure you feel is the *fear* you feel—the fear of doing something you've never done before, and you have no idea if you can do it now."

To handle it, Dryden drew on the same confidence he had developed when he gave a speech at a school assembly in Grade 7, or played in his town's basketball championship game, or started in the NCAA title game as a sophomore.

On the one hand, Dryden knew, "Whatever I had done before in squirts, or juniors, or at Cornell, was nothing like what I was about to face. That's what everybody said, and I believed it. [But] once you take the ice and prepare your crease, and you start taking shots, you find that, 'No, actually, I have been here before, and it's not that different. I can do this.'

"What gets you through these moments is not to focus on anything but what you're doing, in that moment: your angles, your movements, the fundamentals of stopping a puck. You've done this before, and you can do it again. But don't think about all the rest of it—the sweater you're wearing, the sweaters they're wearing, the big names on the ice. None of it matters. Just the fundamentals.

"I'd go through this mental exercise at each step along the way, but I only found words for this later. 'You can never know that you can do something. You just can't know that you *can't* do it.' You cannot know beforehand how it's going to turn out, but that's okay. If you think you know, then you're probably too pumped up about yourself and too arrogant, or you're too fearful of the moment and it will all fall apart before it even begins. That part of it I was actually pretty good at: not getting too high or too low before anything even happened."

Given the opportunity of a lifetime in Halifax, a make-or-break moment, Dryden remained calm, cool, and collected, focusing on the puck and not the famous players shooting it. He knocked back all but one shot from the high-powered Black Hawks en route to a 3–1 victory. He had taken the next step.

Six months later, on March 14, 1971, in the last weeks of a regular season that had seen the Canadiens flounder with goalie Rogie Vachon injured and his backups struggling, the club called up Dryden to start against Pittsburgh. Relying on the same mental approach that had allowed him to take the next step again and again, Dryden won his first NHL game, 5–1. Encouraged, Montreal stuck with Dryden for five more regular-season games—and watched the untested goalie win all five.

What his teammates remember most about Dryden, however, is not his ability, but his intense focus and deep confidence.

"The thing about Kenny was that it didn't matter if it was a Stanley Cup Final or a practice drill," Frank Mahovlich recalls. "He was locked in. He took every shot seriously. When Dryden played five or six games for us at the end of the season, I'm saying to Fergie, 'He's better than Rogie!' And Rogie was a great goaltender!"

"In practice Cournoyer and [Jacques] Lemaire would come down and fire the puck," Frank's brother, Pete, remembers, "and they'd have no idea where it's going—on net, wide, over Dryden's head, whatever. But Kenny never, ever got upset. He was focused. He *hated* to be scored against in practice!"

The Montreal brass made the gutsy decision to ride the hot rookie in the playoffs as far as they could go. In the first round Montreal faced the defending Stanley Cup champion Boston Bruins, who had finished eight wins ahead of the next best team and 15 ahead of Montreal. The Canadiens lost the first game and were losing the second, 5–1, before coming back with six unanswered goals to win, 7–5. Dryden had collected himself to shut out the Bruins for the second half of the game.

"He had great composure," Frank Mahovlich says. "He had *such* confidence."

"Even in the Stanley Cup [playoffs]," Pete adds, "Boston scored five in one game and seven in the other. But Kenny came back to play great in the seventh game, and we won, 4–2."

"[Guy] Lafleur said it best," Frank says. "Dryden was great, but when Kenny played bad, he *really* played bad. But he knew how to bounce back."

"Those playoffs," Dryden recalls, "it was all supposed to be so different from the regular-season games. But it really wasn't. The bigger leap had already been made when we were playing against the Black Hawks in Halifax."

When the Canadiens travelled to Chicago to face Tony Esposito and the Black Hawks in the first game of the 1971 Cup Final, Dryden faced 58 shots and let in only two—but the second was the overtime winner. Entering the sixth game, down three games to two, Dryden let in only three goals for the win, then just two in the seventh game to help secure a 3–2 victory and Montreal's 17th Stanley Cup. The new guy had played only six regular-season games before starting all 20 playoff games to win his first Stanley Cup, plus the Conn Smythe Trophy as the playoff MVP.

The next year, 1971–72, Dryden proved it was no fluke, starting 64 games for Montreal and winning the Calder Memorial Trophy as the league's rookie of the year. In the first round of the playoffs, however, a very strong Rangers squad knocked out Montreal, 4–2.

So, even after putting in a good camp for Team Canada, Dryden did not think it was a given that Sinden would pick him to start the series. The fact that Game One would be played at the Montreal Forum might have been the deciding factor, but Sinden also assumed he could start any of his three goalies and win handily.

Sinden was probably right about one thing: it wouldn't have mattered which goalie he picked.

PART II

Into the Abyss

11

STRANGE VIBES

From the minute Sinden woke up the morning of Saturday, September 2, he started riding a roller coaster of emotions that ran right up to the opening faceoff.

"You try to fortify yourself in case the unexpected happens. A coach not only prepares his team, somewhere in the deepest recesses of his brain, he also gets himself prepared to lose," he recorded that day. "And I don't care who the coach is, or how cocky he acts, unless he's a complete moron he's afraid of losing, no matter how big a favourite he is."

Pete Mahovlich took a different tack. "I figured it's just a game," he recalls.

But his brother, Frank, a natural worrier, was one of the few who sensed trouble. "I was bothered right off the bat," he says. "I had experience with winning teams and losing teams, and I know what each of them do. And the winning teams have a routine, and they stick to it. When I played in Toronto and Montreal, Stanley Cup teams, we were always prepared for the game. You had a time for everything, and you stuck to your routines religiously.

"We didn't have that."

The players who were dressing for the first game went

through a light skate at the Forum from noon to 12:30, while the 16 others attended a luncheon.

"When we went out for our morning skate," Frank recalls, "the Russians were still on the ice. They were already playing games with us, but we didn't seem to care. I thought, 'We're too loose. We're not ready.'

"I didn't like it. It wasn't like being on the Maple Leafs or the Canadiens.

"I go to the Zamboni guy, I say, 'Get them off! And if you don't, *we'll* get them off!' Phil fires the puck right over their net, and the bloody puck's going over their heads, and they don't flinch! They just keep skating.

"I didn't like it.

"I'm looking at our team, and we're going to play four lines, and [Toronto and Montreal] never played four lines.

"A lot of things were bugging me. *The vibe was not right*.

"I didn't like it."

After the morning skate, Team Canada met next door in the Montreal Junior Canadiens' locker room to go over the game plan one last time. Sinden's strategy entailed applying maximum offensive pressure; sticking to their NHL style; shooting early, often, and from every angle to expose the Soviets' shaky goaltending; and being aggressive but avoiding fighting.

Sinden believed if they could hit the Soviets "with a couple of quick goals, they might panic."

"I left that meeting feeling exceptionally good," Sinden wrote. "I felt that if we played just an adequate game by our standards, there was no way the Russian team could beat us. This feeling was with me throughout the afternoon, and I know the players felt the same way."

After the players had a short walk, a nap, and their pre-game meal, they took cabs to the rink 90 minutes before game time. Sinden left a little later because he didn't like to get to the rink more than an hour before game time. He never liked hanging around the players beforehand, either, because he feared that would leave him with nothing to say for his pregame talk.

Shortly before Sinden got in the cab, his emotional roller coaster ran back downhill in a stomach-churning swoop.

"Frankly, I started to be a little afraid at this point," he wrote. "I knew we weren't in the condition [the Soviets] were and I had the feeling maybe . . . maybe we're not quite as good as I thought we were. This is when, about 50 minutes before the game, I felt most afraid of losing."

Sinden planned to spend the last 15 minutes alone, going over the final thoughts he'd soon deliver to his players. But in the middle of his meditation he was interrupted by the official scorer, who asked for his lineup. Since they had negotiated months ago that Canada would be the home team in Canada, and the Soviets in Moscow, Sinden was surprised when the scorer said the Soviets wouldn't give him their starting lineup, which the visiting team is obligated to provide first.

Assuming the Soviets would start their top line, featuring Valeri Kharlamov, Sinden would counter with Clarke's line, "our fastest group," and also the best defensively. But without seeing the Soviets' lineup first, he was stymied.

"This really bugged me," he wrote. "Just one of their cute little tricks."

Sinden told the shaken game official to go back to the Soviets and get their lineup. The Soviets hassled the official again before finally handing it over. When the scorer returned to Sinden, he saw the Soviets weren't starting Kharlamov's line, so he countered by starting the Esposito line, saving Clarke's line for Kharlamov's.

Sinden believed Team Canada's superior talent would make the issue moot. But, he admitted, "I just didn't want them to get away with something that might give them the idea they could get away with anything they liked."

This would prove prescient.

Sinden might have noticed something else: while he would be dressing only five defencemen, Bobrov had decided to dress seven.

Also unbeknownst to Sinden, while he was haggling with the Soviets through the official scorer, his players were experiencing just what he'd hoped they would: a bolt of national pride—at just the right time.

They got ready in the Canadiens' dressing room, adorned with the line from the famous World War I poem "In Flanders Fields," written by Canadian physician and soldier John McCrae: "To you from failing hands we throw the torch; be yours to hold it high."

When they pulled the national jerseys over their heads, they sensed just how special the opportunity was.

"It was very emotional, actually," Ratelle says. "You're playing for your country now. Okay, maybe you think it's going to be easy, but you have to go and play the game. We had underestimated them—no question about that—but I don't think we underestimated what it *meant*."

But then, how could they? The Cold War was everywhere around them, from Reykjavik to Munich to Montreal. In the fall of 1972 the unrelenting battle between East and West seemed to permeate every endeavour.

And this wasn't chess or basketball. This was Canada's sport, arguably the nation's strongest unifying force. Canada's hockey dominance was one of the few things that *hadn't* been questioned since World War II.

When the United States escalated its involvement in Vietnam, its closest ally, Canada, stayed home, increasing tensions between the long-time friends. At a press conference in 1971, Prime Minister Pierre Trudeau opined that the United States posed "a danger to our national identity from a cultural, economic, and perhaps even military point of view."

President Nixon responded privately, referring to Trudeau as "that asshole."

When Nixon's comment went public, Trudeau memorably replied, "I've been called worse things by better people," and won the round.

But Canada didn't need the United States to spark an identity crisis. By 1972 Canada's own identity crisis was well under way.

The design for Canada's flag, one of the world's most instantly recognizable, was actually submitted as a rough draft. But they decided to approve it as is in 1964—just eight years before the series.

In 1967, when French president and World War II hero Charles de Gaulle prepared a speech to be given in Montreal, after years of French Canadians suffering second-class status, he privately predicted, "They will hear me over there. It will make waves!"

He was surely right about that. De Gaulle's speech, delivered from the balcony of Montreal's city hall, rose to a stirring crescendo with this ringing line: "*Vive le Québec libre!*" Long live free Quebec! With those words, he promised France's tacit support for Quebec's separatist movement.

Prime Minister Lester B. Pearson was furious and immediately cut short the rest of de Gaulle's visit, but it was too late. De Gaulle had lit the fuse on a powder keg within the province. Three years later, in October 1970, a terrorist organization called the Front de libération du Québec (FLQ) made headlines around the world by bombing sites throughout the province, kidnapping the British trade commissioner in Montreal, and kidnapping and murdering Pierre Laporte, a Quebec provincial cabinet minister—all part of the FLQ's effort to win independence for the province.

Canada's new prime minister, Pierre Trudeau, invoked the War Measures Act, effectively declaring martial law to quell the uprising. But the nation was still wrestling with this new fissure in the age-old issue of Anglo-French relations in 1972. It raised one tangible question—Would Quebec leave Canada?—and a number of less tangible ones, including: What, exactly, *is* Canada's national identity?

"In Canada, we're always apologizing," Rod Seiling says. "Look at any Canadian town on July 1, and any American town on July 4, and count the flags. It speaks to the point."

What could possibly unify Canada's 22 million people, roughly one-tenth the population of its neighbour to the south, scattered across a land mass 20 percent larger than the continental United States?

Sinden himself had an answer: "Canada is first in the world in two things: hockey and wheat."

And nobody watches wheat.

It is not just because Canadians invented hockey that it's their national sport. They also invented lacrosse, which doesn't have a hold on the people like hockey does. Hockey perfectly reflects Canada's national character, because it has shaped it—and been shaped by it.

Hockey is not easy. Just to play it, you need an unusually high threshold for biting cold and pain. To play it well, you must have the lungs of a runner and the strength of a gymnast, the balance of a skier and the hands of a golfer. Until they start playing water polo with lacrosse sticks or baseball on Rollerblades, no sport requires its players to master as many different elements as hockey does.

The nature of the sport ensures that no single player can dominate a game the way, say, a basketball player can. It's impossible to hang on to the puck for very long, and the game is too exhausting to play more than a couple minutes at a stretch.

Bobby Orr never won a Stanley Cup without Phil Esposito, and Wayne Gretzky never won one without Mark Messier. You need teammates. For decades, most of Canada's best hockey players came from small, cold farming and mining towns, which added to the character of the sport. All these things make hockey players a tough but humble breed—which describes Canada's national identity in a nutshell. Canadians play other sports, and other nations play hockey, but Canada is the world's only country that puts hockey first, second, and third.

There is little question that, in 1972, more Canadians cared about hockey than anything else—their greatest source of national pride, so powerful it transcended the nation's many regional, cultural, ethnic, and religious differences, from Team Canada's players themselves to the sprawling nation they represented. Hockey was the one endeavour in which they would never take a back seat to anyone, the one arena in which they put aside their famously apologetic, self-effacing demeanour and insisted they were the best.

Despite chuckling through Sinden's black-and-white films from the 1958 World Championship in Oslo, right up to the medal ceremony, the players were well aware of the stakes, and their responsibility.

"We were excited," Berenson says, recalling the mood of the locker room before Sinden walked in for his pregame talk. "Prime Minister Trudeau was there. The Forum was *buzzing*.

"We were right in the middle of the Cold War: the Iron Curtain, the race to the moon, Vietnam, and on and on. And it just built from there. But this was *our* part. I don't know how aware we were of the political dynamics we'd be thrust right in the middle of—the series would take on a life of its own before we were done—but everyone knew it was more than a game. It was a test between our system and their system. But this is our sport. *Our sport!*

"With expectations so high, we all thought it was just a matter of how badly we were going to beat them. No one talked otherwise."

═

THANKS to the kerfuffle with the Soviets over the starting line-ups, Sinden didn't have time to collect his thoughts before his pregame talk, but he really didn't need to. They had gone over all this many times.

Sinden kept his strategy session short. "Don't forget," he told them, "we want to play aggressive hockey, but let's not take any foolish penalties. Shoot, and keep shooting."

Then, standing in the centre of the most heralded hockey locker room in the world, a space that had spawned more Stanley Cup champions than any other, Sinden paused before delivering his next message—one he was not at all sure, after his aborted attempt to instill patriotic pride with his grainy, 14-year-old World Championship films, they would listen to. But he still felt it was worth the risk.

He had avoided politics throughout training camp, but now it was time to face the elephant in the room: this was much more than a mere hockey game, and it was foolish to pretend otherwise.

"But most of all," he said, tentatively at first, "I want you to remember this: we're going to play this game for Canada. We're going to play it for the people of the country and for hockey, and what it means to this country. And most of all, we're going to play it for ourselves and our own reputations. I want you to think of how hard you worked these last weeks and what you gave up to be here. Now we're laying our reptations on the line for the world to see. That's why I want any benefits that will go with winning this game and this series to go to you. You've earned it."

Sinden did not know how deep his players' quiet patriotism really ran. But he knew instantly, as any good coach does, that his speech had hit the mark. They were pumped up, and quiet, until Pete Mahovlich let loose a yell that got to everyone.

"We were like caged animals," Henderson wrote. "We were so pumped up, it was crazy. Everyone in the country had been talking about this series for so long that we were at a fever pitch, eager to finally get at it."

When the players started putting on their gloves, Sinden spontaneously started walking around the dressing room to meet each player, one by one, and give them a final message of support—"Good luck," "I hope you perform to the best of your ability," and so on. He always made eye contact, and they returned it.

"I didn't plan what happened, but it became very emotional," he wrote. "I could see clearly that these players—these men who really weren't supposed to care about anything but money—were very touched by this game.

"I had never experienced that kind of a feeling with a team before. It wasn't like a Stanley Cup game where 'the money on the line' is what the players react to. It was 'I'm playing for the postman, the milkman and every other Canadian in the world who ever put on skates and thought about being the best in the world, if only in his dreams.'

"This reaction was a complete surprise to me. I always felt that in order to have a feeling of 'team' among a group of players, they must first experience something together. They must win, win a big game when their guts are on the line, when their courage and ability are being questioned.

"But tonight that feeling of team was there in that room just before the faceoff for only one reason. They were Russia. We were Canada. They were the new guys on the block and we weren't about to let them take our territory from us."

They didn't know it yet, but their preparation had been insufficient, their strategy far off the mark. But their deep sense of national pride had been beating from the start.

12

GAME ONE: WHEN LEGEND BECOMES MYTH

September 2, 1972

When the players stepped onto the ice, with the Forum's temperature already at 23 degrees Celsius (73 Fahrenheit) and rising, they were met by 18,818 screaming fans.

More than 15 million Canadians, out of a population of 22 million, watched from homes, bars, and restaurants, plus millions of Americans and Europeans, and many of the 125 million Soviets, where the game started well after 2 a.m. in Moscow and Leningrad.

"After months of talking about it," Gretzky recalls, "here it was. *Finally.* We didn't have a colour TV, but luckily the first people we knew who had one were our next-door neighbours and good friends, Mary and Sil Rizzetto. They weren't big hockey fans, but they let us come over to watch. It was the first time I'd ever seen a hockey game in colour. Pretty cool, to say the least. I'll never forget it."

But the Gretzkys and everyone else would have to wait, since the organizers had set up 20 minutes of pregame ceremonies. All the anticipation in the world, however, could not erode the dividing lines that five decades of NHL play had carefully constructed, even among the fans.

The players were introduced in numerical order. Because Rod Seiling held rank over the younger Bob Clarke, he wore 16, while Clarke wore number 28, putting him between Frank Mahovlich (27) and Ken Dryden (29)—both Montreal Canadiens. Clarke still remembers Mahovlich getting a standing ovation, followed by dead silence for him, then another standing ovation for Dryden.

"Well," he says with a chuckle, "you knew where you stood."

"Terrible!" Pete Mahovlich says, recalling the same scene. "But the point is, even the fans in Canada weren't fans of *Team Canada*. They were fans of Montreal. So they were booing Clarkie and the Bruins. And that meant that the rest of our team wasn't really playing at home. They were playing an away game in Montreal, just like always."

The fans were living in the same silos the players were.

"I can't recall any game that I've ever been at where you can just *feel* the tension," Foster Hewitt told TV viewers from the Atlantic to the Pacific, "and it keeps building up, and it's very warm in the Forum tonight, and at the same time the fans are really on their toes. They hardly can wait to see the beginning of this game."

For the ceremonial faceoff, Prime Minister Pierre Trudeau walked out on the red carpet to do the honours.

"I remember the opening faceoff," said Vladimir Vikulov, who took the draw against Phil Esposito. "I knew this faceoff was symbolic. I didn't know why, but I really wanted to win it. At the last second, I decided not to fight for the puck. I thought it would look strange."

Vikulov backed off, and Esposito—not willing to let the puck sit there, as is customary—quickly swept it behind him, to outsized cheers.

When Ken Dryden watched the Soviet starting five skate onto the ice for the real opening faceoff, "My lips became tense. My jaw jutted out. My back stiffened. Determination had settled in. I thought I was ready."

But what did anyone know? They were essentially facing the Martians.

"Before the game," Sinden wrote, "I had told anyone who would listen, 'Just let me see them on the ice for five minutes and I'll tell you how tough the Russians are.'"

On the very first shift, the Canadians worked the puck beautifully to send a three-on-two over the Soviet blue line. When Bergman flicked the puck behind the net to the right corner, Cournoyer flew in to take the puck, then fed it to Park sneaking into the slot. The defenceman then passed to Frank Mahovlich on the back door, who banged it at Tretiak. When Tretiak bobbled it, Phil Esposito whacked it out of mid-air, baseball-style, right into the net.

Within 10 seconds, all five Canadian players had passed or shot the puck effectively, validating Sinden's decision to start Esposito's line and save Clarke's line to check Kharlamov's.

"Some of the guys [on the bench] looked back at me," Sinden recalls today, "and I felt like a damn genius."

The players and fans celebrated much more than an opening goal would normally warrant—but this wasn't a normal opening goal. The series would last 28,800 seconds, but it seemed like Canada needed only the first 30 to confirm its superiority. The crowd, the coaches, and the players all reacted as if Esposito had scored with 30 seconds left in the last game, not 30 seconds into the first one.

"I had never seen a bench react that wildly to a goal in the first half-minute," Sinden wrote.

"We scored right off the bat," Dryden remembers, "and you think, 'It's exactly as everyone thought. This is going to be a whitewash.' But then the game started going back and forth, back and forth. And the Soviets were *flying*—no problem keeping up with us at all. That got my attention. They were not taking it to us, but we weren't dominating them, either, as we'd expected. Just a few minutes in, I remember starting to feel that *this was a game*."

Henderson shared Dryden's early uneasiness. "I remember my first shift," he recalls. "I'm panting for air, and I look at this [Russian] guy, and he's not even breathing, and I said, 'Oh my God. Something's up.' You knew it early."

When Sinden recalled his statement that he needed to watch the Soviets for only five minutes to assess how tough they were going to be, he wrote, "I was wrong. I needed only three minutes. In the two minutes following Phil's goal the Russians tore up and down the ice, making beautiful passes, taking beautiful passes, getting their men in position, outskating us to loose pucks, and doing everything but putting it into the net. It was right then I knew the Russians were everything I didn't want them to be, and everything we were led to believe they wouldn't be."

Six minutes and two seconds after Esposito's opener, however, Clarke won the faceoff cleanly back to Ellis, who tapped it toward Henderson, who fired it into the lower right corner for Team Canada's second goal.

"Clarke's line didn't take a while to get going," Dennis Hull says. "They just took off and left. No one was second-guessing Harry on that."

With the Canadians taking a 2–0 lead in the game's first six and a half minutes, the players, the media, and even the scouts all seemed to be right: the Soviets were in way over their heads, with Tretiak looking every bit as bad as the scouts had promised.

"When we scored the second goal," Dryden says, "you think, 'Well, maybe I was wrong. Nothing to be worried about.'"

Sinden now looked like Nostradamus, his plan working to

perfection. As he'd said, if they could "hit them with a couple of quick goals, they might panic."

Now, seeing it all unfold before him exactly as he'd hoped, he was even more certain. "Our rink, our crowd, and a two-goal lead just a few shifts in?" Sinden says. "Are you kidding?"

It seemed all the Canadians had to do was keep pressuring the Soviets and wait for their inevitable collapse. It was all over but the shouting.

But a funny thing happened: nothing. The Soviets didn't panic. They didn't collapse. They stuck to their own game plan and put the pressure back on the Canadians.

"Up 2–0, that was great," Ratelle agrees, "but even up 2–0, they were already better than we thought. You could see that. They could skate. And dressing only five D, that was a mistake! They were in much better condition, and it was very, very, *very* hot. Probably as hot as I've ever seen for a game. And when it *is* that hot, it's the playoffs, and you're getting used to it bit by bit. Here, *boom*!"

When Henderson came back to the bench after his goal, he didn't gloat. He was breathing too hard. When he finally caught his breath, "I remember saying these exact words to Ronnie [Ellis]: 'This is gonna be a looooong series.' You could see it in the first few minutes.

"I was in better shape than most, and I was hustling. *And I couldn't catch them*. And that's when it hits you: we've been sucked in. Duped. The bad scouting, the bad practice they had, their funny skates—we'd bought the whole thing. And now you realize you have eight games of this? It was just a *sickening* feeling."

Henderson's dread soon spread through his teammates, whether on the ice or in the stands.

"I was sitting in the corner of the Forum," Dale Tallon recalls, "just in shock. After Henderson's goal they were barely letting us touch the puck. So it turned out three weeks doing jumping jacks in our underwear wasn't enough? Oops."

"I never watched them practise at all," Phil Esposito says. "Didn't want to. Didn't care. I thought it would be played like the All-Star Games now—no one hits anyone, it's all just for fun, an exhibition. I score the first goal, then Hendie scores. Easy, right? But then a few shifts later we're like, 'Holy Christ!' We weren't in good enough shape to keep up with them. Boy, what a rude awakening. Wow. *WOW!*"

Six minutes after Henderson's goal, the inevitable happened: Vladimir Shadrin passed to Alexander Yakushev in the corner. He fired a slick pass to Yevgeni Zimin on the other side of the net, who converted for their first goal.

"The most important goal in my hockey career was the first Soviet goal of the series," Zimin said years later. "I only played two games but I shall always remember the red light shining behind Ken Dryden's back in the first period in Montreal."

Dryden had gotten so spun around on the play, he ended up falling down, facing the crossbar, and had to pull himself up by grabbing the net.

"They keep coming at us, and finally they score," Ratelle recalls. "Then they took over the game a little bit. We were not used to each other, and we were not in good enough shape. Then it all came down so fast, you didn't have time to think."

"They're passing so sharp, skating so well, and they're picking it up a notch," Clarke says, "a notch we didn't have. For me it was about the 15-minute mark. That's when I knew we were in trouble."

As Sinden predicted, panic ensued—but it wasn't the Soviets who lost their heads. The Canadians started chasing the Russians around the rink, trying to hit anything that moved—exactly what the Soviets hoped they would do.

Still ahead, 2–1, with a few minutes left in the period, the Canadians went on the power play—one of their great strengths, they believed, especially with the offensive powerhouse Sinden had dressed for Game One—with a chance to restore their two-goal lead. Instead the Soviets broke loose on a two-on-one, with Mikhailov shooting and Petrov following up for an easy rebound to tie the game at 2–2 with 2:32 left in the first. Dryden, on his backside, whacked the puck away in frustration—something he almost never did.

"Even after our second goal, they don't go away," he recalls. "It's a game again, going back and forth, and they score, and they score again, and now it's 2–2 at the end of the first."

On paper, a 2–2 game? No problem. But the Canadians already knew better. Two thoughts dominated the locker room: the Soviets' conditioning was light years ahead of the Canadians'; and the yawning gap between the Canadian professionals and the Soviets—a decades-long belief—was not merely grossly exaggerated, it no longer existed. The first epiphany was alarming; the second demoralizing.

"I have a vivid memory," Dryden recalls, "of Harry coming into the locker room, standing in the middle of the room and saying, 'Well, you didn't think it was going to be easy, did you?' And we said, 'Well, no. No! Of course not!' But the truth is: we *all* did.

"In the locker room it was less a feeling of being gassed, though we were, than 'This is a game, a real game. This is a real series—and we have seven games and two periods left.' That's a long way to go."

The same locker room that had been all energy and optimism just a half-hour earlier had fallen dead silent. No one shouted. Few talked. The loudest sound was players panting.

"Christ, I couldn't *breathe* in the first game!" the normally high-flying Gilbert recalls.

It was bad for the forwards, and worse for the blueliners.

"We only had five defencemen," Park says, "and we were sucking wind. We learned pretty quick that there were other guys out there who can play the game pretty well, too.

"One period. That's all it took.

"When Bergie turned to me and said, 'Whaddya think?' I said, 'I think we're in trouble.'"

That sinking feeling had ripples.

"Sitting there, sweating, you knew that our scouting was wrong about everything," Ratelle says. "It was not going to be easy; it was going to be a battle to the end. We had to figure out, *now*: What do we have to do?"

Retreating was not an option. They would have to stand and fight, with what they had, as best they could.

THE score was far less worrisome to the Canadians than the speed of the contest. In the second period the pace never let up, driven entirely by the Soviets—with the heat and humidity getting worse by the minute and approaching lethal levels. According to the *Montreal Gazette*, the temperature in the old Forum soared to a suffocating 46 Celsius (115 Fahrenheit). That softened the ice, which only made everything—skating, stickhandling, passing, and shooting—harder for the Canadians.

"The soft ice just highlighted the superiority of the Soviets' conditioning," Sinden says. "They had trained for this."

Even Sinden, the most cautious member of Team Canada, was shocked by what he had just seen.

"I knew they had good players," he says today. "I really didn't think I had underestimated them. But I didn't think they had *one* player who could play in the NHL. By the middle of the first game, you knew: *every one* of them could play in the NHL. So I guess I was a little off."

Just a couple minutes into the second period, Kharlamov skated in alone on Seiling and Awrey—not the kind of situation that strikes fear into the hearts of NHL coaches, since the forward will rarely get so much as a decent shot off. But when Kharlamov looked as if he intended to split the defencemen, and

Awrey bought it, Kharlamov flew around him to the outside, forcing Awrey to lunge and dive at him going by. Then Kharlamov cut back in on Dryden and snapped a quick forehand into the far corner—3–2.

Phil Esposito and Frank Mahovlich, on the bench, leaned back in amazement.

Eight minutes later, at the midpoint of the contest, Maltsev won the faceoff at the Soviet blue line and Kharlamov picked it up, got Rod Seiling crossing his legs, then fired a "bullet drive" past Dryden's glove to put the Soviets up, 4–2.

"It had Dryden beaten all the way," colour commentator Brian Conacher said. This time Dryden just flicked the puck out of the net, his anger drained.

"Whatever they're doing," Ratelle thought, "they can do it with their eyes closed."

"When we came in after the second period," Berenson says, "I'm looking around the locker room at all the guys sweating and trying to catch their breath—there were some long faces—and I'm thinking, 'We're working our tails off—and we're whipped!' At the start of the series, their fitness was the main difference. They were in playoff shape. We've already hit the wall—and we had 20 minutes to go. You knew then the first period was no fluke. We'd been snookered. That's when I realized we were in trouble—real trouble."

So did Alan Eagleson. After the second period he headed to the dressing room on the double, "to see what the fuck is happening."

Who did he bump into but Gary Smith, the Canadian official who first read about the Soviets' interest in a real series in *Izvestia*.

Smith saw Eagleson and said, "Holy shit, are they ever good!"

Eagleson replied, "'Gary, fuck you, you're a fucking communist. Fuck off!' Last time I spoke to him in the series."

Tensions were a little high.

═

AFTER confronting the stunning gap in conditioning and the mind-blowing fact that the Soviet players were every bit as good as they were—two thoughts hard to swallow in themselves—the Canadians slowly started recognizing through the fog that the Soviets were playing a game they had never seen before.

"*How* they played was something else, too," Berenson says. "The skill level was terrific. They used their feet so well, and were so good with the puck. They'd make five or six passes before they got their shot off—and wow! Where did *that* guy come from? They were making backdoor passes on their off wings, something we didn't do. And the D would join the rush like the forwards. We were not just physically whipped, but mentally whipped, too. All of this was new to us."

"The cycling in our zone," Phil Esposito recalls, shaking his head. "Everyone does it now, but we'd never seen it. We didn't know what the hell they were doing—and we wouldn't know what to call it if we did!"

"I admired their lateral movement," said Pat Stapleton, who sat in the stands that first night. "That's something we just didn't teach or do—maybe because we didn't even think it was a good idea."

The Soviets' endless movement, fuelled by unmatched passing and stickhandling and usually culminating in a wrist or snap shot, was supported by their sticks—different ones than the Canadians were giggling about the day before, when they watched the Soviets practice: Sher-Woods, Kohos, and "Montreal Surprise."

"In Moscow, good sticks are hard to find," Stapleton later learned, "so they didn't want to break them with slapshots. They cut them much shorter than we did, too. Better for puck-handling. For them, passing and wrist shots trumped the slapshot—and we saw a lot of that."

The Canadians were also surprised by the Soviets' truly

foreign habit of regrouping in the neutral zone—a definite no-no in the NHL.

"I played for Punch Imlach in Toronto," Henderson says. "Man, if you *ever* went back [with the puck], he'd kill you! And what are the Soviets doing? Going back and regrouping if they didn't like what they saw—again and again, until they were ready to go in. I'd never seen anything like it.

"They were such a well-oiled machine, you could barely tell the difference between their lines. They all did the same things, and could change all five guys without losing the puck. Nobody in the NHL did that. We didn't know that was something you *could* do.

"Every time we thought they were going to shoot, they passed, and every time we thought they were going to pass, they'd shoot. Never felt so bad for a goalie as I did for Kenny that night. I felt sorry for him—honest to God I did."

"Kenny couldn't go side to side," Phil Esposito says. "But in the NHL he didn't have to. We didn't play that style, and he had D in Montreal to clear the rebounds."

"Kenny's a big guy," Park says, "which is normally an advantage. But the Russians didn't go north and south and shoot when they crossed the blue line like we did. They'd go east and west and east again, and just kept passing until someone was open, then shoot a one-timer off the pass. We never did any of that. Kenny had to make some changes."

But then, they all did. The Soviets had pried the Canadians from their game, rendering Sinden's game plan moot. When the Canadians made one of their countless attempts to line up a Soviet for a big hit, he'd just slip away. When the Canadians forechecked, the Soviets embarrassed them with long passes to start an odd-man rush. And when the Canadians dropped to block a shot, the Soviets simply skated around them and looked for their next pass.

Dryden saw all this, but he was more consumed by the stark

reality that they had just started a really hard series and still had a long way to go.

"The second period only reinforced that feeling at each stage," Dryden remembered, "and they finished us off in the third."

FOR the third period, Sinden decided to sit Jean Ratelle's line—the Goal-a-Game trio that had set the NHL record for scoring just a few months earlier—because they seemed to be the most vulnerable to the skating and passing wizardry of the Soviets.

But that meant three lines would have to play against the Soviets' four during one of the hottest nights the NHL players had ever seen. Since they were dressing only five defencemen, an already hard task became harder.

Nonetheless, eight minutes into the final period, Team Canada showed some fight when Henderson hit Ellis in the high slot; Ellis then shot the puck to the right corner, where Clarke deflected it into the net for the team's third goal. Despite the balance of play, the Canadians were down just 4–3 with 11 minutes remaining, and at home, no less. That allowed the fans to believe this nightmare could still be banished.

A few minutes later Cournoyer came within an inch of tying the game when he hit the post—only to see the Soviets take the rebound and rush down the ice, where Mikhailov waited out Dryden until he dropped first, then pinged his shot off the pipe. Unlike Cournoyer's, however, Mikhailov's went in, causing Seiling to bang his stick on the ice like an axe.

Just like that, instead of a 4–4 game it was 5–3, and the Canadians collapsed.

"The wheels?" Henderson asks rhetorically. "Oh my God, did they ever come off that night."

"Middle of the second period, we're already on fumes, and they're flying," Seiling says. "We're trying to hit everything that moves, and if you're not in shape, that wears you out, too! By the third period you're reduced to a traffic cop, just directing guys past you. But you don't want to embarrass yourself. We were unprepared for a variety of reasons. But you never give up."

No matter how badly the Soviets had ambushed the Canadians, on paper, the game was still in the balance with seven minutes left. But then, as Dryden reflected the next day, "Being down by one or two goals is not a disaster, but we reacted like the sky had fallen."

That helps explain how the Soviets scored three goals in rapid succession by Mikhailov, Zimin—his second—and Yakushev, all coming between 6:28 and 1:23 left in the game. Lafleur had been right: when Dryden was off, he was really off.

Final score: Soviet Union 7, Canada 3.

The Soviets' final three goals didn't change the outcome, but they did change the perception: Team Canada hadn't merely lost; it had been crushed, destroyed, humiliated.

"At the end of the game," Ratelle says, "we knew this was not just a really bad game for us. It was a fiasco. We had a lot of work to do."

"It was a good lesson for anyone who believes that arrogance is the right way to go in sports," Clarke says. "If you're arrogant, it's going to be a lot tougher for you. And we were fucking arrogant."

"In a book called *Twenty-Seven Days in September*," Dryden recalls, "there is this great photograph in a two-page spread. It's taken from behind the Soviet net, up ice toward our net. It's right after a goal, might have been their seventh, with the mist of heat and fog circling our ankles.

"You can see our guys skating back to centre ice for a faceoff. They're bent over and gasping for breath, with a body posture of complete depression, and you can see me at the other end. And I'm leaning on my stick, and behind me the red light is still on.

"It's fantastic, a perfect picture. The whole story is right there.

"It was one of those moments where you think, 'Can I have a do-over here? Can this be five weeks earlier? Can we think about this differently, can we approach it differently, can we prepare differently so we're ready for this?'

"And of course the answer is no. You can't go back. Now we're into something that we're not ready for. It's not the way we imagined it would go, not in a million years, but we have to find a way—a new way—and fast."

13

THE RECKONING

The reckoning was swift and severe—within the team and across the country. Because there was no TSN, talk radio, internet, or Sunday newspapers in Canada in 1972, the coaches and players would be spared the brunt of their nation's scorn for 36 hours. But they would not be spared their own thoughts.

If the locker room had been quiet after the first and second periods, after the third it was a morgue.

"Oh hell," Berenson recalls, shaking his head. "That was 'wow!' You looked around, and no one was talking. No one had to. You didn't know what to say anyway. It was just, 'What the hell just happened out there?' We were in shock. I can think of no better word for it. Everyone who came in the locker room started walking around, dazed, like there'd been a death in the family."

For Team Canada, Game One felt like taking an exam, only to discover you had not studied nearly hard enough—or even read the right books. But in Team Canada's case, they would have to figure out what they had missed during the exam itself, which would resume in two days.

While they sat staring at their skates or looking off into space, they were interrupted by Alan Eagleson bursting into the room, shouting, "Get the players back out there! The Russians are still on the ice, waiting to shake hands with us."

They did as instructed, but by the time they got back to the rink the last few Soviets were leaving the ice. They had created a minor international incident.

When they returned once again to the locker room, the impossible had happened: Sinden's already rotten mood had taken a turn for the worse. His anger momentarily turned to Hockey Canada, which had agreed to the postgame handshake without bothering to tell Sinden or Eagleson. When Sinden confronted the Hockey Canada officials, they said, "Well, we just assumed you'd know."

The embarrassing faux pas served as an almost comical metaphor for the ignorance, arrogance, miscommunication, and poor preparation among the various parties that led to the Game One debacle in the first place.

Sinden, who couldn't bring himself to talk to the players in the locker room after the game, and Phil Esposito still had to face the media.

"That first game shocked the shit out of me," Phil Esposito says. "I remember when Harry and I were walking toward the press conference, and I said, 'Harry, we're in trouble, man.'

"'I know,' Sinden said.

"I said, 'Harry, you've got to pick a team and stay with it. If I'm not in the lineup, that's fine—but you've got to pick your team. The only way to *beat* this team is to *become* a team. They've been together since they were 13 or 14. We've been together one month. We're not a team. We're a bunch of individuals. We don't feel for one another like we can and should.'

"He said, 'It's hard because we promised everyone's going to play.'

"'Yeah, well, I promised my wife I wouldn't fuck around, but I did.'"

At the press conference, Sinden was refreshingly candid. "They outplayed us everywhere," he said. "We offer no excuses whatsoever."

Privately, Sinden said into his tape recorder, "They skated circles around us and, at the end, they were actually laughing at us. That's the only emotion they showed all night.

"A little piece of all of us died today."

Sports Illustrated concluded, "The Russians skated better, shot better, checked better and hit harder than the Canadians. All night long the Russians beat the Canadians to loose pucks, all night long the Russians were in perfect position to take good, high-percentage shots at Dryden."

An unhappy fan leaving the Forum told *Sports Illustrated*, "This is Canada's worst day since winter wheat sank below a dollar during the Depression."

"I recall early in the first game, Canada going up 2–0," Gretzky says, "and my neighbour said, 'It's gonna be a whitewash, eight games to nothing!' Then all of a sudden the Soviets come back, and it's a game—and then it's not a game. Holy cow. I was just *sick* about it. But now you're hooked. You can't miss a game. You have to watch them all."

Leaving the locker room wasn't safe, either.

"We felt like a train hit us," Rod Gilbert said. "After the game, I saw my brother first. He was my mentor. He's six years older than me. He asked, 'What happened?'

"I said, 'I bought you a ticket. You saw the game. They're good.'

"My brother says, 'No, they're not that good, and you were all horrible.' This is from the one who pushed me up. 'And furthermore, I want you to know you're a disgrace to the country.'

"So this hurts. I still remember it."

After the game, they took a bus to the airport for the flight to Toronto. Dryden sat next to Pat Stapleton, who'd watched the first game from the stands.

On the deathly quiet bus, Dryden whispered, "*What happened?*"

"I shrugged," Stapleton recalled years later. "Then I said, 'Maybe we lost our composure.' But it was bigger than that, and we both knew it."

"I tell ya, two things happened after that game," Sinden says. "When we flew to Toronto, I went to the back of the plane and finally talked to the team as best I could after a whacking like that, and struck the chord I wanted them to hear. I told them, 'We were caught by surprise, and it's shocking, but no pointing fingers, and no blaming yourselves. We lose as a team, we win as a team.'

"I couldn't have them dividing, or getting so far down we couldn't get back up. I got it off my chest. Don't know if it helped.

"We were very late leaving Montreal, so we got to Toronto at two in the morning. I said to Fergie, 'Come on up to my room. We've got to change a few things.'"

While Sinden and Ferguson conducted their autopsy, life happily intervened for Brad Park. After the team checked in to the hotel at 2 a.m., Park had a couple beers with his teammates, who were all trying to make some sense out of what they'd just seen. Then he excused himself, slipped back to his room, and called his wife, Gerry, who was now three weeks overdue with their first child.

"You better get here quick!" she told him, and she meant it.

While Gerry's mom took her to the hospital, Park raced to join them. They arrived a little after 4 a.m., and their son, James, was born at 4:52 a.m.—a time Park can still recite.

"I was over the moon!" Park recalls. "In just a few hours I went from the worst day of my life to the greatest day of my life. And thank God."

The next day Sinden had scheduled an optional skate, so Park told Gilbert, James's new godfather, to tell Sinden he wouldn't be there. His alibi held up. A few took it as a good sign that the proceeds of the "baby pool" set up to guess James's birth date went to Tony Esposito, who would be starting in goal the next night.

Dryden was not so lucky. In the wee hours, tired and spent, he dropped his bags and flopped in his room.

"It was the first time I had a room by myself," he recalls. "On some teams the goalies had their own room, but not the Canadiens. So this was new for me, having no one around when I woke up.

"Back then there were no Sunday newspapers in Toronto. There were no all-sports TV stations, either. So there was really no evidence that Saturday night had happened at all. There was nobody else in that room, and so long as I was by myself, the whole thing might not have happened. I stayed in that room as long as I possibly could, because I knew that as soon as I went out of that room, I'd be confronted by what had happened. It would become real again.

"The only thing that got me out of bed was practice. I knew I had to be there. So I had to walk across the street to the old Maple Leaf Gardens for practice. Once you do that, you know it was no nightmare. This had really happened. Now what?"

First, they had to admit that their scouting report was completely wrong. Tretiak was not the Soviets' biggest weakness, but one of their greatest strengths.

"I figure he took at least five goals from me tonight," Phil Esposito told *Sports Illustrated*.

The Canadians had never seen anything like the Soviet team.

"Possum," Bobby Orr mumbled to *Sports Illustrated,* thinking back to the Soviets' practice the day before with their old equipment. "They were playing possum yesterday."

The stunned silence among the players stood in stark contrast to the national panic outside it. A mere 26 years after Anatoli Tarasov had organized the Soviets' first crude pickup game in an outdoor park, his players had beaten the best team in the world—and with a 7–3 blowout, no less, on Canada's most hallowed ice.

The outcome forced Canadians to question everything they had ever believed about themselves. On Monday, when paper delivery resumed in Canada, the headline of a Montreal daily cried, *"Le Canada Humilié!"*

One NHL executive, who apparently hadn't heard of either world war, called the loss "the catastrophe of the century."

In just 60 minutes, Canada's best team had been reduced to the East York Lyndhursts, the Senior B semifinalists who had been the Soviets' first victims in the 1954 World Championship, 7–2. The NHL All-Stars finished only one goal better than the Lyndhursts—while playing at home.

Canada had been the sport's leader for the first century. But when they finally got that chance to send their best players, it was too late: the world had already caught up.

The nation's assumption that it had been hockey's best since the sport's inception went *poof* in one night. If they weren't the best anymore, they would have to ask themselves: How many years ago had they stopped being the best?

TEAM Canada's immediate concern was Game Two, now less than 48 hours away. They would have to re-engineer their plane in mid-flight.

They might have been underprepared and overconfident, and too ignorant of their opponents to respect them. But nobody staring into space that night in the Canadiens' famed locker room was stupid.

The most pressing question was the simplest: What do we do next? There were no easy answers. They knew they could not go back the way they came.

But crucially, they didn't make a desperate situation worse by blaming each other or giving up. Not one player recalls thinking their cause was lost, when many in the media would soon be saying just that.

Their confidence was in their DNA. They would need every strand.

14

22 MILLION CRITICS

The players slept in the next morning, but Sinden and Ferguson left their rooms early to get a cup of coffee in the hotel restaurant—with a side dish of crow. Neither could sleep very well anyway, so what was the point of suffering solo?

"No question I knew they were coming," Sinden recalls, "but not like *that,* and not against the best players in the league. We knew we would have to tear it all apart and start over—and fast."

The duo took a cab to Maple Leaf Gardens ahead of the team to study the film—and it didn't look any better flashing on the screen than it had on the ice the night before. The film confirmed what their eyes had told them: the Soviets' conditioning, speed, and deft passing really were that impressive.

But in the cool light of day a few things jumped out that they couldn't discern when enveloped by the fog of war the night before. The Soviets had beaten the Canadians in one-on-one situations—and sometimes even one on two—*six times,* though some who've watched it have counted 10.

"You'd have to go to 20 NHL games to see a team get beaten one on one just twice in the same night," Sinden wrote, "and here were guys walking right by us like nothing."

This confirmed their decision not only to bench Awrey for the third period but also to make sweeping changes for Game Two.

If the coaches were tempted to take some solace in the official shot totals, which actually favoured Team Canada, 32–30, these two seasoned hockey men knew better than to distrust their eyes.

Shots on goal, one of the few statistical measures they used 50 years ago, can be quite misleading. Bouncing a shot at the net from the far blue line counts, but a two-on-one that finishes with a shot just an inch wide does not—though clearly the latter is the far more threatening play. To get a better sense of what happened in this series, I asked Evan Hall, the analyst for the University of Michigan's hockey team, to run these eight contests through the same statistical measures NHL teams use today.

Their primary tool is a metric called "scoring chance plus-minus." First, a scoring chance is defined as a "significant scoring opportunity," not necessarily a shot on net, and is therefore a judgment call. The shot from centre ice doesn't count, but the barely missed two-on-one does. Another way to think of it: if you were defending the play, you'd feel lucky to escape without giving up a goal.

The plus-minus aspect is even more sophisticated, requiring the analyst to determine if each player contributed to the play that led to the scoring chance—for or against. For example, the player would get a "plus" if he made the shot or the pass that led to the shot, but so would the player who created the turnover that led to the pass, or even the hit that led to the turnover. A player would get a "minus" for any of the mistakes that led to a quality scoring chance against. When you break all this down by even-strength, shorthanded, or power-play chances, it becomes even clearer.

While each individual call can be tough, if you have a skilled analyst who is consistent throughout the game, by the end of the contest, Hall says, "those statistics will tell a story, one that more accurately reflects how a game actually went than shots on goal."

For example, Awrey came in at minus-2 on even-strength plus-minus scoring chances—and his stats would likely have been worse had the coaches not benched him for the third period. Seiling was not so lucky, as he then had to play every other shift in the third because they were now using only four defencemen.

"What really stands out," Hall concludes, is Seiling finishing at minus-5 on even-strength quality scoring chances. "I have him partially or directly responsible for four of the seven goals against. His [lack of] foot speed was very evident and I am sure the Canadian coaching staff saw the same thing, which relates directly to his playing time the rest of the series."

In fairness to Seiling, who was a top-shelf NHL defenceman, he had been dropped into a fundamentally different competition for which no one was prepared.

On the other end of the defensive spectrum, Park tied for third on the team with three quality even-strength scoring chances, most among the Canadian blueliners, but he was also on the ice for three quality chances against, to finish even. That night, that was good enough to lead all Canadian defencemen.

On offence, modern analytics tell us the GAG Line's Ratelle came in at plus-1 on even-strength chances, while Gilbert was even and Hadfield was minus-2, justifying Sinden's decision to bench them for the third period. In contrast, the trio of Frank Mahovlich, Esposito, and Cournoyer totalled plus-10, thanks largely to Mahovlich's plus-6 on even-strength scoring chances, which would tie the high-water mark for the Canadians for all games in the series—a remarkable accomplishment during the otherwise horrific first game.

What's truly striking, however, is how well Sinden and Ferguson divined all these patterns without the benefit of modern measurements. Their eyes and intuition were working well—two assets Team Canada would need if they were to dig out of the hole they'd created.

═

WATCHING the film the morning after, Sinden and Ferguson realized they had made a central mistake: they'd put their fastest, most skilled offensive players on the ice, yet they still couldn't outskate or outscore the Soviets. Well, Sinden reckoned, if *that* lineup couldn't outskate the Soviets, no one could. So, for Game Two, Sinden and Ferguson took the opposite approach: they would put in their grinders and defensive specialists to slow the game down and keep the score low, in hopes of wearing down the Soviets.

"Smart move," Park says.

The next challenge: breaking up the Soviets' tic-tac-toe passing plays, which resulted in too many great chances at close range. Sinden and Ferguson decided they would try to clog the slot and force the Soviets to shoot from outside. To do so, they would make an unconventional switch: instruct their wingers to cover the Soviet forwards instead of their defencemen, and move Team Canada's centre up high to cover *both* Soviet blueliners. They hoped this move would force the play to the Soviet defencemen, whose slapshots weren't particularly threatening, instead of down low to their crafty forwards.

These strategic flips dictated a dramatic change in personnel, starting with the number of defencemen they would dress—a question Seiling, Savard, and other defencemen had entertained before Game One.

"How come a smart guy like Harry dressed only five defencemen the first game?" Savard asks. "I was a versatile defenceman. I would love to play that first game in Montreal. I love that kind of game, up and down. I like Harry. He did a real good job. But the biggest mistake he made was dressing five defencemen in Montreal. If you dress six D, we might have lost, but not 7–3.

"But then I think, if the Russians don't win the first game 7–3, do I dress for the next game? *Any* of the games? I don't know."

Looking back, Sinden concedes the point. "Honestly, I don't

know why I played five D in the first game. Yes, we made a promise to play everyone, and we had a lot more forwards than defencemen. But we might have been victims of our own overconfidence."

For Game Two, the coaches pulled Don Awrey and Rod Seiling—thereby taking out one of the best defensive pairs at training camp, and giving priority to what they'd just seen the night before instead of what they had thought the previous 17 days. They replaced them with the reliable Chicago pair of Pat Stapleton and Bill White, and added Serge Savard, who wouldn't have been available if Ferguson hadn't insisted on inviting him to camp. The coaches paired him with his Montreal teammate Guy Lapointe. Savard, healing leg and all, would get his chance.

Sinden and Ferguson left intact only the Park-Bergman pair, which had proven to be the team's best the night before. Their strong play and good chemistry was one of the few impressions from training that held up under live ammunition.

"In Game One, Harry dressed only five defencemen," Park says. "That was a mistake. In Toronto, he dressed six, and from then on, we had a solid six that played most of the rest of the games."

On offence the coaches concluded that their third-period decision to bench the famed GAG Line had been correct, so they kept them out for Game Two. They also dropped Detroit's Berenson and Redmond to make room for a sixth defenceman and another forward, but dressed their linemate, Pete Mahovlich, a decision that would prove crucial.

They replaced those forwards with Stan Mikita and three unglamorous grinders: Wayne Cashman, Bill Goldsworthy, and J.P. Parisé, among the last players picked, who hadn't expected to see much ice time.

"I felt Parisé, Cashman, and maybe Pete Mahovlich would be the type of players who would be useful in a battle, a little more dogged," Sinden recalls. "They were not as highly skilled as the others, but they were tough and their energy and determination stood out. They were welcome additions."

Sinden made another change at Phil Esposito's request.

"I said, 'Don't put Frank [Mahovlich] with me," Esposito recalls. The Hall of Fame winger had been Canada's best forward by modern measures, but Esposito worried about how much Frank had been shaken by the Soviet onslaught. "He was a basket case! I said, 'Give me Cash.'"

Since Esposito and Wayne Cashman had already been linemates for five years in Boston, it made sense to put them together. Sinden acquiesced, added Parisé to Esposito's line, and put Frank Mahovlich with Mikita and Cournoyer.

One of the few pleasant surprises in Game One had been the play of Clarke, Ellis, and Henderson, who had wedged their way into the lineup through sheer hard work. They finished at plus-6 in even-strength scoring chances, while accounting for five of the team's eight points, including two of the team's three goals. They had been an unknown quantity in camp, but the secret was out when the media selected Bobby Clarke as Canada's player of the game.

"The NHL must've known how good of a player Bobby Clarke was," Gretzky says, "but when the tournament started, *we* didn't know. But he really stood out—how well he played, how *hard* he played, and how important he became to the team."

When Sinden dressed them again for Game Two in Toronto, the line achieved one objective that had driven them during 17 days of training camp: Henderson would get to play in front of his mom at home.

The elephant in the room could not be ignored: goaltending. The Soviets might have had more good scoring chances, especially down low, but they didn't have 133 percent more, as the final score would suggest. Tretiak had been as spectacular as Dryden had been bewildered.

With Tony Esposito subbing for Dryden, Team Canada had swapped out eight out of 19 players, or almost half the lineup—the kind of luxury you can only afford when you're carrying 35 players.

Berenson held no grudge. "Harry made the right calls," he says. Not everyone would take Sinden's decisions with such team spirit.

If Sinden didn't like telling 16 top-notch NHL players they weren't going to dress for the first game, telling eight All-Stars that they'd be sitting out the second game after a blowout was even less appealing.

"Making the lineup with Fergie over coffee is one thing," Sinden says. "Telling the players is another."

If Canada's national identity was shaken to its core by the loss of the first game, some of the players' personal self-worth, so attached to their prominence as hockey players their entire lives, would be tested by sitting out for Game Two. To soften the blow, Sinden told all the players, before announcing the lineup, that being benched didn't mean they'd blown it. He reiterated his mantra: "Last night was a team effort."

But Sinden knew he needed to make some major lineup changes, not only to counter the Soviets' speed and conditioning but also to convince everyone this game was going to be different.

"The players were really interested in our changes," he recalls, in an understatement. "And you have to give them a reason we weren't going to lose again. You can't just say, 'Do this,' without explaining why. I thought we were able to get our reasons across. They had to have something to hang their hat on after a loss. 'Oh yeah, we lost, but if we do this . . .' Whether it helped or not, it helped!"

Sinden's belief in change for change's sake is supported by research: when a factory paints the walls, installs new light bulbs, or adjusts lunchtime, it usually results in a bump in productivity, however temporary. The players needed reasons to think things would be different, and Sinden had given them a dozen.

"We changed our style and our lineup," he says. "After the first game, they couldn't very well object. If Fergie and I came out and said, 'We'll do it the same way tonight and hope for the best,' they'd be right to object!"

But when Sinden decided to sit the best line in the league, Hadfield—who had scored 50 goals the previous season, then signed an eye-popping $200,000-a-year deal—did object, forcefully.

"First of all, the whole change took place after the adversity of the first game in Montreal," Rod Gilbert recalled. "And now we're in Toronto, and we see the three of us are not on the board to dress for the second game. So all three of us go into Harry's office, and Harry's sitting on the front edge of the desk.

"Vic says, 'Are you fucking blaming us for the loss?'

"Harry says, 'No, I'm not blaming you. But we have a lot of players and that style isn't working here, so I need to make a change."

"Vic says, 'You can't change! I'm not getting paid for this. You're *embarrassing* me. I've got my whole family here in Toronto!' Vic took it personally, instead of thinking about what was best for the team. But that was Harry's job."

"Vic was very upset about that," Park recalls. "But Harry stuck to his guns."

"Vic *was* really upset," Sinden agrees. "But the reason I sat him was because he was too slow for this kind of hockey. Simple."

"Harry is very smart, and he never panicked," Ratelle adds. "That's the reason why he did *everything*: whatever's best for the team. Probably one of his best qualities. No matter what happened, he always had a plan for the players and he'd tell us, 'This is what we're going to do.' Same thing in this series. Harry was really good at that. He always had something good for us to go on."

Scratching Hadfield for Game Two attracted the most attention, but one of the biggest moves Sinden made was one of the quietest—unknown to almost everyone. During Game One, Ellis chased a loose puck in open ice, with a Soviet player rushing toward the puck from the opposite direction. Right before Ellis reached the puck, another Soviet player tripped him from behind, sending him falling forward. On his way down, he turned and the back of his head—with no helmet—hit the thigh of the oncoming player.

"It felt like hitting a brick wall," Ellis says. "My first thought: 'I'm hurt, and the series might be over for me.' Then I thought, 'I've just *got* to get up.' You don't want to let them know they hurt you, right? So I got up, got off the ice, and got through the game. But the next morning, I couldn't move my neck."

When Ellis arrived at the Toronto locker room the next day, he mentioned this to the trainer, who summoned Sinden and told him, "Ron's neck's bad and I certainly don't like this one."

"The trainer said I'm out," Ellis recalls. "I told Harry I couldn't shoot the puck. But Kharlamov had scored two beautiful goals, which I'm sure was on Harry's mind. He said, 'We've got to shut down Kharlamov. Can you skate with him?'

"I said, 'If that's what you want me to do, that's what I'll do.' Remember, Paul and I *really* wanted to play in Toronto. So I was back in the line-up to cover Kharlamov.

"And that's what happens in these situations," Ellis continues. "Players have to be willing to take on whatever role the team needs. These guys are All-Stars. But you can't play like 20 offensive All-Stars and expect to beat the Russians."

The Clarke line, at least, was already a model of team spirit.

AFTER all the drama of the past 24 hours, Sinden was anxious to see a strong effort in practice, which he had closed from the press, the Soviet coaches, and everyone else who had casually watched them skate in Montreal. He was relieved when the players put in a "really good practice. We had their interest."

Their largely positive energy might have concealed some

problems. Gilbert Perreault and Rick Martin were still peeved to be out of the lineup, Hadfield was positively furious, and Dryden, standing near the boards while Tony Esposito and Eddie Johnston took shots, was wallowing in a rare spell of self-doubt.

"I was not used to this," he says today. "It might have been the lowest day of my entire career."

Sinden's good mood quickly soured when he was leaving the ice, looked up into the stands, and saw the two Soviet coaches, Bobrov and Kulagin, taking notes.

"It was bullshit," Sinden wrote. "I was so mad I could have taken a bite right out of the boards."

It didn't get better for anyone after practice when Sinden walked the team through the game film, which Dryden described as a "horror movie." Jaws dropped, heads fell into hands, some groaned, but no players spoke. No one had to.

If the Soviet scouts and film session took some of the wind out of Sinden's sails, reading Monday's papers would have finished the job. The crescendo of criticism started from the top and cascaded downward.

For reasons hard to fathom the 71-year-old president of the IIHF, Bunny Ahearne, whom you'd expect to bend over backwards to appear neutral, released the following statement: "The moral of the story is that you don't have to be a Canadian to be a top-class hockey player . . . I don't think the Canadians will wake up. They're too small-minded. Now they'll start to think up alibis."

If Ahearne was trying to hide his anti-Canadian bias, he was doing a poor job of it. But the Canadian newspapers were even tougher. Yes, the same writers who had mocked the Soviets and anyone who dared to praise them just two days earlier, while smugly asserting that Team Canada wouldn't break a sweat in dispatching their new foes in eight straight games, didn't hesitate to pivot their cannons 180 degrees to pound the very players they had just extolled, and even the system they played in. They delivered their broadsides without a trace of self-awareness.

Although the teams took only four minor penalties each—the refs were almost invisible, which would not be the case as the series progressed—the Canadian press berated the players for playing dirty after the game was out of reach.

The column by the *Globe and Mail*'s Scott Young, father of famous singer Neil Young, was representative of this vein: "The thing that shamed me, and I guess many of us, was not the loss. That was nothing—one team playing hockey at its best and deserving to win. Also, the loss could be reversed as early as tonight. But when grown Canadians wearing their nation's name on their backs get chippy, cheaply chippy, I feel badly for us. The night when we show we can't dish it out, we show that we can't take it, either."

Other criticisms were fair, if unpleasant for the players and coaches to read. The *Montreal Gazette*'s Ted Blackman included himself—and perhaps the press, by proxy—among those who woefully underestimated the Soviets.

"To say we took Russia lightly is to hear General Custer ask: 'What Indians?' We spotted the challengers playing dates most favourable to them and the least favourable to us, clucking confidently that we'd clean 'em anyway. Our invincible image now lays bare, a myth."

The *New York Times*'s Gerald Eskenazi referred to the opening game as a "shock to Canada's nervous system," and who could argue?

Perhaps the most painful cut came from the *Globe and Mail* headline writer who plastered the following across their September 4 edition: "Canada mourns hockey myth."

Dick Beddoes, the *Globe and Mail* columnist, had famously promised that if the Russians took even one game, he would eat his column "shredded at high noon in a bowl of borscht on the front steps of the Russian embassy."

"Well, to his credit, Dick literally ate his words," recalls *Sports Illustrated*'s Mark Mulvoy, who had been one of the few to predict Canada would actually lose one game. "We were there, all the scribes, in front of the embassy, and watched poor Dick dip his column in borscht and, to his word, he ate it."

The deluge of criticism even got to Gerry Park, who had other things on her mind just hours after giving birth to her and Brad's first child.

"I was talking with my dad about our new son on the phone," she recalls, "and he couldn't help but bring it up, that first loss. My family, their neighbours in Winnipeg, everyone was just so disappointed. Everybody thought it would be so easy, and now nobody could believe it. We definitely felt that the entire nation's reputation was on the line."

No matter what happened next, the status of the NHL players as invincible had been decimated in just 60 minutes. But how much of their reputation could still be salvaged remained an open question.

The Canadians could harbour no delusions about the skyrocketing stakes. But they still couldn't tell just *how* good the Soviets really were. Were they truly the equal of the Canadians—and perhaps better in some ways? Or were they simply a good team in great shape that caught the reigning kings off guard? Game Two would have a lot to say about all of that—and everyone watching knew it.

"It was supposed to be eight friendlies," *Sports Illustrated* wrote. "Once the Soviets won the first one, 7–3, the friendly part disappeared."

It was only Game Two, but 48 hours after believing the entire series would be a lark, the Canadians already knew they were playing for everything.

"If you lose Game Two," Sinden says, "now you're down 0–2 and your guys start looking for excuses. 'We didn't want to be there anyway.' 'We were never interested in this series.' And now you've lost it."

In only the series' second game, failure was not an option.

15

GAME TWO: JUST A BAD DREAM?

September 4, 1972

After peaking at 28 degrees Celsius (82 Fahrenheit) on September 1, by Monday, September 4, Toronto's temperature had cooled down to 21 degrees (70 Fahrenheit), removing at least one problem the Canadians had in Game One.

But the Soviets picked up where they had left off, firing seven high-quality shots in the first period at Tony Esposito, who stood firm.

"My brother saved us in the first period before we got going," Phil Esposito says. "And then we got going good. But Tony was responsible for Game Two."

The first period of the second game also ended in a tie, but 0–0 this time, not 2–2. The Canadian locker room felt very different during the first intermission than it had in Montreal. There were no wide-eyed looks, no staring off into space, no whispered wonderings about what the hell was going on out there. Sinden's many changes, in personnel and tactics, had worked as he had hoped. The Canadians had kept up with the Soviets this time, firing 10 shots on Tretiak, and didn't feel like they were drowning between periods—all considerable improvements. They had even killed two penalties. But no one was taking anything for granted.

Seven minutes into the second period, Cashman took out Vladimir Lutchenko, retrieved the puck, and dished a deft little pass to his Bruins linemate Esposito, right on the doorstep—the kind of play familiar teammates make. Esposito pulled it across the crease to his forehand and around Tretiak for a 1–0 lead, his second game-opening goal.

The Canadians outshot the Soviets, 16–5, in the second period and 26–12 through the first 40 minutes. With six seconds left in the period, the Soviets' Yuri Liapkin took a minor for slashing, and the great Kharlamov a 10-minute misconduct, which would give the Canadians a golden opportunity to open things up in the third. But hanging on to a one-goal lead going into the last stanza, which had been their Waterloo in Game One, didn't provide much comfort.

"We were just getting to know each other," Park recalls. "We were on the power play, and there was a faceoff. Yvan [Cournoyer] comes up to me and says, 'Brad, Brad! Watch me—I go!'"

Esposito recalls Park passing this information on to him right before Esposito took the faceoff. "Parkie said, 'If Cournoyer goes full blast, no way they're going to catch him.' I knew he was right, and we knew what to do."

Esposito didn't win the draw, but the Soviets threw the puck into the Canadian end, which had the same effect. Park started behind the net with the puck, then built up speed alongside Cournoyer.

"And sure enough," Park says, "Yvan takes off and I send it to him, and he's gone!"

Flying past the Soviet defencemen like they were standing still, Cournoyer popped the puck between Tretiak's leg pads for a 2–0 lead, and the crowd erupted.

The Canadians' satisfaction ended a few minutes later when the refs gave Clarke two minutes for slashing. It took the Soviets only 38 seconds for Yevgeni Zimin to get loose on a breakaway. When he shot wide, Liapkin grabbed the loose puck and dished to Yakushev in front, who cut the score to 2–1 with 14:07 left.

Just 21 seconds later Pat Stapleton took an uncharacteristic hooking penalty. If the Soviets had been waiting for the perfect chance to crush the Canadians' spirit, this was it. But the Canadians were not content to play defence and survive the two minutes—nor were they confident enough to think they could afford to take such a passive approach.

As Pete Mahovlich recalls, "Harry comes over to Espo and me on the bench and says, 'You guys go kill it. And look, we're going to try to rag it as much as we can. No dumping it in if we can avoid it.'"

Esposito remembers taking Sinden's idea and cranking it up a notch. Before skating in for the faceoff in the Canadian zone, Esposito told his teammates, "'If I win the draw, Parkie, you launch it, and Pete, you go.' I felt we needed to score. I didn't win the draw, but I got the puck in a battle and knocked it off the boards. Pete picked it up and just *took off*."

Pete's brother, Frank, who had been sitting on the bench a few feet away, recalls, "Pete gets it just outside our blue line. He picks up a head of steam and it seemed like he could have gone through the whole damn team out there, deking and diving, a great run."

"Phil dumps it off the wall," Pete Mahovlich says, "and I pick it up and I decide I'm going to go to force the play. I'm going to fake the shot and go to the middle of the ice and rag it to kill some time, just like Harry said. But when I wound up for the fake, [Soviet defenseman Yevgeny Paladiev] flinches and stands up straight, like I'm going to shoot. And now I'm not *thinking* about what I'm going to do next. I just *do* it."

Esposito loves Pete's description almost as much as what Mahovlich did next.

"Watching the players today," Esposito says, "they play like the robots the Russians were. They come out of cookie moulds. I think the instinct for the game is gone. But Pete," he says, shaking his head in admiration, "man, he *had* it."

Mahovlich wound up, freezing Paladiev, then sucked the puck back just out of reach of Ragulin's stick and went right around him to his right. Now only Tretiak remained.

"Tretiak stayed back in the net way too much," Esposito says. "But when Pete comes down, Tretiak finally comes out a bit, and Pete faked him like he faked the D: left, then right. Here we go with the instinct again. He shows the shot, but then he tucks it in, and then he reaches *all the way around him* on the backhand, and right behind him. He beat Tretiak with his wingspan.

"Holy fuck! That was great! The best fucking goal I've ever seen. I *jumped* in Pete's arms, and that sonofabitch is strong, too! And he just tossed me around like I was nothing."

"I was so elated!" Pete says. "The emotion. Unbelievable. I didn't celebrate a lot of goals, but I celebrated that one!"

A half-dozen teammates, some pouring over the boards, trapped him in a group hug right in front of Tretiak.

"I remember Game Two distinctly," Gretzky recalls. "The whole country wanted to win so desperately. You could see it on the ice. You could see it in the stands. You could *feel* it. Then Pete Mahovlich scores that beautiful short-handed goal. I don't have to rewatch that one; I can still *remember* it, clear as day. That kind of changed the series. You could see the enthusiasm and the interest of the Canadian people come back."

"My most famous goal?" Pete asks. "No question. Years later I'm working for the [Florida] Panthers. We trade for [Jaromír] Jágr, and I'm responsible for him, so I meet him for the first time in Montreal. He comes up to me and he says, 'I know you! I thought that was my move, but it was *your* move!' And he tells me about that short-handed goal in Game Two, then takes a great picture with me and him and his wife."

"Phil's right," Frank says. "It was instinct. The most famous goal of the series."

Game Eight would have something to say about that, but everyone agrees Pete Mahovlich's goal was the prettiest of the series, which is saying something.

"Listen, we *needed* to win that game," Henderson says. "I don't think there's any way around it. So there's your backdrop for the greatest goal ever scored at Maple Leaf Gardens. And I can still run that one over in my mind, clear as can be. They've got a power play, they're down one, and *we* score? Oh man. That broke their backs."

"Now we're up, 3–1," Pete Mahovlich says, "and Mikita gets the puck in the corner and finds Frank in front. Bangs it off the pipe and in—4–1."

Even with a three-goal lead and 11:01 left, the Canadians weren't about to let up, and this time they had the momentum and the emotion to secure the 4–1 victory.

There are three goals from the Summit Series that everyone remembers. Pete Mahovlich's short-handed tally in Game Two was the first.

"I remember guys in the locker room saying, 'Great game. Now take care of yourselves tonight,'" Esposito says. "Nobody had to tell us to be in early."

"If we lose that game, Game Two," Cournoyer says, "I think we would have been done. Down 2–0? Four games in Moscow? Too much. Might get ugly. We *had* to win. And for me, that game set up the mentality: *now we can beat them*."

It was a bona fide victory, right down to the 36–21 shot differential. Nothing fluky about it, with the Esposito brothers sharing player-of-the-game honours.

"Just ask yourself," Savard says, "how did we win, 4–1, just 48 hours after losing, 7–3? Were we in that much better shape? Did our strategy change so much? No. We had six defencemen—that's a big difference."

Sinden had also changed half the lineup, and virtually the entire playbook, while the players put everything they had into every shift—all of it necessary to win.

"That game we won strictly on emotion—and desperation," Clarke says. "That's all we had. But then a little bit of the arrogance creeps in and you're desperately hoping you're right, that the Russians really weren't as good as they looked in the first game."

But to extrapolate from one game that all the shortcomings the Soviets had exposed in Game One had been fixed, all Team Canada's problems had been solved, and now all they had to do was duplicate that effort in the six remaining games, that was fool's gold.

Running the game through our modern analytical filters, we see that two of Canada's four goals were created by great individual efforts on the rush: Cournoyer's and Pete Mahovlich's. In full-strength play in the neutral and defensive ends, Canada's defence still struggled to keep up with the Russians. But Tony Esposito's great work—including several crucial saves early on—concealed the Soviets' ability to exploit Team Canada's defence on odd-man rushes.

But if Game Two was fool's gold, the players had little choice but to buy it. Without that victory, so rarely appreciated in retrospectives on the series, the rest of the games could have been reduced to a death march.

THE media covering Game Two eagerly jumped back on the bandwagon as fast as they had jumped off it after Game One, ignorant of the irony.

"WE DID IT!" exclaimed the *Toronto Sun*.

"The Russians claim to have conceived everything from pizza to applejack," the *Montreal Gazette*'s Ted Blackman wrote. "Well, they can add another discovery now. Footsteps. Bobrov's Bobcats came face to face with intimidation last night in an old-fashioned game of river hockey. Hmm. Saturday's supermen were Monday's mortals, with 20/20 hearing to boot."

The same physical style that the journalists had criticized two days earlier as a flaw in the national character, they now celebrated as a show of Canadian grit.

"Does anybody really think that the NHL will—or should—turn their backs on the game they have played all their lives just because the opposition happens to be the friendly Soviet Nationals?" Red Fisher wrote. He added, accurately, that the Soviets had played plenty rough themselves. "Who says the NHL All-Stars have a lock on elbows, sticks and muscle?"

What the writers had to say would have no impact on the coming games. But when Andrei Starovoitov, head of the Soviet hockey federation, claimed, "The American referees let the Canadian players perform like a bunch of barbarians," it wasn't accurate—Team Canada took five minor penalties to the Soviets' three, plus Kharlamov's misconduct—but it would carry far more weight in the days ahead.

It took the Soviets one game, which they had lost fair and square, to start working the refs. They had only just begun.

16

FOOL'S GOLD

On Tuesday, September 5, the players woke up in Toronto to the breaking news that something had gone horribly wrong in Munich.

Taking advantage of Munich's intentionally lax security, intended to help visitors forget the nightmare of the Nazi police state, a little-known terrorist group called the Palestinian Liberation Organization broke into the Olympic Village and held all 11 members of the Israeli Olympic team hostage.

The players didn't have much time to watch the news. They had a practice in Toronto that morning, followed by a flight to Winnipeg, and Game Three the next night. The brief spell of peace and joy the team had earned with the 4–1 victory didn't last long.

Vic Hadfield, still stewing over not playing in Game Two, confronted Sinden by the players' bench right after practice. As Sinden recalls, Hadfield gave him an ultimatum: "I'm not going [to Winnipeg] unless I'm going to play." That the team had been trounced with Hadfield in Montreal, and won by three without him in Toronto, did not seem to factor into his calculations. By then, Sinden knew enough not to make any more promises he might not be able to keep. Winning the series could no longer be taken for granted, so that imperative precluded all else, including the feelings of the league's best players.

Sinden didn't flinch. "Well, there are no guarantees," he replied. "You do what you want to do."

After practice, Sinden learned that NHL president Clarence Campbell had blasted Sinden and his team in the paper after the first game.

"I don't want to second-guess and I don't like to second-guess," Campbell said, then proceeded to second-guess everything Sinden had done, right down to starting Dryden in net—a decision that was easy to criticize only in hindsight.

"Campbell came out to say how bad we were," Eagleson recalls. "We sure needed help like that! Christ, we had enough problems. And how does that benefit him? I never understood that."

One possible factor: once Sinden had left the NHL, he'd become a lame duck in the eyes of Campbell and others, powerless to object. He was no longer in the club.

"I think that's fair," Eagleson says today. "All I know is any NHL executive or coach who complained about Harry in the papers wasn't much of a help to us."

When Sinden saw the papers, he was livid. "The whole thing was really bush league," he wrote. "Can you imagine a guy of Campbell's stature doing something like that? Here's a guy putting down some of the best players in the league—*his* league—because of one game."

Once again, Sinden held his ground and confronted Campbell directly.

"Listen," Sinden told him, "you don't have any control over me or Team Canada. So to me, you're just another fan. If you want to get carried away and be critical of us over one loss, that's your right as a fan."

Campbell claimed he had been misquoted but didn't apologize.

Dryden was as mad as Dryden gets. "Here we are down and

defenceless, and he kicks us in the teeth," he wrote. "I'm burned up about the whole thing."

If Sinden needed a third front to add to Hadfield and Campbell, the fans provided one by sending more than a hundred telegrams, all but one "very nasty."

Living in a democracy comes with a price.

BEFORE leaving for Winnipeg, Dryden met his older brother, Dave, then playing for Buffalo, for lunch a few blocks from the team hotel. This provided Ken the rare luxury to discuss his craft in confidence with someone who could actually help.

Ken told his brother that his style—standing up and coming out to challenge the shooters—was effective in the NHL, where the players often crossed the blue line and fired, but far less so with the Soviets, who worked the puck down low with tic-tac-toe passing until the defence finally left one of them open for an easy tap-in. The Dryden brothers realized that the style of Tony Esposito—staying back and dropping for most shots—was better suited to countering the Soviets' offence.

So, what to do? Amazingly, they decided Dryden would have to change the style he had perfected his entire life—within a matter of days. He would need to do the opposite of what had gotten him there: to stay back in the net, stay low, and move laterally with the Soviet passes, denying them the easy goal.

It was a lot to ask, with no guarantee it would work. But what choice did Dryden have? They had already seen what his normal style would get him against these guys.

The therapy session helped, and by the time they landed in Winnipeg, Dryden felt ready to take on his new challenge.

"So there will be a new Dryden in the goal from now on," he wrote. "I hope it will be a new Dryden, anyway."

AFTER Sinden's unsatisfying encounter with Vic Hadfield before practice in Toronto, which left Sinden unsure whether Hadfield would be flying with the team to Winnipeg, Sinden asked Eagleson to do him a favour.

"Harry said, 'Vic is going to go to Ratelle and Gilbert and bitch to them, and try to convert them,'" Eagleson recalls. "'I want you to sit with Gilbert and keep him with us, because we're going to need him.'"

Light duty, Eagleson figured, because "I always liked Rod Gilbert. Handsome, debonaire, could speak both languages smoothly, and always had a big smile. But I never knew what kind of a guy he was." Pretty boy or team player?

On the plane, Eagleson got right to it. "What about Vic?"

"He's already unhappy," Gilbert said.

"Okay, here's all I want to know. Never mind Vic. I want to know where you stand."

Gilbert didn't hesitate. "Al, I signed on for the duration. If they want me to play, I'll be ready to play. If I don't play another game, it means our team is winning."

Looking back, Eagleson says, "Before that week I had Vic on a pedestal, a character guy, and Gilbert as a happy-go-lucky type, but not necessarily a team player. I was wrong about both. We didn't know about Vic yet, but Gilbert was no dilettante. He was with us, 100 percent."

The coaches could have just asked Brad Park's wife, Gerry, about Gilbert. "He would call for Brad but when I picked up we'd just talk and he'd ask, 'How are you, how are you doing?' and he meant it. He always had a way of making everyone feel special—just a super, super guy. I loved him to death. We all did."

Because the team once again split up to take two planes as a precaution, Sinden didn't know whether Hadfield had gotten on the other plane or stayed home until he saw him in Winnipeg. Sinden then asked Gilbert himself how he felt. After all, the entire line had sat out the second game, not just Hadfield.

"Listen, Coach," Gilbert told him, "do what you think is best. You're the coach and I'll go along with it."

THE day of the third game, Wednesday, September 6, 1972, started grimly.

"Our worst fears have been realized," ABC's Jim McKay famously said. "They have now said there were 11 hostages. Two were killed in their rooms, yesterday morning. Nine were killed at the airport. They're all gone."

Fearing for his safety, Jewish-American swimmer Mark Spitz, who had just won a record seven gold medals, left Munich in secret. The IOC stopped the Olympics for 34 hours, marking another tragic event in an unsettled time, when it seemed like almost anything could happen.

AT the morning skate, Sinden made only one change to his Game Two lineup: sitting Bill Goldsworthy in favour of Hadfield's centre, Jean Ratelle.

"So Vic came to Winnipeg, and didn't play," Sinden says. "If he had a different attitude, I probably would have played him. You couldn't ignore his Goal-a-Game Line. But I didn't think caving in to pressure, no matter where it was coming from, was going to help."

From the outset, Sinden had planned to start Dryden in Game One, Esposito in Game Two, then whoever was playing better in Game Three. As Dryden had let in seven goals and Esposito just one, it wasn't Sinden's toughest call. But Tony's brother, Phil, was still surprised.

"I thought they were going to put Kenny back in the net," Phil says. "Tony wasn't in shape." But then, who was?

The mood in the locker room for the morning skate in Winnipeg was relatively light. When Dryden couldn't find his skate before practice, "I looked in my equipment bag, under the bench, all over the room," Dryden recalls. "Finally, I noticed my skate was being used as a stop to keep our door open. The blade was wedged between the bottom of the door and the floor."

Berenson couldn't resist. "Well, Dryden, that's the first thing you've stopped all week." Everyone laughed—a good sign. It's a safe bet that if they hadn't taken the second game, nobody would have been laughing. But they had not only won, they had beaten the Soviets soundly, playing old-fashioned Canadian hockey, suggesting the first game must have been a fluke, after all.

With Ellis covering Kharlamov, the Soviet star managed only three shots on net all night, and only one at even strength. The earth had been righted on its axis, all was well with the world, and the future was bright.

"We really felt that we were going to take the series over," Henderson recalls, "just like we were supposed to. Harry had lots of confidence in us, and we felt that."

Another feel-good moment: on the ice that day, Ferguson skated up to Henderson and said, "We're counting on you, Hennie." That was all, but it was enough. "When you hear that, from Fergie," Henderson says, "then you know your job, and you know it's important. I told my wife, 'Can you believe him coming up to *me* and saying that?' It's flattering, and you feel like you need to respond."

After practice Sinden had yet another unpleasant encounter, this time with Soviet hockey federation head Andrei Starovoitov and head coach Vsevolod Bobrov. Although the two teams were supposed to alternate picking officials for each game, the Soviets were still angry about the officiating in the second game. Though it had been handled fairly, and quietly, by NHL standards, the Soviets pressured Sinden and Ferguson not to use the American referees from Game Two again in Game Four, when Canada got to choose again.

Since Sinden and Ferguson thought the Game One refs had also done a decent job, they agreed to use those referees for Game Four.

"Sometime," Sinden said at the time, with an almost touching naïveté, "we'll ask the Russians to reciprocate in some way."

═

THE fans at Maple Leaf Gardens helped make it one of the old building's best nights—but then, 24 of the 35 players on Team Canada had grown up in Ontario. Nine hailed from Quebec, but only two were from the west: Red Berenson from Regina, Saskatchewan, and Bob Clarke from Flin Flon, Manitoba. Alberta, British Columbia, the Territories, and the Atlantic provinces had no representatives.

How fans in Winnipeg would respond to Team Canada was harder to predict. The city had a well-earned chip on its shoulder, one created by repeated slights from the IIHF and the NHL, and carefully nurtured by the locals since.

Winnipeg already boasted one of Canada's richest hockey traditions. The Winnipeg Victorias claimed the Stanley Cup in 1896, 1901, and 1902, and their successors, the Winnipeg Falcons, won the first Olympic hockey tournament in 1920. In 1965 the CAHA picked Winnipeg to host the newly formed Canadian national team, managed by Father David Bauer. Over the years Manitoba has produced a staggering 400-plus NHL players, from Turk Broda, Terry Sawchuk, and Andy Bathgate, to Butch Goring, Reggie Leach, and the Hextall family, to current stars Duncan Keith and Jonathan Toews.

Nonetheless, when the NHL doubled from six teams to 12 in 1967, then added six more over the next seven years, the NHL kept bypassing Winnipeg in favour of American cities like Los

Angeles, Atlanta, and Washington, D.C., that had no hockey history and had never produced a single serious player.

Finally, in 1972 the World Hockey Association recognized Winnipeg as a major-league hockey town worthy of a franchise. When the Jets pulled the great Bobby Hull from Chicago with a record-breaking contract, it seemed that Winnipeg had finally arrived. Until, that is, NHL president Clarence Campbell squeezed Team Canada until it dropped Bobby Hull from the roster. How Winnipeg would react to the arrival of so-called Team Canada was anyone's guess.

17

GAME THREE: WHO *ARE* THOSE GUYS?

September 6, 1972

They showed up in force, some 9,800 fans packing Winnipeg Arena. They would alternate between robust support, indifference, and mild hostility, but they started out as strong as the team did.

On the first shift for Esposito's line—still with Cashman and J.P. Parisé, a late addition to the team—Parisé did what he did best, digging the puck out of the corner to Esposito, who passed it to Bill White at the point. He fired on net, where Parisé reappeared to bang home the rebound for a 1–0 lead just 1:54 into the contest. The Winnipeg crowd rewarded them with a loud standing ovation.

A minute later the refs called Valeri Vasiliev for elbowing. But instead of Canada mounting an early 2–0 lead, Petrov intercepted Frank Mahovlich's ill-advised pass at Canada's blue line, took a few strides, then wound up to beat Tony Esposito between his pads. 1–1.

Team Canada then got a boost from another Sinden addition for that game, Jean Ratelle, who would have a fantastic night, combining with Frank Mahovlich for a plus-9 by our modern "scoring chance plus-minus" metric. After Henderson took out Yuri Lebedev at mid-ice, Gary Bergman passed to Cournoyer, who slid a simple little pass to Ratelle flying past the defenders. Ratelle then popped the puck into the upper left corner of the cage to give Canada a 2–1 lead. At the first intermission, Canada also had a solid 15–9 shooting advantage, more proof that Game One was an aberration.

"We're up 2–1," Henderson says, "and we're thinking, 'These suckers are not going to score on us!' That was our focus. I never thought about scoring goals. Never once did I think about scoring in this series—until the very end.

"It goes back to what Fergie had said to me on the ice that morning: 'They're counting on us. Know your job, and do your job.' Our line played a lot against Kharlamov's, trying to shut down their top line. We were fine with that role. Look, you have to be honest with yourself: if we're on a team with Espo and Cournoyer and Ratelle and Gilbert, nobody expected us to be the scorers. We would have been happy if we didn't score a single goal if we could just stop Kharlamov's line."

They were doing just that, keeping Kharlamov's potent threesome off the score sheet in five-on-five situations for a game and a half since Montreal.

Four minutes into the second period Esposito's line once again took over the game. Parisé won another battle for the puck in the corner and tapped it to Cashman, also in the corner, who passed to the high slot—Esposito's office—where he ripped it to the top right corner for his third goal in three games.

"What a competitor!" Sinden wrote. "At times in training camp I wondered how he was going to play without Bobby Orr. Those two complement each other so beautifully that I felt Phil might not be the same super player without Orr. But he's shown me and anyone else who might have had the same doubt . . . He just keeps going no matter what the situation is."

By the modern scoring chance plus-minus measurement, Esposito would post an impressive plus-5 in Game Three.

With a 3–1 lead, Sinden admitted, "I really thought we had 'em." He had reason to think so when Team Canada went on another power play, but they whiffed again. Through two and a half games, Team Canada's power play had produced exactly one goal—the same as its penalty killers—nowhere near the level they expected or needed.

Just a minute past the midpoint of the second period they got another chance when Lebedev went off for tripping. After seeing the Soviets score short-handed goals in the first game and in the first period of Game Three, however, Sinden warned his players about the Soviets' strategy of sending a forward flying out of the zone as soon as their defenceman got the puck.

As Frank Mahovlich recalls, "I take this guy out in the corner, and Phil's right there. I mean, I finished my check. But he moves the puck to his partner [defenceman Gennadi Tsygankov], who just *whips* it off the far boards, no hesitation, and it bounces right out to the red line. That's when we see Kharlamov, going 100 miles an hour, swoop in—then we look up and the puck is in the net!

"That's when you know they can play. I'm convinced that was a set play. They were doing things we'd never seen before."

The Soviets' second short-handed goal of the night cut Canada's lead to 3–2. Burned again, Sinden put out Clarke's line to stop the bleeding, and once more they overachieved. Ellis and Clarke got the puck up to Henderson breaking in. With the puck still on its side, he fired anyway, ripping it past Tretiak for his second goal of the series to restore Canada's two-goal lead, at 4–2.

Just when the Canadians thought they had the Soviets figured out, "they put out a line I'd never seen before," Sinden says. "A bunch of young guns."

Their names: centre Vyacheslav Anisin, 22; right winger Yuri

Lebedev, 21; and left winger Alexander Bodunov, 21—all two or three years younger than the youngest Canadian to play so far, 24-year-old Guy Lapointe. Anisin was making his second start of the series, but his wingers were making their debuts. After the Soviets scored only one goal in Game Two, Bobrov also replaced a defenceman with a forward.

With 5:01 left in the second period, 23-year-old defenceman Valeri Vasiliev and Anisin set up Lebedev for a tipped goal to cut Canada's lead to 4–3. Then, with 1:32 left in the second, Anisin passed across the slot to Bodunov, all alone, who beat Esposito before he could get back into position, tying the score at 4–4.

"Their 'Kid Line' scored two crucial goals," Sinden recalls. "They were the best players on the ice! I turned to Fergie and shouted, 'Who the hell *are* these guys?'"

Sinden was quoting a famous scene from *Butch Cassidy and the Sundance Kid*, a movie that had come out three years earlier. After the two cowboy renegades ride into the night to shake the posse chasing them, they let one horse run away as a decoy, then both hop on the remaining horse and ride it through a river to lose the scent. But when they look back down the mountain, they're alarmed to see the mysterious posse hasn't fallen for their trick and is still coming after them. Paul Newman's Butch Cassidy, exasperated, turns to Robert Redford's Sundance Kid: "I couldn't do that! Could *you* do that? How can *they* do that? *Who are those guys?!* They're beginning to get on my nerves."

The Canadians didn't know who the mysterious Soviets were, but they couldn't seem to shake them, and they were beginning to get on their nerves.

Sinden wasn't finished ranting to Ferguson: "What the hell is going on here? They're all over the place. Are they putting eight guys out there or something? Why the hell is this happening to me? I'm just a little guy from Rochester."

In his journal he added, "Here were these guys who all look

the same, skate the same, shoot the same, the whole game without ever changing expression. They just keep coming after you and the only thing different about them is the number on their backs. I've never had to contend with anything like this in my life before!"

Despite outshooting the Soviets, 31–17, over two periods, the Canadians returned to the locker room for the second intermission frustrated, bewildered, and wondering if they had enough gas in their tanks to avoid another Montreal-style third-period collapse. All the doubts they thought they had banished after Game One were creeping back in.

The Canadians could manage only six more shots in the third period. Wayne Cashman's second slashing penalty of the night, which came with a 10-minute misconduct, didn't help. The referees, who'd probably read the Soviet officials blasting them in the papers for being too loose, were watching the Canadians more closely.

"I've seen Cash tailed by cops," Phil Esposito cracked, "but never by a referee before."

Now getting outskated to loose pucks all over the ice, the Canadians were no longer trying to win the game. They were trying to hang on for a tie.

"You can win one game on emotion," Clarke says, "but you can't win three. You can't keep it up for that long. We still didn't have the legs, the conditioning. It's another game at that level. We could go for a while like that, but then it started falling off."

"In the final 10 minutes of the game, our guys were gone physically," Sinden wrote. "They just didn't have anything left to give. I thought for sure the Russians were going to beat us near the end . . . If they had shot more when they had the opportunities they could have won. Geez, I'm glad they didn't."

Neither team could break the 4–4 tie, thanks partly to outstanding goaltending by both Tony Esposito and Tretiak, who was named the Soviets' player of the game for the second contest in a row—thus cementing Team Canada's scouting report as worse than useless.

A 4–4 tie a week earlier would have been shocking, but the Canadians now considered it a moral victory.

"Now *that* was a hell of a game," Pete Mahovlich says, and it was.

If the victory in Game Two doesn't get the respect it deserves, the Canadians tying Game Three is surely underestimated, too. If they hadn't, the last three games in Moscow wouldn't have mattered nearly as much, since the best they could do was tie—which would have made it one of the most miserable weeks in Canadian history.

HAVING studied the Soviets for a full 180 minutes, the Canadian coaches and players could see beyond the yawning gap in conditioning to analyze what their mysterious foes were doing, peeling back layers from the obvious to the finer points.

Unlike the NHL teams, which typically ran their forward lines and defensive pairs separately, the Soviets sent out their players in five-man interactive units. And that wasn't all: their defencemen played like forwards, jumping into the play whenever they smelled an opportunity, an integrated part of their offence.

The Soviets also eschewed the NHL habit of dumping and chasing in favour of endless passing and regrouping in the neutral zone, until they could cross the blue line as a five-man unit with the puck fully under their control. They favoured skating over standing, and passing over shooting, putting them in constant motion. While the Canadians got sucked into watching the puck carrier, Stapleton recalled, "the guy behind you comes flying up and they send the puck over to him, and he rips it. But they wouldn't shoot until they saw the whites of your eyes."

When they did shoot, they didn't bother with big, booming slapshots from beyond the faceoff circles, either, but waited until the off-wing was wide open, then set him up for a quick one-timer—enough to drive the Canadians crazy.

"I don't recall anyone in the NHL one-timing it back then," Dryden says, then gives the refrain: "All this was news to us."

"They had a style, a consistent style, one we had never seen," Sinden says. "I remember thinking to myself, 'How did they learn to play hockey like this?' We didn't play that way. We played a lot differently. Nothing wrong with the way we played, either. But it had nothing to do with the game they were playing."

ALTHOUGH tying Game Three would prove crucial, in some ways it shook Canada more deeply than losing Game One. To be surprised on opening night, under far from ideal conditions . . . that was bad. But to see that they could not shake the Soviets, even playing their best, was far more unnerving. They could no longer kid themselves that the Russians weren't for real and that Game One had been a fluke.

"The 4–4 tie was heartbreaking," Sinden says. "It was. It was."

If most players on Team Canada couldn't name a single Soviet player before the series started, after three games they knew many of their names from hearing the announcer pronounce them after their 12 goals and 13 assists—names like Valeri Kharlamov, who scored three goals in the first three games; Boris Mikhailov, who might have looked like Charlie Chaplin but played as tough as any Canadian in the corners; Alexander Maltsev, a smooth skater and passer; and agile, quick, strong defencemen like Lutchenko and Ragulin, who could join the rush. But the one who stood out for most of the Canadians was not the famed Kharlamov, but a sturdy six-foot-three left winger named Alexander Yakushev.

"Yakushev was great," Pete Mahovlich says. "He was their Jean Béliveau, flying from one end to the other."

"Yakushev," Phil Esposito says. "I thought he was the best player on their team. My brother said he had a harder shot than Hull. When Tony caught it, it *hurt*."

"Before that series," Berenson asks, "who would have known Kharlamov was their Cournoyer, and Yakushev was one of the best in the world? Not us!"

WHILE the players had been humbled repeatedly, and acted accordingly, no such self-reflective contrition had seeped into the press box. The reporters once again jumped to the front of the parade, this time to castigate their countrymen as they had after Game One.

Winnipeg's hockey writers, already bitter at the NHL's treatment of their city, had been waiting years for their chance to vent their spleens about it. When Team Canada's 1–1–1 record gave them an opening, they didn't waste it. Maurice Smith of the *Winnipeg Free Press* wrote, "Maybe now, other centres in Canada, particularly those with NHL franchises, will come to realize that hockey doesn't have to be a game of fisticuffs, clutch and grab, shooting the puck into the defensive zone and chasing after it. If nothing else, the Russians are teaching us that the game of hockey can be beautiful to watch and that to be entertaining blood and mayhem need not be part of it."

Under a screaming headline, "THE BIG, FAT NHL HAS LOST ITS PATENT ON THE GAME OF HOCKEY," the *Winnipeg Tribune*'s Jack Matheson wrote, "If this is Team Canada, I want no part of it. It's Team NHL, and we've all been sucked into a monstrous trap. We have sundry things to be proud of in this country, but the NHL isn't one of them."

Team Canada didn't fare much better with reporters back

east. In the *Globe and Mail*'s front page story, under the headline "Russian play in 4–4 game shows hockey belongs to both countries," Dan Proudfoot wrote, "One of the 10,000 fans at Winnipeg Arena last night left behind a sign which read, 'It's Still Our Game.' It ended up in a pile of litter, an appropriate resting place for the idea."

Not to be outdone, Ted Blackman of the *Montreal Gazette* added, "No matter how this world showdown turns out, and at the moment it doesn't appear the result will be cheered hereabouts, the NHL image has suffered a mortal blow. For years, in defeat at the international level, we hollered, 'Wait till you meet our pros.' This self-accredited invincibility has been shattered, and with it the myth the National Hockey League was the temple of hockey."

The unquestioned superiority of the NHL was gone, and probably forever.

But Game Three raised another question: If no longer dominant, could the Canadians still claim merely to be the best by any margin?

18

LOOKING FOR A LEADER

The morning after Game Three, Team Canada practised at Winnipeg Arena before boarding its two flights to Vancouver for Game Four, to be played on Friday, September 8.

During a drill, Red Berenson's slapshot hit Serge Savard in the right ankle. It didn't seem like much at the time. Berenson doesn't even remember it. A few hours later, Savard walked onto the plane without much difficulty, but during the flight his foot swelled up like a grapefruit. By the time they landed, it had gotten so bad he had to get off the plane in a wheelchair.

"Maybe Red noticed *that*?" Savard says today, laughing.

"Serge is just lucky it was my shot," Berenson says, "and not Dennis Hull's. Then he'd be in real trouble."

The X-rays told no lies: Savard had suffered a hairline fracture. They didn't know if the savvy defenceman, who had been quietly effective in Games Two and Three, could return to the series. But he was definitely out for Game Four, a tremendous blow for a team struggling to put the pieces together. Savard's unlucky injury marked the first domino to tumble in Sinden's carefully reconstructed lineup. Fatigue was another factor, as were the officials.

"Three games in five days was too much for some of our guys to handle at this stage of the season," he said. "The games had all the fury and heavy skating of Stanley Cup play, only our players didn't have 85 games to build themselves up to that kind of pace."

The referees had become a variable, too. After Canada won Game Two, Sinden wrote, "the Russians beefed in the newspapers about the officiating. And referees read the papers. So they were on Cashman's back all night in Winnipeg," giving him two minors and a misconduct.

Sinden had already started regretting how Hockey Canada had let the Soviets dictate the terms of the series, from the dates to the rules to the referees.

"They have the biggest advantage of all playing us this time of year, which is the worst time for us . . . If we had to give away the dates in their favour, then we should have at least been allowed our own rules" and NHL referees.

Sinden hadn't seen anything yet.

He thought it smart to swap out a few guys who'd already played, simply to keep the officials from picking on the same players. Because Sinden clearly considered Cashman a marked man, he sat. But despite the overwhelming evidence that the Soviets were for real and the outcome uncertain at best, Sinden stubbornly held to his original pledge to the players.

"Even though we tied in Winnipeg," Sinden says, "I thought Vancouver might be the best opportunity to put in some of the guys who hadn't played before. That game, I tried to live up to my promise that everyone would play a game."

Add it all up, and Sinden would switch eight of his 19 players for the second time in three games. At the team meeting the next morning, Sinden said that, with Savard out, he would go with five defencemen: Park and Bergman, the only pair that had played every game; Awrey and Seiling, figuring one of the top pairs in camp would fare better than they had in Game One; and

Pat Stapleton, who'd played well in Games Two and Three. But when the defencemen reminded Sinden what had happened in Game One with only five defencemen, he agreed to add Bill White to play with Stapleton. This meant Guy Lapointe would also sit. Thus, Savard's injury cost Canada two of its best players.

On offence, perhaps inspired by the success of the Soviets' explosive Kid Line in Game Three, Sinden put down the name of the first player the Buffalo Sabres drafted in franchise history two years earlier: Gilbert Perreault. But Sinden stopped short of putting together Canada's own Kid Line, keeping Rick Martin and Marcel Dionne in the stands once again.

Instead he dressed Dennis Hull, one of the most popular players on the team. Because Hull is also one of the funniest, people tend to underestimate his commitment to playing serious hockey. Over the previous four seasons in Chicago, he had averaged almost 30 goals and 63 points a year. But what impressed coaches and teammates more was his steadfast backchecking, making him one of the NHL's best defensive forwards before the league awarded trophies for such things.

A few years later, when Montreal forward Bob Gainey was rightly celebrated for his defensive play, while scoring 20 goals just four times with powerful linemates, Yvan Cournoyer joked, "You know, the best defensive player on the Black Hawks scores 40 goals a year."

Like Pete Mahovlich and Tony Esposito, Hull played in his brother's shadow. But if Hull needed a chance to show what he could do, Sinden had given him one.

Sinden also gave Cashman's replacement, Bill Goldsworthy, his first start since Game Two—plus a pregame lecture about avoiding the kind of dumb penalties he was prone to take—and put Hadfield and Gilbert back into the lineup for the first time since Game One. Sinden hoped these moves would mitigate the fatigue of his already stressed troops.

Finally, Sinden told Dryden he would start in Vancouver—on the dual assumptions that Tony Esposito needed a break and Dryden's horrible first game had to be an aberration. The local papers ripped Sinden for this decision, since Tony Esposito had played quite well in his two games, but Dryden felt he had something to prove and was eager to prove it.

—

DESPITE its catchy name, Team Canada was still anything but: just a collection of All-Stars with inadequate conditioning, weak team spirit, and uncertain internal leadership. Canada's lineup had already featured 24 different skaters occupying 17 spots, a jumble of a squad with no focal point.

Of the team's four alternate captains, Mikita would play in only one more Summit game, while Mahovlich and Ratelle were quiet, "lead by example" types. That works well over a long season, but the team needed more in a short series, especially with their backs against the wall. No, to get out of the jam they needed a fiery front man unafraid to take on everyone from his teammates to his countrymen to the NHL's leaders and even Soviet players and officials, whatever the cost, and unify everybody for a singular mission.

They were about to find him.

—

PHIL and Tony Esposito's grandparents left Italy for a better life in Sault Ste. Marie, Ontario, where their father was born. When their father turned 14, he went to work for Algoma Steel, the town's main employer, as a welder.

"His nickname was 'the Bushel,'" Phil Esposito recalls. "He was maybe five foot ten, but man, was he barrel-chested, and his forearms were so big—jeez! He arm wrestled Tony *and* me, when we were in our 20s, *at the same time*, and he'd beat us both! Christ! My old man was something, I tell you.

"My dad got kicked out of hockey at 13 for punching a ref. I think that's where I got my disdain for officials. But off the ice he was a different guy. He had a big heart, and he was very diligent, very deliberate. My brother has my dad's personality, and I definitely have my mother's. If she had something to say, she said it. That's me."

For the Espositos, hockey was the fastest way out of a tough town dominated by shipping and steel. Although Sault Ste. Marie, Ontario, shares the St. Mary's River with Sault Ste. Marie, Michigan, the Canadian town is five times larger, with about 75,000 people today. It has produced the Maki brothers, Ivan Boldirev, Ron Francis, and Marty Turco, and four Hall of Famers—a testament to Canada's hockey culture.

"I learned how to play hockey on the streets of Sault Ste. Marie," Phil says, "how to stickhandle, pass, and shoot, by playing with a puck on the street in the winter and a ball in the summer. You don't need ice."

Phil's skating was always a liability, and it almost cost him his chance. After the Chicago Black Hawks signed him in 1960 at age 18, they sent him to their top junior team, the St. Catharines Teepees. But the Teepees concluded he couldn't help their club and sent him to the Bruins' junior affiliate in Niagara Falls. A mere two laps into Esposito's first practice, the coach told him, "If you can't make it in St. Catharines, what makes you think you can make my team? Pack up your shit and get outta here."

A despondent Esposito called Bob Wilson, a famous scout.

"Go to the Junior B team in Sarnia [Ontario]," Wilson told him, and he did.

"I tore the league apart," Esposito recalls, scoring 47 goals and 61 assists in just 32 games. He even notched 12 points in a single playoff game.

His scoring knack and fierce competitive spirit got him a ticket back to St. Catharines. Now 19, old by junior standards, and pudgy at 217 pounds, Esposito again drew attention at his first practice that August. When coach Rudy Pilous saw Esposito skating, he barked, "Hey Fatso! Come over here! How much do you weigh?"

"I don't know," Esposito lied. "Two ten?"

"Come back at 200 on October 3. You lose that, I'll give you a contract for 60 bucks a week."

Avoiding bread and pasta, the staples of his mother's cooking, Esposito dropped 16 pounds in two months and came back at 201.

"You didn't make it to 200," Pilous said.

"Ah, c'mon, Rudy!"

"Okay, I'll give you $57.50, docking you $2.50 for that one pound."

"And that," Esposito recalls, "is how my career started."

Esposito's prolific scoring in St. Catharines earned him a sweater on Chicago's top minor-league team in St. Louis. The Black Hawks brought him up to Chicago midway through the 1963–64 season, centring a line with Bobby Hull.

"Bobby taught me more about the game, and about life, than anybody," Esposito says. "Everything from eliminating my bad grammar—'It's "doesn't matter," not "don't matter"!'—to how I signed my name. 'Always sign your name so it's legible,' he told me. And boy, I still do to this day. Absolutely."

Four years after getting cut from two Junior A teams in the same month, Esposito established himself as a top scorer in the NHL's fiercely competitive Original Six. In 1967 the Black Hawks traded Esposito to Boston, where he joined Bobby Orr and became the first player in NHL history to score 100 points in a season. He would do it six times, winning two Hart Trophies as league MVP and two Stanley Cups.

Esposito turned down Sinden's invitation to play on Team Canada until Orr made the case. Phil relented, and got his brother to play, too. Phil was the team's leader from the start, but he admits he didn't take it seriously—until it turned serious. Once that happened, nobody worked harder.

Without the Esposito brothers, it's a safe bet Canada would have lost Game Two—when the brothers were named the two players of the game—and perhaps a couple more.

But Phil Esposito's finest hour would arrive at the team's lowest point.

19

GAME FOUR: TOUGH CROWD

September 8, 1972

After the Vancouver Millionaires (later known as the Maroons) competed in five Stanley Cup Finals between 1915 and 1924, winning one, the city was relegated to minor-league status from 1926 until 1970, when the NHL created expansion franchises in Vancouver and Buffalo.

Perhaps to the surprise of Vancouver's visitors, who invariably find the people as friendly as the city is beautiful, NHL players maintain it's one of the harder places to play. No one knew this better than Dale Tallon, one of Ferguson's pickups, who served as Vancouver's consolation prize after Buffalo picked Gilbert Perreault first overall in the 1970 draft.

"They wanted Perreault," Tallon says, "and I can't blame them. That guy's really good! No wonder they were pissed off."

Despite Tallon being Vancouver's lone representative at the All-Star Game in each of his first two seasons, "They booed me pretty well when I was playing there," he recalls. "Their hockey fans are really involved—*not* laid-back. I was probably the only guy on Team Canada that understood that."

It didn't help that Vancouver, like Winnipeg, resented being constantly overlooked by the "Eastern elites." Getting an NHL franchise certainly helped, but the locals weren't too pleased to see the Canucks' two Team Canada delegates, Dale Tallon and Jocelyn Guèvremont, in the stands for their fourth straight game, while Buffalo's star, Gilbert Perreault, would be playing his first. Throw in Team Canada's underwhelming start, which had the entire country grumbling, and you had a crowd poised to pounce before the puck even dropped.

"They had an awful group of fans there," Pete Mahovlich says. "During the player introductions, same thing happened that happened in Montreal: booing everyone but the home guys."

And, in Vancouver's case, there were no home guys.

"The booing didn't surprise me—let me put it that way," Tallon says.

"Oh yes," Rod Seiling says. "Never forget it. Disappointing. But not unexpected. See, the media had fed Canadians this expectation of an easy 8–0 sweep. None of *us* said that. But when that didn't work out, the media was embarrassed. Their so-called expertise, how much they really knew about hockey, was obviously in question." But instead of admitting their mistakes and explaining how they had been misled, "The media turned on *us*. Now *we're* the bad guys. The Canadian people felt let down, and the media fed that line, and that was very hard to take."

The Vancouver fans took it one step further when they cheered the Soviets.

HOURS after the game, Dryden would say, "It's hard to say that a team feels defeated before the game, but, well, we seemed to have a sort of a 'let's get it over with and get to Moscow' attitude about things in the dressing room."

It soon became a self-fulfilling prophecy.

Vancouver fans had barely finished booing the Canadians, cheering the Soviets, and taking their seats when Bill Goldsworthy jumped over the boards to cross-check a Soviet player 84 seconds into the contest. Thirty-seven seconds later, Petrov passed to Lutchenko at the point, who paused while his forwards set up down low, then fired on net. Boris Mikhailov deflected the puck between Dryden's pads for an early 1–0 lead.

Sinden was beside himself. "What are you doing?" he asked Goldsworthy. "That thing was a penalty all the way. I didn't tell you to do that. Let's wake up out there."

Goldsworthy told Sinden not to worry, but on his very next shift he jacked a Soviet with his elbow and went off again. The Soviets ran the exact same power play: Petrov to Lutchenko, whose shot Mikhailov deflected into the corner of the net. Just seven minutes and 29 seconds into Game Four, the Soviets had a 2–0 lead.

Penalties are usually the result of contact with the puck carrier, a skirmish behind the play, or jostling after the whistle. The latter two are usually stupid and selfish, gaining the culprit's team little advantage even when they go uncalled—and those were the kind Team Canada was taking.

"We were shameful," Clarke says. "We couldn't keep up with them, and we resorted to taking one penalty after the next—for no reason—which is a sign that your team is not good enough and you're not in good enough shape. These penalties weren't for being tough or smart. They did no damage to the opponent. They just gave them a power play."

"Goldy took two bad penalties," Henderson says, "and they scored twice, just like that, and that took us out of the game. Down 2–0 early against a good team, you start taking chances you shouldn't. And you know you're not playing the game the way you should, but you can barely help yourself."

"We took some bad penalties," Esposito says, "and we learned real quick you just can't do that against them. They had a killer power play, and we paid."

Were they headed for another Montreal-style blowout—perhaps even worse? The Vancouver fans certainly thought so.

"I was up in the stands for this one," Pete Mahovlich says, "and it was embarrassing. The booing started early. In the middle of the first period you heard a smattering of boos, then it just grew and grew and grew. It got pretty ugly. You had to remind yourself we were playing at home."

After one week of games, the Canadians were in better shape, but still awed by the Soviets' incredible conditioning, stamina, and skating. They would learn years later from the Soviet players themselves that, like many Eastern bloc athletes, they had been put on performance-enhancing drugs. "I was strong in my upper body," Park recalls, "and I had to work harder to move them than I ever did NHL players. They could only test the Canadian players for hops—and we'd test positive."

"I remember Dennis Hull in that game, his first," Sinden says. "Like a lot of NHL wingers, he'd been trained to go up and down his lane. One time [when] he came to the bench, he said that his guy would leave the ice and be replaced by another guy with fresh legs, and sometimes a third guy. He said, 'I've got to get a transfer to another train.'"

In the second period, Team Canada outshot the Soviets, 8–4, all but squelching the Soviet offence—yet the Soviets put two of those four shots past Dryden, who never looked comfortable, to take a 4–1 lead. The Canadians' lone tally came from the youngster, Perreault, who bounced one in off a Soviet defenceman.

The Canadians should have been credited with another goal when, down 3–1, Hadfield passed to Gilbert in front and the puck bounced off his skate and in. The referees ruled incorrectly that Gilbert had kicked it, and disallowed the goal.

But the Canadians weren't giving up, coming out for the third period as determined as ever. They hammered Tretiak with an incredible 23 shots—enough for an entire game, some nights—while allowing a meagre six against Dryden. Yet they could only get two past Tretiak—the first from Bergman to Esposito to Goldsworthy, to cut the Soviets' lead to 4–2 with 13:06 left, only to see Shadrin expand the gap to 5–2 with 8:55 remaining. A final goal from Goldsworthy to Esposito to Hull with 22 seconds left made the final score more palatable, at 5–3, but it didn't mean much.

"I was in the stands," Berenson recalls, "and holy smokes, were the fans ever booing. You couldn't even hear the PA announcer give Dennis's goal—*our* goal. And I didn't blame them. By the end of the game, we'd played four games in Canada, and lost two convincingly. It wasn't working out the way we thought it would."

"Of all the people on that team, I was probably the most ready for the fans," says Tallon, "but I still didn't think it would be *that* bad. It got to be pretty severe."

As distracting and disappointing as the jeering might have been, the Canadians knew the fans weren't the problem, but the symptom.

"Ohhh yeah," Clarke says. "We deserved them, we *earned* them, by playing the way we did. They wanted us to win, and they came to cheer us on. But we played shitty. We didn't uphold our end of the deal. We got our asses kicked. It's not that our emotions were off, it's that they weren't enough. Look, you can work your ass off and still do fuck-all, and in that game that's exactly what I did."

For the first time in the series, Clarke's line didn't account for a single point.

"I was struggling all night," Henderson recalls, "and our line just didn't click."

"I was always a guy who believed that after training camp was over, the game was 90 percent mental," Esposito says. "I never underestimated my opponent. But I did in '72—a *huge* lesson. And I never underestimated my opponent after that."

The booing reached a crescendo when Team Canada left the ice in defeat.

"All I remember," Dryden wrote, "are the boos."

"Goldy was giving it his heart and soul all night," Esposito says of his linemate that night, "and he was devastated, the way he was treated."

The night's bizarre backdrop set up one of the most dramatic moments of the series: the TV interview with Phil Esposito, who had scored one goal and assisted on Canada's other two, while notching a team-best plus-5 on scoring chances. The next closest were Clarke, Henderson, and Ellis, who were all at plus-2, despite their shared disappointment in their play.

═

"I was coming out on the ice to take the player of the game award with Mikhailov, and shook his hand," Esposito says. "But I wanted to get my stick and jam it down their throats. Still gets me! But what really set me off were these three teenage kids standing behind the Zamboni, looking at me and yelling, 'Communism is better! Admit it now!' Oh man! I can still see those kids. I get hot even now just thinking about it!"

Nobody else remembers those teenagers, but everyone remembers what came next: an impromptu speech that would change the tenor of the series.

"During his interview," recalls Serge Savard, who missed the game with his fractured foot, "he's sweating so hard, it's dripping off him. Phil never sweated like that in his life!"

No matter how prepared a coach or player might otherwise be, the one moment nobody can rehearse comes immediately after a loss, which is why it's the most likely time to say the wrong thing. Emotions are high, your guard is down, and the reporter suddenly sticks a microphone in your face. A lot can go wrong, and things rarely go right. CTV's Johnny Esaw put that microphone in front of Esposito just seconds after the game ended.

"Honestly, I don't even remember what his question was," Esposito says. "But once I started, it just flowed and flowed. Came right from my heart and my guts."

His comments run only three paragraphs, but they tell a story.

"To the people across Canada," Esposito said, face drawn and dripping sweat, "we tried, we gave it our best. And to the people that boo us . . . geez. I'm really . . . all of us guys are really disheartened and we're disillusioned, and we're disappointed in some of the people. We cannot believe the bad press we've got, the booing we've gotten in our own buildings. If the Russians boo their players . . . then I'll come back and I'll apologize to each one of the Canadians, but I don't think they will.

"I'm really, really, I'm really disappointed. I am completely disappointed. I cannot believe it. Some of our guys are really, really down in the dumps. We know, we're trying. But hell, I mean, we're doing the best we can, and they got a good team, and let's face facts. But that doesn't mean that we're not giving it our 150 percent, because we certainly are . . .

"Every one of us guys, 35 guys that came out and played for Team Canada, we did it because we love our country, and not for any other reason, no other reason. They can throw the money for the pension fund out the window. They can throw anything they want out the window. We came because we love Canada. And even though we play in the United States, and we earn money in the United States, Canada is still our home, and that's the only reason we came. And I don't think it's fair that we should be booed."

Johnny Inchot, the producer of the telecast, later told Esposito that "his guys were telling him, 'Wrap it up! Wrap it up!' and he says, 'No fucking way! He's on a roll—let him go!'"

Inchot clearly made the right call. It was great TV.

"I'll never forget that as long as I live," Gretzky says. "Sweat was just pouring off Phil, and then he let his heart out. It was so impactful because he was just being spontaneous. He wasn't prepared, he just spoke from the heart, and even an 11-year-old watching on TV could sense that. They let him talk—and it was very emotional. I don't know if I've ever heard a speech I remember better than that—not so much the words, but how it *felt*. He brought the country together."

But was it great motivation? Only those players sitting in the stands saw it live, while those who'd played that night were already in the locker room. Some didn't find out about it until the next day.

"I was sitting in the stands for that one," Ratelle says. "I recall everything! I listened to Phil's speech going out on the PA system. And when he's talking, I'm thinking, 'Way to go, Phil! It's right on!' I knew the guys tried as hard as they could, but the Russians just won the game. Phil's speech was important because the people were booing us, because they thought we were going to win easily. And they were fooled just like we were."

When Esposito finished, he wiped his face with a towel CTV had provided, and had no idea if his talk had any impact whatsoever. When he returned to the locker room, thick with defeat, he admits, "I thought all the guys would think, 'He was showboating.' Then Jean Ratelle came in and said, 'Guys, guys! You gotta see what Espo said!'"

"So Phil came in after that," recalls Ellis, "and he says, 'Guys, I told them what it was like, all right. But I told them the truth.' Really, at the time I don't think we had any idea what had just happened."

"I was dressing beside Phil that night," Henderson says, "and the locker room was pretty bleak—as bad as it gets. Guys complaining that they'd wasted their summers for *this*? And then Phil sits down and tells me, 'I really teed off on the people.' I didn't see that speech. They should have shown us in the dressing room. But honestly, it was a relief just to talk about something else."

The players didn't give it any more thought—and why should they? They had problems of their own, down 1–2–1 with four games left in Moscow and a completely different style of hockey to figure out. But it was the kind of moment where you had to be there—as Ratelle had been, and thousands of fans, and millions watching on TV. The 18 players back in the locker room would soon feel the ripples.

"We didn't know what Phil said for quite a while," Ellis says. "All we knew is they definitely picked the right guy to interview. He was so emotional. And he spelled it out beautifully, that 'hey'—without crossing the line, right?—'we're doing our best, we're playing our best. But these guys are good!'

"And some of the guys may not agree with me, but I've said this many times since: I believe the next morning when people across Canada were sitting at their breakfast table reading this, they were saying, 'Hey, what do you think of Phil's speech? Maybe the Russians are better than we think. Maybe we should get behind this team.' Hey, it changed the topic! And that's when the mailbags of telegrams and everything started coming in to Moscow, waiting for us when we arrived. We really had no idea."

"I didn't hear about Phil's speech until the next day, in the papers," Clarke says. "I agreed with what he said, but I also felt bad, because I had let my teammates down, our fans down, and I think a lot of players thought that. We let ourselves down. I don't think Phil's speech helped me as a player. I played shitty and needed to play better. That was on me. But I think what he did united the country on our side. We *needed* the fans on our side, and that really helped do that."

"One thing for sure: that's when Phil became the leader of that team," Sinden says. "There was no question after that."

Sinden never named a team captain, but from that night forward he didn't have to. After Esposito's impassioned defence of his teammates—when he was already the team's leading scorer with five points and could have pointed fingers elsewhere—no one had any doubt who their leader was.

That was important, because after winning just one game out of four on home ice, they had reason to doubt just about everything else.

═

Not surprisingly, the media gave it to Team Canada even harder than the Vancouver fans had.

In a column titled "Russian series destroys NHL's credibility," the *Montreal Star*'s Red Fisher wrote, "I've had this idea fixed in my mind that the NHL was the strongest league in the world and its players were the most proficient hockey players in the world. Now, in what amounts to a one-week wipeout, the idea has been erased. If it hasn't been erased, it's close to it."

Fisher's colleague at the *Star*, John Robertson, added, "As of today the Russians are No. 1 and we are Brand X."

In the *Winnipeg Free Press*, Maurice Smith piled on: "For years Canadian hockey fans have been fed a steady diet of publicity extolling the greatness of the National Hockey League," and "fans didn't expect to see the superstars humbled by players from a country that has been playing the game for only 25 years."

Harsh, perhaps, but who could say a single word wasn't true?

Frank Mahovlich added, "After seeing what the Russians did to us at our game here in Canada, I'm afraid nothing in sports is sacred anymore. If someone gives them a football, they'll beat the Dallas Cowboys and win the Super Bowl in two years."

"We knew what had happened," Seiling says, "but other than playing on heart, and hoping for time, we were at a disadvantage.

"That's why Sweden became so important."

20

LONG WEEKEND

No hockey team had ever been placed on so high a pedestal, nor fallen so far, so fast.

A couple hours after suffering one of the most demoralizing defeats in hockey history, some of the Canadian players boarded planes headed for their hometowns or NHL cities, while others flew out the next morning. All were eager to start their much-needed three-day break before they reconvened in Toronto on Tuesday, a day ahead of their departure for Stockholm. Some would spend the break at Toronto's Sutton Place Hotel; others dispersed to homes in Montreal, Boston, and Rochester, to name a few, where they would pass the time with their wives and kids and sleep in their own beds for a few nights.

On the midnight flight from Vancouver to Montreal, the players were surprised to see the Soviets. A nightmare for some, perhaps, but for Dryden, an opportunity to meet players he now greatly respected—or it would have been, if he knew how to say more than "thank you" in Russian.

Thanks to the distance and time zones, Dryden's flight would land in Montreal at 10:30 a.m. on Saturday, September 9. He stumbled off the flight tired, haggard, and beaten, dreading the days ahead—when he realized he had fallen asleep on the plane with his contact lenses still in, now stuck to his eyeballs. They felt like someone had "rubbed sandpaper on them."

Jocelyn Guèvremont gave him a ride from the airport to the Montreal apartment where Dryden stayed during the season. After getting a prescription for a special ointment, Dryden opened the door to his apartment, dropped his bags, applied the ointment, and fell asleep. According to the prescription, he had to keep his eyes shut for the rest of the day and could not open them again until the middle of the following day.

Perhaps the doctor's orders were merciful. There was nothing the Canadian players could read or watch that would have made them feel any better about their situation. In the seven days since Team Canada flew out of Montreal, hours after the 7–3 opening night debacle, the team had gained only one victory—and the contempt of 22 million fellow Canadians, starting with the journalists.

IF the players wanted to kill some time, they could watch the United States basketball team take on the Soviet Union for the Olympic gold medal—though they probably wouldn't have found it very relaxing. The Americans had a 63–0 all-time record in Olympic basketball, but the Soviets had medalled in the previous five Olympics, with four silvers, and entered the final game in Munich with a perfect 7–0 record. With the U.S. down 49–48 with three seconds left, Doug Collins hit two free throws to give the U.S. a 50–49 lead.

Inbounding the ball from under their own basket, the Soviets failed to get a shot off, and the buzzer ended the game. Or so it seemed, until an official, who had no jurisdiction over the situation, emerged from the stands to insist they do it over. They did, with the same result—then the same official said they had to do it again. The third time was the charm for the Soviets, who tossed the ball into the bucket as time expired. Final score: USSR 51, USA 50.

The Americans boycotted the medal ceremony. It remains the sport's most controversial finish. To this day the U.S. players have refused to accept their silver medals, which remain in a vault in Lausanne, Switzerland.

A day later, on Sunday, September 10, Frank Shorter appeared to become the first American to win the marathon since 1908—until an imposter entered the stadium first. Although the imposter was soon pulled from the track, the boos continued as Shorter entered the stadium for his final lap.

In September of 1972, it seemed that no international competition between East and West—be it a basketball game, a marathon, or a chess match, which ended in Fischer's favor when Spassky forfeited with a call from his hotel room, drawing international condemnation—could be settled without controversy.

To the Canadian players waking up that morning, however, those dramas seemed very far away. Their own problems were all too near. The three-day hiatus had been planned as a nice respite before the trip to Europe, but the shocking results had turned their homes into purgatories filled with hostile newspapers and TV and radio programs wherever they turned.

"There was no point trying to hide from it," says Seiling, who returned to his family home in Waterloo, Ontario. "I don't hide from things. When you ignore things, it doesn't make them better. Might as well face it. That said, I didn't go out and buy *more* papers. I didn't need to read 10 papers to get the point: they were disappointed. They were mad. Well, we were, too!"

Even if the media had magically fallen silent for three days, their own thoughts provided plenty of unpleasant noise.

"That was not good," Henderson says, lost in a bad memory. "That was not good. We were embarrassed. This was going to be the best time of our lives, we were going to put these Russians in their place—and now it's the most miserable."

In the quiet of their homes, often the first notion that popped into their minds was how woefully unprepared they were compared with the Soviets.

"We start camp August 14, and we had to play on September 2," Frank Mahovlich says. "We're not ready—not for *this*. We had just gone through a lot of emotions—most of them bad—and it was tough. It was exhausting, and we were exhausted."

Harry Sinden, on the cusp of his 40th birthday, returned to Rochester, New York, to see his wife and four daughters. This gave him time to think—maybe too much. It occurred to him he had tried to walk away from hockey three times—when he turned down the Bruins camp and later the Cleveland Barons' offer as a player, and when he left coaching the Boston Bruins days after winning the Stanley Cup. But he hadn't anticipated how much he would miss the game.

"As I sit here in my backyard making this tape," he said at the time, "the sun shining on my face on a bright September afternoon, I have come to believe that hockey never leaves the blood of a Canadian. You like to think you're more mature than that, that a game shouldn't mean that much, but it does.

"Why else would the people react the way they did to the Russians beating us last week? Their pride was hurt. This is the Canadian game and now someone is trying to take it away from us. To a non-Canadian this might seem absurd, but in Canada, hockey is *the* game."

That's what most of the players concluded: however knotty their current predicament, the game meant too much to them, and to their country, to walk away now. They had to find a way out of this mess. If the media offered mostly castor oil for the players, in that unsavoury stew they discovered a plum: Phil Esposito's speech after the Vancouver game, which had been covered by every major media outlet.

"Phil was speaking for all of us, truly," Seiling says. "And there was nothing that you would want to retract—or as they say in today's lexicon, 'walk back.' It was great that he said it. It came from the heart, and it was all well said. We had gotten dealt a bad hand, but we were trying our best.

"I knew the job we had to do. I still believed we could turn it around, and I never doubted that. I *never* doubted that. I knew what I could do, and I knew what the guys in that room could do. All we needed was a chance to show that."

ON Tuesday, September 12, Team Canada's players, coaches, and officials said goodbye to their children for the rest of the month to embark on their longest road trip. Whatever happened overseas, they knew the world would look different when they returned: either in a defeat that would reverberate for the rest of their lives, or somehow in a great triumph, which now looked as unlikely as it would be welcome.

They returned to Toronto a month after they had arrived for camp, and attended a reception at Labatt, the brewer that had paid a then-extraordinary $800,000 to run its ads throughout the series. The executives at Labatt, at least, were not complaining. The ratings were already setting records.

WHEN the Canadian players looked at the schedule months earlier, the week-long stint in Sweden looked like a mini-vacation at best, and an extravagant waste of time at worst. But it now looked like an oasis, a chance to regroup as a team before taking on the biggest challenge of their hockey lives.

"Leaving was a relief," Sinden remembers.

"We needed time away from the fans and the media," Berenson recalls. "It was like two losses meant hockey had never existed in Canada—like it was over, and we were all personally responsible.

There wasn't any good news from anywhere back home. The sooner we got out of Canada, the better.

"By then we knew this wasn't just a hockey series anymore. It was now about the identity of the NHL, of Canadian hockey, and really, even of the country itself. That's enough pressure for anyone.

"With all that, you had to feel that at least the guys in the locker room were on your side. So our team really had to come together."

PART III

Becoming a Team Overnight

21

AN OASIS OVERSEAS

To once again appease their NHL overlords' fear of losing all the league's best players in a single accident, the team took two planes across the Atlantic—one through Paris and the other through Frankfurt, with a seven-hour layover—then met up in Stockholm on Wednesday, September 13. Sinden made sure all the potential partiers were on Ferguson's flight, since Sinden knew none of them would risk bothering the former enforcer. But neither flight carried Frank Mahovlich, who had stayed behind to talk with his doctors.

It marked the first trip overseas for most of them, and it showed. Back when you needed only a driver's licence, if that, to cross the Canada–U.S. border, the Esposito brothers managed to lose their new passports on the flight to Frankfurt, and were saved by an Air Canada agent who found them on the floor, under some seats.

After landing in Stockholm, the Canadians were bused to the five-star Grand Hotel downtown. The Sutton Place might have been Toronto's hottest new hotel, but the Grand has been one of Europe's finest since 1874. Located on an inlet of the Baltic

Sea, with yachts docked in front of the entrance, the 300-room hotel sits next to the National Museum and directly across from the Royal Palace. It had already played host to Sarah Bernhardt, Albert Einstein, Ingrid Bergman, Igor Stravinsky, the Rolling Stones, and presidents and royalty from around the globe, as well as the recipients of the Nobel Prizes since the awards were created in 1901. In short, it was just the place for a band of world-weary players to relax and become a real team.

And skate—hard. On the morning of Thursday, September 14, the team hopped on a bus to travel six kilometres (about three and a half miles) to the 8,000-seat Johanneshovs Isstadion. Built in 1955 as an outdoor rink, it was enclosed in 1963 for the World Championship—the one that started the Soviets' 10-year winning streak. Far more important to the Canadians, the rink itself had Olympic dimensions, similar to their next stop, Moscow's Luzhniki Palace of Sport—15 feet (4.5 metres) wider than an NHL rink, with deeper corners and more space behind the net.

"It was so critical to play on the Olympic sheet," Paul Henderson says. "We didn't know anything about it. Heck, for most of us it was our first time overseas."

Today, the national junior and under-18 teams of the big six hockey nations—Canada, the United States, Sweden, Finland, Russia, and the Czech Republic—all play on Olympic sheets and travel to international tournaments. But in 1972 a team made up of NHL All-Stars could count only three players who'd ever experienced the Olympic rink: Red Berenson, Rod Seiling, and Ken Dryden.

An extra seven and a half feet (2.5 metres) on either side might not sound like much, but if you're a goalie accustomed to calculating angles based on the boards, blue line, and hash marks, or a defenceman who knows exactly when you can shut the door on the forwards when they cross the blue line, it's more than enough extra room to throw all your calculations off. Suddenly the door jamb is seven feet (a couple of metres) away, and you look foolish watching your man drive to the net, untouched. A less heralded side effect of the bigger sheet was fatigue, because players have that much more ice to cover.

"It's easier going from a big rink to a small rink than the opposite," Yvan Cournoyer says. "For the Russians, the change was easy. For us, it was hard. I never played on a big rink before! Big rinks like that give you a big advantage."

Knowing this, Sinden wisely set up rigorous two-a-day practices on their first two full days in Stockholm.

"When Harry was skating us hard, no one complained," Seiling says. "I'd go so far as to say that if Harry had *not* skated us ragged, we would have been on his ass, because by then we knew that's what we needed."

ACCLIMATING to the Olympic rink was necessary, but not sufficient. The Canadians also had to counter how the Soviets were putting all that extra space to use.

"What we had the most trouble getting used to," Ellis recalls, "was the way the Russians would regroup in the neutral zone. But Harry had some ideas about that, too."

"I had a bunch of drills that were kind of interesting," Sinden says. "Things they had never seen before. On one drill, I wouldn't let them shoot the puck until I blew the whistle, so they had to keep passing and controlling the play until I did. On another they had to keep regrouping until I blew the whistle to send them charging into the [offensive] zone. We had another where we played with no offsides, then nine guys a side, and so on."

Sinden wanted his players to break a lifetime of habits the old Canadian system had developed, "things we never even thought about, we just did," so they wouldn't be surprised by what the Soviets were doing. If they got these concepts down, they might even be able to surprise the Soviets with some new tricks.

Esposito remembers Sinden's new drills very well. "He blew the whistle, and wherever you were, you stopped and skated as fast as you could back to the neutral zone, to show us how we'd have to regroup and backcheck against the Soviets. I remember that distinctly. Very, very ingenious. We did it in Russia, too. Hey, let me tell you: Harry wasn't stupid!"

"To me, the single biggest factor in that series was Harry's decision to play a new system," says Dale Tallon, who four decades later would help construct Chicago's three-time Stanley Cup champion roster. The Soviet defencemen "rarely shot the puck in those days. With the bigger ice, they'd beat you down low, so Harry put our two wings down low and put the centre up high, to clog up the middle. Then he got us doing the same things, passing down low instead of shooting up high, and regrouping until we could go into the zone together."

Unstated was the confidence Sinden showed in his players to make such a dramatic change—one that was all or nothing: if the players were smart, worked hard, and invested themselves in Sinden's strategy, they just *might* be able to get it all down before Moscow. But if they weren't sharp enough to rethink the game from the ground up, or willing to commit themselves to doing so, it would fail miserably—and there wouldn't be enough time to go back the way they came.

"Look, that's a big-time decision," Tallon says. "It fails, and Sinden's the one they blame—and he had to know that. Changing our system was the biggest gamble he made—and he made a few. To adapt like that on the fly, that's pretty rare. Harry was *way* ahead of his time—certainly in Canada. I love that guy."

Sinden bet all his chips on these new ideas, but none of them would have worked if the players weren't ready to listen. By September 14, they were. Several players say that if Sinden had tried the same drills a month earlier in Toronto, the players wouldn't have bought in. As Berenson said, "Somehow the same thing in Toronto sounded different in Sweden."

A few players noticed Ulf Sterner, Sweden's best player, watching the Canadians practise. Sterner, then 31, had already played in eight World Championships and two Olympics, winning a gold, five silvers, and a bronze, and he'd win another silver in 1973. A forward with great puck-handling skills who invented the now-common stick-to-skate-to-stick move, he had actually been the first European to make it to the NHL, playing a grand total of four games for the New York Rangers in 1965. But he finished with no goals, assists, points, or penalty minutes, just a lot of bad memories of his opponents and even his teammates, who were not ready to accept a European taking one of their jobs.

Even without bullying, the NHL was simply much tougher than international hockey, which didn't allow bodychecking in the offensive zone until 1969. Sterner played 68 games in the American and Central Hockey Leagues, scoring 30 goals and 35 assists, then returned to Europe, where he played until 1990, at the age of 49.

When Dryden played against Sterner in the 1969 World Championship, "he seemed very nervous." But then, Dryden wasn't feeling much better himself in 1972.

"I'm playing very stupidly," he wrote of his first practice in Sweden. "It seems that I've hit rock bottom. I'm doing everything wrong. My confidence is zilch. I've forgotten how to play the game."

The second day of practice, Dryden scrimmaged a full 20 minutes without allowing a goal. But when his dad, who had flown in from Canada, joined him for dinner that night, his son told him "not to expect any miracles in Moscow." After allowing 12 goals in his first two games, he didn't expect to play in Moscow anyway.

By then it had also become clear that Bobby Orr wouldn't be playing in Moscow, either. When he skated at practice, his knee would swell up afterward, so scrimmaging was out, and even walking downtown was hazardous, causing his knee to lock up and almost send him to the ground. Yet he still attended all meetings, practices, and games to support his teammates.

"If we have Bobby Orr, we're certainly 10, 15, 20 percent better," Savard says. "The way he skated, and carried the puck all over the ice, he would have had a *big* advantage if he played on the big surface."

"We were missing Orr and Hull," Ellis says. "If we had 'em, we might not win every game—the Soviets *were* that good—but I bet we'd go 6–2."

With Orr out for good, Savard now looked like an essential piece of the puzzle if they were going to fight back. Could he return? And if so, when?

IN the days before the internet, the *Montreal Gazette*, the *Globe and Mail*, and other Canadian papers could not be easily found in Stockholm, so the players could ignore the deluge of criticism raining down on them back home. The Swedish media, who traditionally took pleasure in describing Canadian amateurs as "animals," gave Team Canada the first break it had received from just about anyone that month, writing respectful stories about the players and the historic nature of the Soviet series. It helped that Team Canada's two exhibitions that weekend would cap the 50th anniversary of Swedish hockey, twice as long as the Soviets had been playing.

But a team can't bond merely by omission, just removing annoyances. With the notable exception of Game Two, the team's last 10 days in Canada had been joyless. Sinden and other team leaders knew that had to change. To forge a true bond requires everyone to let their guard down and trust each other.

"The difference between today's players and players in our era," Park says, "is that in my day, after practice you'd all go out for lunch. If you didn't know a guy, you'd get a meal and a couple beers, and you learned to like your teammate. Today's teams, they don't necessarily do that. After a game, they get on a charter and go straight home, but we'd stay over, spend a night in Detroit, Toronto, or Chicago, go to a bar, and shoot the shit and talk about the game, then fly home the next morning."

After the first practice in Sweden, the team accepted an invitation from Margaret Meagher, Canada's ambassador to Sweden, to a reception at the ambassador's impressive lake home just outside Stockholm. The event turned into a surprise party for Sinden, who turned 40 that day—though, as Dryden noted, "I'll bet he has aged about 20 years in the last month."

But the real fun started afterward, when they all went out to the bars together for the first time as a team.

What broke the ice?

However big a hole the players had dug for themselves, however despised they were at home or abroad, they knew one thing: no one else in the world could know how it felt to be *them*, playing in a pressure cooker like no other.

In their case, another element completed the chemical reaction: beer.

"In Sweden we had no interruptions of family and friends," Park says. "No media. Just us. We were forced to spend a lot of time together, and we started to hang out and talk to each other—really, for the first time. The old [NHL] system had to be broken down. It's amazing what seven or eight beers will do!"

"We all went out together, as a team, and we included everybody," Seiling says. "I can remember in one bar, Billy White got up and started emceeing some musical entertainment—the kind of thing you'd never do in Canada, or with guys from other teams. By the time we get to Sweden, in case you had any doubts where we stood, it just reinforced the fact that the only friends we had were the guys in that locker room. Exclamation point. Full stop."

The day after the visit to the ambassador's home they endured two more hard skates, then received the much-anticipated news that Guy Lapointe's wife, who was already 10 days overdue, had just given birth to a healthy baby boy, Guy Jr., at 7:07 a.m. in Montreal.

"Guy was going to leave the team to be with her, and I made him change his mind," recalls Serge Savard. Instead of skipping the training camp to stay home with his pregnant wife, as Jacques Laperrière had done, or flying back home in the middle of the series, as others might have, Lapointe stayed. He wouldn't see his wife and newborn son until he got home two weeks later. His teammates loved him for it.

"We became a team when Guy Lapointe's wife gave birth," Esposito says. "We got a bunch of beer and walked across the street to a park, and we got drunk, telling stories and laughing and toasting Guy and his wife and his son. We had a ball!"

"It takes a long time to build a team, and we didn't have a long time," Clarke says. "I believe through the coaches, and a couple of the guys—Espo and Savard—they brought us together."

SINDEN could no longer ignore, massage, or postpone one element that threatened to burst this happy bubble: the lineup.

"In the beginning, we didn't have the synchronization," Jean Ratelle says. "We couldn't have. We didn't know each other, and the lineup was changing every night. For me, the problem was between the defence and the forwards. I was a centre, so I'd come back to help on D, but you have to know who you're playing with. In Sweden, Harry started to settle the lineup, especially on D. We are going to do or die with these guys. That was the right move."

"I felt sorry for the guys who couldn't get into the games in Canada, when we were losing," Henderson says. But like his teammates, he knew it would be foolhardy to keep trying different lineups and expect to win. They had to whittle their roster down. "So who are the guys who are going to play in Moscow?"

Sinden would have to make some hard decisions that were bound to upset some of the players. At the same time, Sinden knew that the two games in Sweden represented his next-to-last chance to get some players in, the last being the final exhibition game in Prague after the Summit Series ended. Another consideration: there was no substitute for game experience.

"You've got to get in *game shape*," Seiling says. "Until you start pushing and shoving in the corners and in front of the net, you're not fully ready. That's where you get in shape, where you get to expend the energy but also recover from it."

Sweden would also serve as a final tryout of sorts. No one said it, but everyone knew it.

After only two nights in Stockholm, on Friday, September 15, a couple players were already sufficiently unhappy that they asked to meet Eagleson in his room. Eagleson agreed, but when they showed up, led by Vic Hadfield, they brought seven more teammates with them. That totalled nine, or one-quarter of the roster. (Eagleson has vowed never to divulge the names.)

As Eagleson remembers it, they expressed their concerns about Sinden's decisions, particularly lines, playing time, and strategy.

"We don't think we'll win another game over here," one said. "You gotta do something," another said, then a third dropped the bomb: "You've got to get rid of Harry and Fergie."

Eagleson recalls, "One of them got smart, seeing how far they were going with this, and said they didn't speak for him. I suspect there were some fellow travellers along, too, but most of them meant it."

Eagleson listened without arguing before responding. "Look, guys, this is a team matter. I'll have a chat with Fergie and Harry."

Right when it seemed like they were finally coming together, a quarter were on the verge of breaking them all apart.

22

BABIES, BEERS, AND BRAWLS

For the two games against the Swedish national team, Harry Sinden recalls, "I made sure all the players who hadn't played got in."

He was still trying to do his best to fulfill his initial promise to the players. The Swedes wouldn't be the same as the Soviets, but they would turn out to provide far more serious competition than anyone anticipated—including the Swedes themselves.

For the first game Sinden wrote in Jocelyn Guèvremont and Brian Glennie on defence, filling in for Guy Lapointe and the injured Serge Savard, plus forwards Mickey Redmond and Marcel Dionne. Notably, Sinden kept Brad Park and Gary Bergman together, and Pat Stapleton and Bill White, two pairs that had solidified their status as regulars, plus Phil Esposito and the Ellis-Clarke-Henderson line, hoping to keep his most effective players sharp.

Sinden put the GAG Line back together for the first time since Game One to appease Hadfield, give them another look, and perhaps restore their status as the team's top unit. This experiment took on greater importance that day, Saturday, September 16, when Sinden learned that Frank Mahovlich would be rejoining

In 1946 an unorthodox, supremely confident Russian visionary named Anatoli Tarasov started a tiny outdoor rink that would produce Canada's first real hockey rivals. Tarasov rebuilt the sport from the ground up, not for kids to have fun but solely to catch the Canadians as swiftly as possible. In 1954 the Soviet Union stunned the hockey world by beating the Canadian amateurs for the World Championship. YURI KARMANOV

Anatoli Tarasov often said, "To copy is always to be second best." He did not try to outmuscle, outrush, or outshoot the Canadians—all losing bets. Instead, he determined his players would train more and skate better than their Canadian counterparts, and eschew individual play for selfless teamwork—creating the perfect model for Soviet socialism. YURI KARMANOV

While the Soviets trained in an army barracks 11 months a year, and started preparing for the Summit Series on July 5, Team Canada started working out on August 14. The camp was much harder than any NHL training camp they had seen, but they were far behind the Soviets. "So it turned out," Dale Tallon says, "three weeks doing jumping jacks in our underwear wasn't enough?! Oops."
FRANK LENNON/*TORONTO STAR* VIA GETTY IMAGES

The day before Game One, Team Canada saw the Soviets practise for the first time. "My first thought: 'Their equipment is horseshit!'" Brad Park recalls. "*These* guys are supposed to give us a run? I don't think so." But it was a smokescreen. The next night they wore new equipment. As Pat Stapleton said, "I can see what I couldn't see then: we'd been suckered—and we bought it, hook, line, and sinker." MELCHIOR DIGIACOMO/GETTY IMAGES

"I can't recall any game I've ever been at where you can just feel the tension," Foster Hewitt told TV viewers from coast to coast, "and it keeps building up, and it's very warm in the Forum tonight, and at the same time the fans are really on their toes. They hardly can wait to see the beginning of this game." HOCKEY HALL OF FAME AND MUSEUM

"We were like caged animals," Paul Henderson said. "Everyone in the country had been talking about this series for so long that we were at a fever pitch, eager to finally get at it." Six minutes into Game One, Henderson scored Canada's second goal. But he didn't gloat. He was breathing too hard. "I remember saying these exact words to Ronnie [Ellis]: 'This is gonna be a looooong series.'" MELCHIOR DIGIACOMO/GETTY IMAGES

When Team Canada's scouts watched Soviet goalie Vladislav Tretiak in Moscow, they didn't realize he had a hangover from his bachelor party. With him in net, they reported, Team Canada would enjoy "a five- or six-goal advantage." The opposite proved true: Tretiak was world class. "I figure he took at least five goals from me tonight," Phil Esposito said. PETER BREGG/CANADIAN PRESS

Ken Dryden was arguably the NHL's best goalie, but the Soviets scored seven times in Game One. "Every time we thought they were going to shoot, they passed," Paul Henderson recalls, "and every time we thought they were going to pass, they'd shoot. Never felt so bad for a goalie as I did for Kenny that night. I felt sorry for him—honest to God, I did." CANADIAN PRESS

Harry Sinden coached Boston to the Stanley Cup in 1970, at age 37—then left hockey for a construction company. When that collapsed, Sinden became Team Canada's coach, which quickly became an all-or-nothing proposition. Lose and he'd be out of hockey for good. Nonetheless, "Harry gave us a chance to win," Bob Clarke says, "because every decision he made on and off the ice was to help us win—nothing else. Sinden was outstanding." HOCKEY HALL OF FAME AND MUSEUM

In Game Two, with Team Canada holding a 2–1 lead in the third period and short-handed, Pete Mahovlich fooled the defenceman, then deked Tretiak on a great move. "Best goal I've ever seen!" Phil Esposito says. "I was so elated!" Pete says. "The emotion. Unbelievable. I didn't celebrate a lot of goals, but I celebrated that one!" To this day, all Mahovlich's teammates can recall it vividly. HOCKEY HALL OF FAME AND MUSEUM

If Team Canada had lost Game Two, Yvan Cournoyer says, "I think we would have been done. Too much. We had to win." They did, 4–1. "We won strictly on emotion—and desperation," Bob Clarke says. "That's all we had. But then a little bit of the arrogance creeps in and you're desperately hoping that the Russians really weren't as good as they looked in the first game."
PETER BREGG/CANADIAN PRESS

In 1968–69 Serge Savard became the first defenceman to win the Conn Smythe Trophy for playoff MVP. The next season he shattered his left femur, then broke it again in 1971, but Team Canada assistant coach John Ferguson insisted he come to training camp. "I consider Serge Savard one of the top five defencemen of all time," Phil Esposito says. "Savard has calmness. Calmness. I didn't realize how important that was, but in Moscow everyone could see what Serge added, and how much we needed that." HOCKEY HALL OF FAME AND MUSEUM

Named one of the NHL's top 100 players of all time in 2017, Brad Park made one mistake: being born the same year as Bobby Orr. Park finished second for the Norris Trophy (NHL's best defenceman) a record six times, four of them behind Orr. But when Orr couldn't play in the Summit Series, Park showed just how good he was, being named the Series' best defenceman. HOCKEY HALL OF FAME AND MUSEUM

After Canada fell back 1–2–1 after four games, the media blasted the team for four days before the players flew to Europe. "Leaving was a relief," Harry Sinden recalls. Before the series, the week-long stint in Sweden between Games Four and Five looked like an extravagant waste of time. But it now looked like an oasis, a chance to regroup as a team before taking on the biggest challenge of their hockey lives. BARRIE DAVIS/*THE GLOBE AND MAIL*/CANADIAN PRESS

After the Soviets threatened to house the Canadian players' wives in a different hotel, the players voted unanimously not to play the remaining games, and the Soviets backed down. In Moscow the players' suitcases and rooms were searched, and they were followed wherever they went. When Red Berenson, touring Moscow with his wife, Joy, focused his Super 8 movie camera on a band of old women trying to sweep the streets with twigs, a hand came over his lens and a man just said, "No." Berenson recalls, "All I could think the whole time was 'Get me out of here!' I just found the whole place incredibly depressing."
MELCHIOR DIGIACOMO/GETTY IMAGES

Vic Hadfield had just scored 50 goals on a record-setting line with Jean Ratelle and Rod Gilbert, but after sitting out two games he decided to leave Moscow before Game Five, and three others followed. "The last three games," Henderson says, echoing his teammates, "all our lines worked together like a hand in glove. It clicked. When the guys left, I gotta say, it made things easier."
MELCHIOR DIGIACOMO/GETTY IMAGES

MELCHIOR DIGIACOMO/GETTY IMAGES

The 11,000 Russian spectators wore black and brown, rarely cheered, and never stood up. Brad Park's wife, Gerry, recalls, "They had soldiers with guns lined all the way around the rink—very, very intimidating. This seemed serious." They were easily drowned out by 3,000 Canadian fans wearing colourful clothes, waving the newly minted Canadian flag, and chanting, "Da, da, Canada!" and "Nyet, nyet, Soviet!" When Soviet officials scattered them through the stadium, it backfired; the Canadian fans cheered even louder, creating the illusion that the rink was surrounded by Canadians, not Soviets.

MELCHIOR DIGIACOMO/GETTY IMAGES

Before Game Five, the first in Moscow, Phil Esposito slipped on a flower and fell to the ice. Most players would have been mortified, but Esposito took a knee, cradled his stick like a sceptre, and pretended to bow to the king. "You have to be confident, really confident, to play that off the way he did," says Mark Messier, who watched as an 11-year-old. "There's no preparing for that." AP PHOTO/EET/CANADIAN PRESS

In Game Five, Team Canada had a 3–0 lead. "And then," Jean Ratelle said, "it came . . ." Esposito gave up five goals in the third and Canada lost, 5–4. "Look, this one wasn't that complicated," Bob Clarke says. "A game like that is when you don't have enough [defensive specialists like] Ron Ellises. And that's how you lose a game like that."
VIKTOR BUDAN, VIKTOR SHANDRIN/TASS/CANADIAN PRESS

After blowing a 4–1 lead in Game Five, Team Canada had to win three straight games to win the series. Sinden told them, "Don't think about Game Seven or Game Eight. Just win your shift, then get ready for the next one." Pete Mahovlich bought in. "I never, ever played on a team that was good enough to win that didn't win. I always felt: just get me to the final game. I don't lose." MELCHIOR DIGIACOMO/GETTY IMAGES

"When people were saying, 'The Russians are going to beat you,' that really scared me," Yvan Cournoyer said. "And when you're scared, you're a good player. I've always been afraid to lose. Maybe that's why I won so much." Despite taking 31 penalty minutes to the Soviets' four, Team Canada played its best game, including Dryden, and they won, 3–2, to stay alive.
MELCHIOR DIGIACOMO/GETTY IMAGES

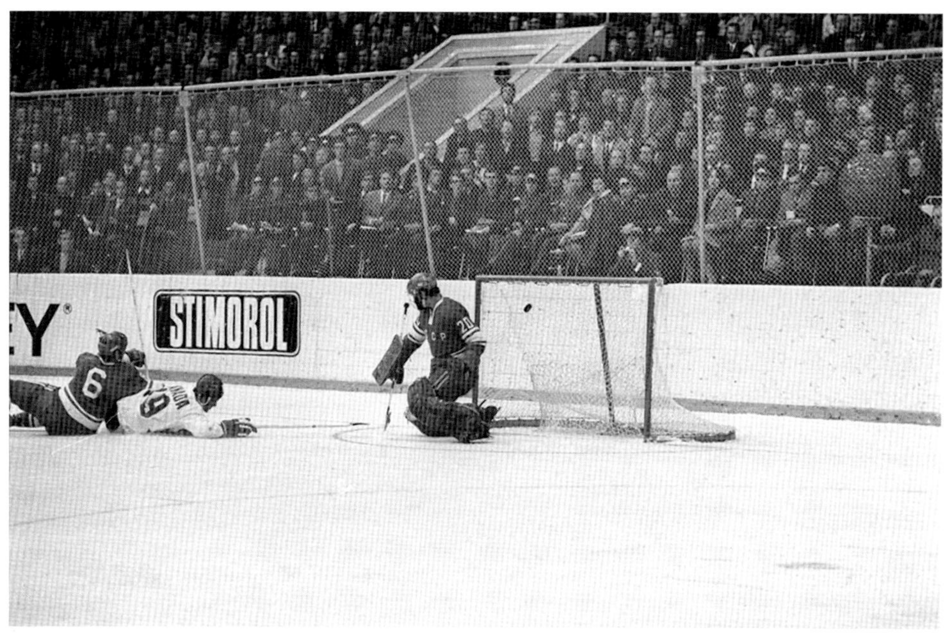

With two minutes left in Game Seven, Paul Henderson kept repeating to himself, "We need a goal, we need a goal." He went around two defencemen, then popped the puck over Tretiak's shoulder as he was tripped. When Henderson returned to their hotel room, "I told Eleanor, 'I will never score a bigger goal in my life! I can die a happy man now.'" He was only half right. FRANK LENNON/LIBRARY AND ARCHIVES CANADA, E010933339

Bob Clarke, Ron Ellis (both pictured here) and Paul Henderson were the last forwards to make the 35-man roster, but they decided to outwork everyone and force Sinden to play them. "Why wouldn't it work?" Clarke asks. "We worked our asses off, and a lot of guys didn't. We didn't assume anything. We couldn't afford to. We just wanted a chance to prove we could play." They proved to be Team Canada's best line at both ends. HOCKEY HALL OF FAME AND MUSEUM

During negotiations, Canada's representatives conceded too much control over officiating. As a result, they got stuck with West Germans Franz Baader and Josef Kompalla, whom the players nicknamed "Baader and Worse." While Canada received 63 more penalty minutes than the Soviets—the equivalent of a full game short-handed—even the cool-headed Paul Henderson couldn't take it anymore. He's seen here arguing with Kompalla, a full-time discotheque manager and part-time referee.

MELCHIOR DIGIACOMO/GETTY IMAGES

After being called for a dubious interference penalty by Josef Kompalla—Canada's third penalty in the first 4:10 of Game Eight—J.P. Parisé hit his stick against the ice, prompting Kompalla to give him a 10-minute misconduct. Parisé went berserk, threatening to bring his stick down on Kompalla's head. After 15 minutes of mayhem, Parisé was ejected, and Pete Mahovlich took his place.

FRANK LENNONV/LIBRARY AND ARCHIVES CANADA, E010933347

After Parisé was ejected, Esposito, Gary Bergman, Frank Mahovlich, and Guy Lapointe complained to Czech official Rudy Batja (15) and Josef Kompalla (16). "Kompalla was so upset," Batja said, "I refereed the rest of the game. [Kompalla] was on the ice, but for nothing." Batja called only seven more penalties that game, four on the Soviets. Parisé's outburst probably helped even the calls.

FRANK LENNON/LIBRARY AND ARCHIVES CANADA, E010933344

Rod Gilbert recalled, "We're losing, 5–4, with nine minutes to go. I got an idea to pick up the team. On the faceoff I came up and smacked [Evgeni Mishakov] right on his nose. But he didn't go down! He wasn't happy with me. And now we're going." It was Gilbert's only fight—and he broke Mishakov's nose. Pete Mahovlich said, "What a great team player Rod is. Big heart. You could see it every game." MELCHIOR DIGIACOMO/GETTY IMAGES

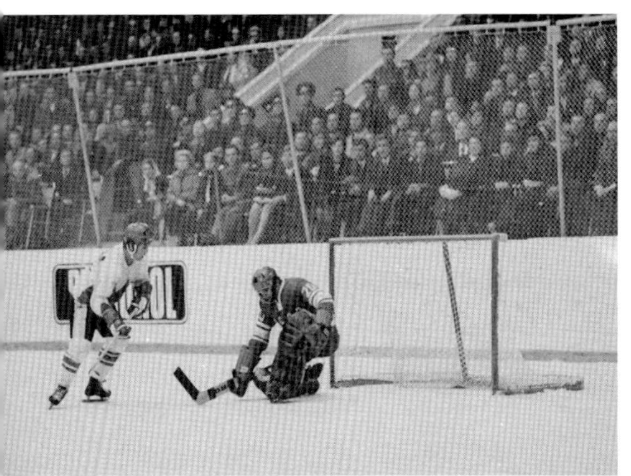

With the game tied, 5–5, and one minute left, Paul Henderson "did something I never did before in my entire 18-year career, and would never do again: I started yelling for another player to come off. I cannot tell you what possessed me, except this feeling that if I could just get out there again, I would score. Complete certainty."
FRANK LENNON/LIBRARY AND ARCHIVES CANADA, E010933341

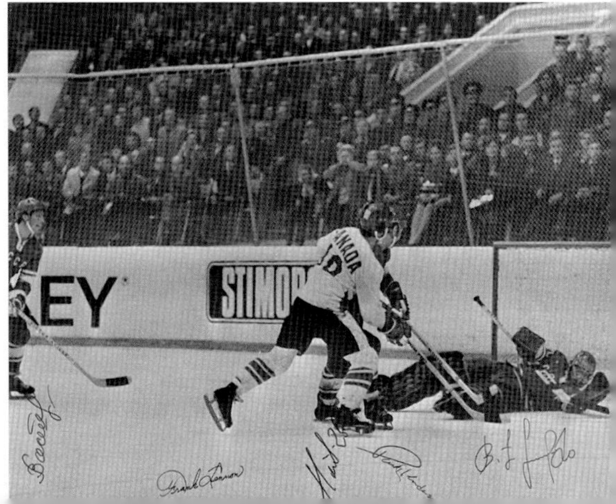

Henderson's premonition was correct. With 34 seconds left, he banged home his own rebound to give Canada a 6–5 lead. Foster Hewitt made the call: "Henderson has scored for Canada!" Not just "scores," or even "scores for Team Canada," but for Canada, the country, and all its native sons and daughters. They were all watching.
FRANK LENNON/LIBRARY AND ARCHIVES CANADA, E010933342

“Everyone in Canada knows where they were when Paul scored,” Dale Tallon says. “You were invested. How could you not be?” The picture of Yvan Cournoyer picking up Henderson is one of the most famous hockey photos of all time, featured on a stamp. After the goal, Henderson told Sinden not to put him back on the ice. “I would have been petrified to play the last 34 seconds. I was done, and I knew it.”

FRANK LENNON/*TORONTO STAR* VIA GETTY IMAGES

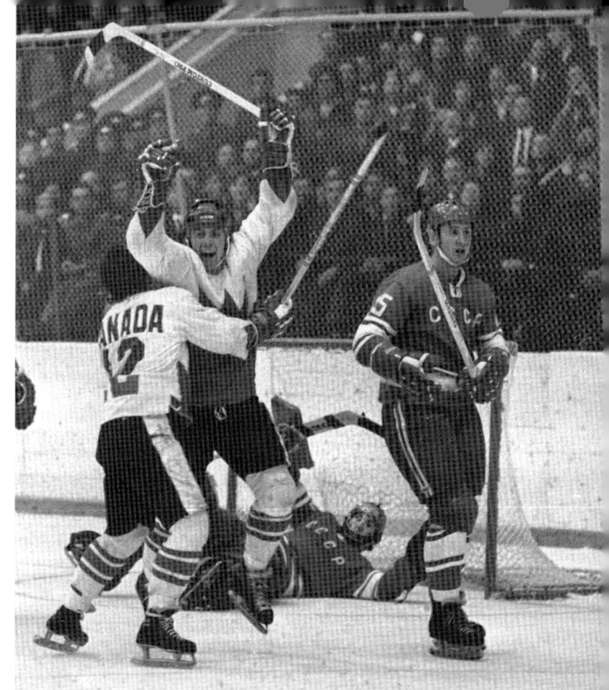

After Paul Henderson’s goal, Ken Dryden wrote, “It was, without a doubt, the longest 34 seconds I have ever played. It seemed like 34 days, but after everything we had been through, we weren’t going to let anything crush us now. It was over.” Bob Clarke says the Soviets “played the last 34 seconds like they just wanted to get the game over and get out of there. The heart—in the end, that was the difference.”

FRANK LENNON/LIBRARY AND ARCHIVES CANADA, E010933343

Bob Clarke says of Paul Henderson, “I’m sorry, but you do not score three goals to win three straight games by luck. In that series, Paul was simply that good of a player.” Phil Esposito recalls “looking over at Paul. He looked so worn out, like he’d played 20 games in a row and couldn’t play another. He’d used it all up.”

FRANK LENNON / LIBRARY AND ARCHIVES CANADA, E010933346

Two weeks earlier, the players had been booed by the fans and ripped by the reporters. After they won the series, they were met by thousands of fans cheering in the pouring rain. "We really had no idea of the impact back home," Dale Tallon says. "All we knew is we were gangsters, the bad guys, from Montreal to Moscow. We kinda liked being the good guys again!" PETER BREGG/CANADIAN PRESS

"There is something special about this team that's very hard to describe," Yvan Cournoyer says. "We were only together for a short time, but every time we meet, it's like we were teammates for life. When I shake hands with Phil Esposito, I shake hands with a teammate from '72, not a Boston Bruin. We don't talk about all the playoff games. We talk about '72." GEORGE PIMENTEL/GETTY IMAGES

"Over the years, we've spent a fair amount of time with the Russians," Brad Park says. "We have a great deal of affection for them." When they see the Soviet players again, Serge Savard says, "We talk about everything—what everyone was doing, what we remember. And every time we see those guys, it feels like you knew them forever. How can that happen?" VLADIMIR BEZZUBOV/KHL PHOTO AGENCY VIA GETTY IMAGES

the team before it left Stockholm, which put more pressure on Hadfield to perform.

The Canadians didn't know any more about the Swedes than they had about the Soviets, but they now knew enough about European hockey in general to take them seriously. If they couldn't name any of the players on Sweden's roster, they would soon know them as opponents and teammates, including Inge Hammarström, Börje Salming, Anders Hedberg, and Ulf Nilsson, all of whom would go on to successful NHL careers—names familiar to any hockey fan of the era.

Shortly after the 9:30 p.m. faceoff, in front of a full house, Team Canada took the lead when Ron Ellis set up Paul Henderson just 1:45 into the first period, and ultimately walked away with goals from Bob Clarke (assisted by Ellis), Park (unassisted), and Wayne Cashman (from J.P. Parisé)—many of the same grinders Sinden had relied on in Games Two and Three—for a solid 4–1 victory. Ulf Sterner scored the lone Swedish goal, assisted by Salming. The GAG Line didn't notch a point, and none of the young stars stood out, confirming Sinden's judgments.

But that wasn't the story.

Canada outshot the Swedes comfortably, 34–24, with Tony Esposito knocking out 23 of those shots. But the most telling statistic was Canada's 26 penalty minutes, with eight minors, to the Swedes' eight minutes on four minors—despite the fact that the Canadians, almost to a man, agreed with Phil Esposito's assessment: "Dirtiest players I ever played against were the Swedes."

Even Ken Dryden, the Canadian most likely to view European players favourably, was appalled by the Swedes' play, which he watched from the stands.

The Swedes weren't aggressive, looking for fights, or even physical. Quite the opposite; they avoided tough play in almost all its forms, instead resorting to hacking, whacking, interfering, spearing, checking from behind, and even kicking—all skilfully done while the refs looked the other way. When hit by the Canadians, they would dive, flop, and generally carry on as if they'd been shot by a sniper in the stands—the opposite of the Canadian ethos, which dictated the better part of valour was to ignore injuries, not exaggerate them like a World Cup soccer player.

The officials, two West Germans named Franz Baader and Josef Kompalla, called a game unrecognizable to the Canadians. They ignored the Swedes' cheap tactics, which would have been whistled by NHL referees or squashed by enforcers, while penalizing the Canadians for routine physical play.

In Sinden's estimation the first period was the worst the Canadians had played since Game One, but they soon adjusted to the Olympic rink. "But," he added, "there was no way we could adjust to the officials, [who] were absolutely terrible. They couldn't even skate. They were miles behind the play all night and didn't know the damn rules. Their incompetence helped the game become very bitter."

The Swedes came away from their first encounter with NHL players with a decidedly different reaction. "It was a door opener," Hammarström said. "We talked after the games and we realized that we had a good chance to make it in the NHL."

Unlike the Russians, the Swedes knew that if they were good enough to play in the NHL, there would be nothing stopping them. This had not occurred to them before—just another ripple that flowed from this eventful month—and those ambitions would ratchet up the intensity the next night.

While the players slept after the first game, the Grand Hotel received a bomb threat. After Munich, no one took such things lightly, and they were evacuated.

"And then I got a couple of death threats," Esposito recalls. "I didn't tell anyone about them, but I walked around with Cash on one side and Tony on the other. They said, 'What the hell are you doing?' but I never told them."

Despite everything, the trip helped the players *and* the coaches bond.

"I remember coming in late with Cash and Cournoyer," Esposito says, "and we're hiding in the lobby so the coaches don't see us. Then I see Harry and Fergie coming back and they're shit-faced drunk! Well, they couldn't get mad at us!"

"Harry was in charge," Clarke says. "It wasn't like he didn't know what we were doing. We weren't drinking together to avoid hockey, but to become a better team. He could have shut that down, but he didn't—and that was the right call."

FOR the second game, on Sunday, September 17, Sinden again gave some players another look, and got in others who probably wouldn't get to play in Moscow.

On defence, he kept Lapointe and Savard in the stands, hoping Savard would recover in time to help against the Soviets. He also rested Bergman for the first time that month, and White for the second. This allowed him to put the Seiling-Awrey pair back in for another chance, while giving Guèvremont his second game in a row, and Dale Tallon his first.

On offence, Sinden sat four players who had proven so valuable, to the surprise of the experts, that he thought it best to give them a rest before Moscow: Clarke's line, marking their first game out, and Pete Mahovlich, who'd played all but Game Four. With Frank Mahovlich in transit, Sinden had the space to give the GAG Line another chance to show what it could do after a disappointing effort the night before. He put Bill Goldsworthy, J.P. Parisé, and Dennis Hull back in; gave veterans Stan Mikita and Red Berenson their second starts each; and let young guns Gilbert Perreault and Rick Martin show off for the Swedish crowd.

But it's worth noting that Sinden never let Phil Esposito or Brad Park sit for any of the games. They were too important to the team, whether the stakes were high or low. He gave Esposito his Boston linemate, Cashman—which, for entirely unforeseen reasons, would be their last game together overseas.

In net, Sinden tabbed the affable Eddie Johnston for his first start, with Dryden backing up and Tony Esposito in the stands. But Sinden had no control over the two most important men on the ice: referees Baader and Kompalla, who would have a greater impact on the contest than all the players combined.

THE second game in Sweden started out about the same as the first. Halfway through the opening period, Team Canada took a 1–0 lead on a snap shot from the slot by the overdue Vic Hadfield—a good sign.

But that was the Swedes' cue to start their cheap tricks. Still unchecked by the refs, they resorted to more sinister tactics in the rematch—but only after the Canadians were called for a variety of penalties: Parisé for holding, then Goldsworthy for cross-checking and, when a Swedish player skated in front of him moments later, another for jamming the toe of his stick into the Swede's chest, plus a misconduct, all in a few seconds.

If Goldsworthy was trying to show that his costly penalties in Vancouver were an aberration and he could be trusted, his efforts fell well short of reassuring his coach. The Swedish fans stopped their incessant, derisive whistling only to cheer each individual Canadian penalty as they were announced. Sinden didn't protest the Canadians' penalties—committed in broad daylight, NHL-style—but he was outraged by the uncalled Swedish infractions, delivered behind the play, the back, and the legs—inevitably luring the Canadians to retaliate and go to the box.

"Again it goes back to the debate, and I'll be kind, about no fighting, and what the by-product of that is," Seiling says. "In a contact game, tempers are bound to flare—it's part of the game.

I wasn't known as a fighter. It wasn't my game. But when you take fighting out of the game, the stickwork takes over. So if one doesn't happen, the other will."

After seeing the ugliness of the Swedish games, even Sinden, who had believed before the trip that hockey would be better without fighting, conceded that if the result of eliminating self-policing was the Swedes' brand of hockey, it was better to allow fighting to keep everyone honest.

With 18 seconds left in the first period, Sterner was skating on the right wing when he received a pass, which was whistled offside. But Cashman, one of the NHL's toughest players, kept skating toward him. When Sterner looked up and saw Cashman coming, he raised his stick, blade first—which went straight into Cashman's mouth, splitting his tongue down the middle like a snake's forked tongue.

Whether it was intentional is still debated a half-century later. Sinden believes it was; others say it was a spontaneous reaction.

"I think Sterner panicked," Park says. "Cash was going to hit him, and Sterner put his stick up out of fear, kind of to protect himself, and it went right into Cash's mouth."

Cashman casually circled back to pick up his glove from someone on the other side of the boards, then skated toward the Canadian bench, giving Sterner a pantomimed gunshot along the way, before sitting down.

Watching the play today, if you didn't know what had happened you'd never realize that Cashman had been injured, let alone how seriously. Even Cashman's teammates didn't understand what had occurred until, Sinden recalls, team doctor Jim Murray "pulled Wayne's mouth open and I nearly vomited on the spot. His tongue was just dangling."

A few seconds later the horn blew, ending the period. One beat later, Esposito cross-checked one of the Swedish players to the ice, then slashed his finger across his own throat—a not-so-subtle gesture he would repeat in Moscow. When players from both teams and the refs all headed toward the same exit, mayhem ensued.

"Cash chased [Sterner] into the dressing room—and I followed!" says Esposito.

With one of the refs trying to keep Esposito away from the Swedes, Esposito started pointing his stick at Sterner, who hustled off. With the players clogging the wide gate, they started pushing and shoving, and even goalie Eddie Johnston, who had made 10 high-quality saves that period, dropped his gloves and mixed it up.

Sinden caught up to Baader and Kompalla under the stands to accuse them of protecting the Swedes, ignoring their dirty play, and basically picking on the Canadians. While Sinden was making his case, a Swedish coach called Phil Esposito a chicken—probably not the smartest move—to which Esposito responded by yelling a few carefully selected words and giving him a shove. The Swedish photographers, who had skewered the Canadians after the first game, got some shots of the Canadian ogres bullying the Swedes, prompting a few of the Canadian players in street clothes to grab their cameras. The Swedish police, in turn, literally brought in the dogs to rescue the photographers, ending the drama for the time being.

"Cash had gone to the locker room," Clarke recalls, "and then there was a huge ruckus, both teams going at it in the tunnel. But we all stuck up for what happened to Cash. We were all in this together.

"All of a sudden, we had become a team. I felt that at the time, not just looking back. We were caring about each other—and not just how we as an individual played and all that shit. We're sticking up for each other. The old 'Fuck you guys—we're a team.' I don't think the Swedes had ever seen anything like that before."

While all this was going on, Cashman's tongue started swelling and bleeding profusely, threatening to block his breathing.

When the dust settled, Dr. Murray had given the two-inch cut 40 stitches. Cashman was done for the series.

In the second period, Ulf Nilsson tied it up at 1–1, then Don Awrey countered to give Canada a 2–1 lead while the tensions continued to rise. In the third, the refs called Team Canada for hooking, tripping, hooking again, a major for high-sticking (Hadfield), and another minor for roughing, while calling the Swedes for just one penalty: Sterner, for roughing, his first penalty of the night.

In all, the refs called Team Canada for eight minors, one major, and a 10-minute misconduct—31 minutes total—dwarfing the four minors they charged the Swedes, for a total of eight minutes.

"They were the dirtiest players I've ever seen," Tallon says today, echoing Esposito. "They kicked you in the back of the calf with their blades, jabbed you in the back of the knee with their stick, every little nasty thing—but always behind the refs, and never to your face. What threw us off is, I don't think we *expected* it."

If September's first surprise was the Soviets' conditioning, the second was the Swedes' dirty play. The Canadians hadn't anticipated any trouble in this miniseries, but whenever they went into the corners first they were followed closely by a Swede sticking their calves or shoving them headfirst into the boards—things you just didn't do in the NHL if you wanted to keep your job, or your head.

"I did things I never would have done, *ever*, in that game," Tallon continues. "I think I swung my stick at Ulfie Sterner. Never did that before or since. That was never my role. I didn't make any money sitting in the box. But I lost it because of what happened to Cash. That's what pissed me off."

Early in the third, the Swedes, who had replaced their awe of the Canadians with their new-found belief they could actually beat them, tied the game at 2–2. Just 16 seconds later, Martin shook his man behind the Swedish net with a nifty move, then found his Buffalo teammate Perreault in front of the net. Perreault deked the goalie to put Canada ahead, 3–2—a hint of the French Connection line to come.

The Canadians still weren't too happy with—well, just about anything, and became even less so when the parade of penalties resulted in two Swedish power-play goals, the second by Hammarström, giving them a 4–3 lead with 8:44 left.

Would Canada suffer yet another embarrassing setback? While killing off Hadfield's major penalty for high-sticking, the Canadians would often daringly send three men in deep. With a minute left, Johnston made a clutch save on a two-on-one and Tallon quickly dished a pass to Esposito, who weaved his way around the Swedish blue line to find some open ice, fired, and tied the game at 4–4.

In the final 47 seconds, the Canadians were not just trying to hang on—as they had been in the 4–4 tie in Winnipeg—they were playing to win. They were flying around the Swedish zone, led by Yvan Cournoyer, who got off a strong backhand that forced the goalie to stack his pads. But they couldn't score again.

This time, the Canadians at least knew to stick around for the handshake line.

"THE Swedish press was just brutal on us," Sinden recalls. "When the second game was over and the players were in the locker room, the Swedish press wanted to go in. I said, 'Well, let me go see if they finished feeding the animals yet.'"

After the game, the players once again retired for a few beers—together—to commiserate about everything that had happened that night.

"Our group didn't come together until we went to Sweden," Pete Mahovlich says. "All of a sudden, we're forced to work together, and we didn't have to worry about our wives or the press, so what are we doing tonight? This is where I got to know Tony and Phil and Serge. There was no *talking* to these guys before!"

"I watched them sew up Cash in the dressing room," Dennis Hull says. "Looked like a lot of work. When we went to the bar after, and Wayne walked in, he could hardly talk—and that man can talk! I had a little fun with it. I said, 'Wayne, I can't understand you!' and he said, 'I always wanted to speak French.' And then he's getting pissed, so he starts writing on a cardboard beer coaster. But he was one tough guy—you better believe it."

After a long night out, the players woke up the next day to fulfill a promise made long ago to visit a rink 30 minutes outside Stockholm in Södertälje, home to a Volkswagen factory. There they skated for 80 minutes in front of 4,000 locals, many of them kids, then played a mock game against a group of peewee players. Marcel Dionne, the team's shortest player, listed at five foot eight, got on his knees to face off against one of their players, about the same height as Dionne on his knees, and the crowd roared. Guy Lapointe got some laughs skating like a drunken sailor, and all the guys gave the peewees some tips, a few laughs, and a lot of autographs.

The visit reminded them how much they loved the game, how simple it could all be, and how they were still heroes to many—the role they were used to playing before they had been labelled entitled losers and worse. Sinden stacked a couple cases of beer on the bus back to Stockholm, and soon the players were "singing songs like a bunch of camp kids," Sinden said.

The timing couldn't have been better; that very morning, at every Stockholm newsstand they passed, the headlines blared about the Swedes' historic 4–4 tie and the debauchery of the Canadian goons, complete with photos invariably depicting a Swede being mugged by a Canadian.

"The headlines in Sweden were saying we were the Mafia, and worse!" Esposito recalls. "Hell yes, I remember it!"

"The Swedish media was really giving it to us," Dale Tallon

confirms. "Oh my God, we received the wrath of the entire nation. 'Gangsters.' 'Mobsters.' 'Thugs.' You name it. But after Phil's speech, and everything that happened in Sweden, we got close, really close."

The Canadian media joined the pile-on. Pierre Gobeil of *Montréal-Matin* wrote, "I am ashamed to be a Canadian."

"We were depicted as gangsters and vicious and all that," Park recalls. "Even the *Canadian ambassador* publicly sided with the Swedes! But by then we weren't going to let anyone get to us. We weren't in any mood to back off. Our attitude was 'Okay, if that's what they think we are, fine—but we'll be that *together*.'"

That evening, their last in Sweden, the players went out again en masse and got their money's worth. Yet the next morning, they turned in what Sinden called "the best practice session we've had . . . We gave them the most strenuous skating drills we've had and they were dragging when they left the ice, but they seemed happy. We're in better shape than we were at home.

"Our players must be superhuman. Let's face it. Could the Russians stay out all night drinking and carousing like our guys do and still skate their butts off the next day? Never."

A team meeting later that day sealed the team's new bond.

"There were two things that did it, that made us a team," Sinden recalls. "Eagleson put together a meeting. Just the members of the team, the doctors, the trainers, about 50 people. No outsiders. By this time we had been pretty well castigated by every news media outlet in Canada, Russia, and Sweden, so we needed to circle the wagons. That's what Al did."

Eagleson started by listing some things to avoid on their upcoming trip to Moscow. Don't trade rubles. Everywhere you go, someone will be watching you. And watch out for the women, who were often working with the KGB.

And then, as Eagleson recalls, he delivered this finale, addressing the secret meeting nine of them had with him four days earlier: "A few of you guys have chatted with me about the problems with the team. Well, we've got 50 guys in a boat, and they're all in this room, but we're hitting each other over the heads with our oars. We've got to get our oars back in the water and get everyone pulling the same way and get back to shore. We won't get there any other way. If you want to get out of the boat, you gotta get out now."

He was as direct as he was correct: it was them against the world; no one outside that room could save them; until they were all pulling in the same direction, they weren't going anywhere; and if anyone wanted out, now was the time to jump.

"I remember it well," Sinden says. "I suspect everyone does. 'There's 50 of us here, and that's all that's left, so let's pull together and win this thing.'"

It was the right message at the right time, and apparently it sank in. Most confirmed they were on board—while a few prepared to bail.

"The second thing that made us a team," Sinden says, "was the wives."

In the same meeting, Park recalls, "Eagleson told us the Soviets had just informed him our wives would have to stay at a different hotel in Moscow. By that time, Espo had basically taken over as the spokesman for the team, and he stood up."

"I asked Al and Harry to leave," Esposito recalls, "then I asked the guys, 'Boys, whaddya think? We can say okay, or we can say, 'Fuck it,' and go home if they don't stick by the deal."

"We knew if we went to Russia and the wives were not in the same hotel with us, they'd be miserable," Park says, "and we wouldn't be able to play a bit. Being Canadian husbands, we're thinking, 'How's this gonna fly at home?'

"So we tell Espo: either the Russians honour the original deal, or we don't go at all. It was kind of our way of telling them, 'Don't fuck with us.' By that time we were *together*, and we were going to stand up for ourselves and for each other. We all voted if that was what they were going to do, we're not coming—*to a man*.

"And that was it right there: the united front that we'd been looking for. At that point, we're a team. That was kind of a turning point."

When Esposito summoned Eagleson and Sinden back into the room, he informed them of their unanimous vote. Eagleson gave his commitment that their wives would stay with them.

From the series' inception, Alan Eagleson would prove to be as central to the team as he was controversial. But he would prove invaluable during the many tense standoffs with the Soviets over everything from the trivial to the vital.

"When the Russians said the wives aren't coming," Berenson says, "Eagleson told them, 'Then we're done. No more games.' They backed down pretty fast. He was the only one who understood that you don't negotiate with these guys. You dictate terms, or you'll get nothing."

The Soviets would try to rattle the Canadians and their wives many times in Moscow, but round one had gone to the Canadians.

"It all started with the vote in Sweden," Park says.

THE trip to Sweden had initially been scheduled as a vacation for the players, and then looked like an annoying waste of time. Upon departure it had proven to be an absolutely essential week of conditioning, acclimating, and team bonding.

"If we don't go to Sweden before Moscow, we lose," Cournoyer says. "*I know this!* We had to learn how to play over there."

If there is one opinion every player shares, Cournoyer coined it.

"I agree 100 percent," Ratelle says. "It was important for us to keep in good shape. We needed to get the lines together and it was going to be no one else but us."

"Yvan's right," Ellis says. "We didn't have enough time to become a team without Sweden."

"I couldn't agree more!" Esposito says. "That's where we became a team."

"I believe it, too," Hull says. "While we were walking to get on the plane to go to Moscow I said to Harry, 'We're really in a tough spot here.' And Harry turns and says, 'No, we're not. We became a team in Sweden. We're going to be fine.' That's exactly what he said, and that's why he's such a great coach."

Before they left Sweden Sinden and Ferguson had a beer, looked back on their week, and came to three conclusions: "One, refereeing will be our biggest problem in Moscow," Sinden said. "Two, if we don't start playing better, we're going to lose. Three, what happened here might be a blessing in disguise."

Even Sinden could not have imagined just how right he would be on all three points.

23

STRANGERS IN A STRANGE LAND

On Wednesday, September 20, the players said goodbye to the free world, boarded two planes for a two-hour flight to Moscow, and jumped two time zones along the way.

En route, Ted Blackman, the columnist for the *Montreal Gazette*, anxiously circulated among the players to get as many quotes as he could. Dryden asked him, "What's your rush?" After all, he said, they'd have plenty of chances to talk during their 10 days together in Moscow. Blackman replied, "No, we don't." He knew the players' wives would be bringing their husbands the stories on the Sweden series that had run in the Canadian newspapers.

"When you guys read them," Blackman said, "you won't talk to us again."

When they landed in Moscow they were seven hours ahead of Montreal and Toronto, but it might as well have been the moon.

Unlike the Soviets, who were accustomed to playing across Europe, North America, and even Asia, only a few Canadian players had travelled overseas, and none had been to Moscow—a place that was not just foreign, but strange and scary, not the kind of environment an already rattled roster needed. As soon as they landed Air Canada parked the plane at the far edge of the airfield for two or three hours, in the dark, to allow Soviet officials to go through all of Team Canada's bags. Although Eagleson had prepared them for this and other intrusions, it still got the players' attention to see it start before they had made it inside the airport.

But now, at least, they were surrounded almost entirely by true teammates.

"Fortunately, I've never gone to war," Seiling says, "and I can't say what kind of bond you build in the military, but I would imagine what we had was very close. You knew what was at stake, that it wasn't just a hockey game. And if it needed any reinforcing, landing in Moscow and being taken to the back end of the airport, where there was a squad of Russian soldiers with their guns out, made it clear. It was a war to us—our way of life versus communism—and it was built up that way."

They looked forward to getting to the hotel, where their wives, 300 Canadian steaks, and a pallet of Labatts would be waiting for them. If a Canadian hockey player could be said to have a security blanket, that's what it would look like: his wife, a thick steak, and a cold Canadian beer.

Gerry Park made the trip, just 16 days after giving birth to Jamie.

"Brad called from Sweden and said, 'I really, really want you to come,'" she recalls. It wasn't going to be easy, requiring an expedited passport and new clothes, since her wardrobe was in New York. She would also have to deal with public criticism—"How could you leave your baby behind?"—but she knew her mother, a nurse, "was more than capable of looking after a newborn.

"But when your husband calls, and he needs you, you come," she says. "The guys just felt they needed all the support that they could get. I think that's why Brad was asking me to come. It was important that I went, that all the wives went."

The second the players walked into the lobby of the Intourist Hotel, designated solely for foreigners, they were welcomed with warm hugs and kisses from their wives, which they had expected. But they also received booming cheers from some 3,000 raucous Canadian tourists, which they definitely had *not* expected.

The Canadians, *Sports Illustrated* reported, came "supplied with beer, Scotch, mineral water, steak, Coca-Cola, towels, soap, toilet paper, miniature maple leaf buttons, regulation Canadian flags, enough gum to dam the Moskva River, and enough clothes to outfit the Soviet Army for the next 10 years."

The Canadian travel agents had gotten the fans into the hotel the day before the players arrived, and they seemed to have spent the entire 24 hours getting a head start on the hotel's ample supplies of world-class vodka. It was immediately clear that the hearty souls who made the rigorous and expensive trip were hard-core fans. There were no lightweights in that lobby.

Before meeting up at the Toronto airport for their flight, the wives knew only the women whose husbands played for the same team. The spouses effectively lived in the same silos the NHL had built for their husbands. But unlike their husbands, these women didn't hesitate to get to know each other, so by the time they landed in Moscow they had already made lifelong friends. They'd also made a few friends among the fans, who had been starting their ascent well before the plane's.

"We were put on the plane with 200 drunk Canadians who already had their bottles," recalls Joy Berenson, who had to leave her four children, between two and 10 years old, with her mother. Despite the disappointing start to the series, "None of the fans gave us any hard questions, and everyone was very kind to us, very respectful. No one asked us what had happened in the Canadian games."

When the players heard 3,000 fans give them a raucous reception, after they had been hounded by the fans and media in Canada and Sweden, it got to them.

"Over the years, I guarantee you I've talked to at least a thousand of them who went over there," Henderson says. "About 10 years after the series, Eleanor and I were in Windsor [Ontario] when two women came up to us to say they found out that they could go to Russia for 500 bucks, 'And we had the time of our life, just on a whim. The time of our life!'

"Our little village of Lucknow, with less than a thousand people, had folks going. Our next-door neighbours came over to Russia. You look around that lobby at a few thousand Canadians you didn't expect to see and you think, 'Holy crap, these guys must've spent a lot of money over here!' Other people who passed up their chance to go tell us, 'Dammit all! We missed the chance of a lifetime!' And they did!"

When Sharon Seiling ran up to her husband to give him a hug and a kiss, he recalls, "It gave you a sense of home."

Most of the players hadn't been home since August 13, more than a month earlier, and they wouldn't be back until the end of September.

"We were used to long road trips," Seiling adds. "That's not out of the ordinary. But these were not ordinary conditions."

Sharon told him, with a mischievous grin, "Just wait till you see our room!"

"Well, tell me about it," Rod said.

"No no—just wait till you see it."

"So we go up to our room," Seiling says, "and it's just one of the worst rooms I'd ever seen. We had two beds basically made out of plywood, and what they called a mattress was an inch thick. I just looked at Sharon and said, 'Just one more thing.'

"'It's like a Third World country!' she replied. "'But it is what it is, so let's make the best of it.' It wasn't like someone else got a better room."

Actually, the Ratelles did, for a simple reason: Nancy was noticeably pregnant, so the hotel gave them the only room that seemed to have heat.

"Our rooms were freezing cold!" Gerry Park recalls. "They regulated the heat—like everything else. But they had these beautiful down duvets that you could snuggle down into—a nice, big, warm, fluffy blanket. The hotel looked like an office building—just a big concrete box, that's all it was. There was nothing to it. It certainly wasn't a tourist hotel you'd want to go to. It was a culture shock, for sure."

"We were told not to bring magazines or any reading material that was current," Joy Berenson remembers, "and when you got there, you understood why: they didn't want us showing the Russians what life was like in the West, so they could see how far behind they were. The curtains they had on the windows were just like the kind my mom had removed from our house in Regina when I was six—and our house didn't have indoor plumbing!"

The Soviets had been constantly insisting that the hotel was one of the best in the world, but Team Canada knew better. They'd just stayed in two of the world's great hotels, in Toronto and Sweden—and this wasn't it.

"It was a fleabag hotel," Seiling says. "So you look around, and you want to laugh. You start to unpack, and you can tell your bags have been searched, and you're quickly back to the reality of the situation: you're in hostile territory—and not just Boston Garden, but an entire nation. Well, good to have your wife and your teammates with you!"

"I was so glad they let the wives come over," Red Berenson says. "When they met us in Russia, it was like, 'Oh my God!' Whether we were more homesick or they were, it helped both of us. The players really appreciated that. It kind of gave us some stability. The wives were a godsend."

Sinden and Eagleson allowed players with serious girlfriends to bring them, too, a move ahead of its time. But the single guys had been warned by Canadian officials that any woman who might approach them at a bar or the hotel would almost certainly be a prostitute, a KGB spy, or both—and the Intourist Hotel was teeming with them. Any encounter would likely produce pictures intended to blackmail or extort them—which would be even easier to accomplish if they were married—something no one needed with the biggest games of their lives in front of them. These unique circumstances ensured the guys would be sticking together on this trip, which had the side effect of making them even closer.

NEXT to the elevator on each floor, the Intourist had stationed two women behind a table whose job it was to—well, it wasn't quite clear what their jobs were. Ostensibly, they were there to clean rooms and fulfill guest requests, but they spent more time arguing with the guests than helping them, and more time digging through their bags than cleaning their rooms, reporting anything untoward.

"They wore these nylon stockings," Park recalls, "and you could see the hair on their legs coming through. Big babushkas. Like weightlifters. They were very, very intimidating."

Seiling described one on their floor thusly: "A 300-pound gorilla."

Nonetheless, some of the players chatted with the floor ladies when they were waiting for the elevators, which took "forever," Berenson recalls. "By the elevators they had a little black-and-white TV that looked like it was from the 1950s, with strips of coloured cellophane stuck to the screen to substitute for actual colour TV. I'd ask her, 'Is that a colour TV?'

"'We have real colour TV,' she replied, defiantly.

"'Oh, this is a real colour TV?' I'd say. Every day we'd have an argument at the elevator. The next day I'd ask, 'Can you leave here if you want to?'

"'If I want to go, I can. But I don't want to go.'

"'Well, I don't think so,'" Berenson replied, but there was no point in arguing.

"We all felt like we weren't in control of anything," Berenson adds. "The Soviets took our passports when we got there, and wouldn't give them back until we left. Even in our hotel, you had to turn in your key to the babushka when you left, and you couldn't get it back until you returned. We were at the mercy of the system."

The first night at the hotel, Phil Esposito remembers, one of the Canadian fans broke a mirror in his room, for which he was thrown in jail and threatened with a long trip to Siberia. As absurd as it sounds to us now, the young man had good reason to take the threat seriously, and he did.

The feeling of being watched by Big Brother followed the players into the streets. Berenson brought a Super 8 movie camera with him. One day, he saw a band of old women trying to sweep the streets with brooms of twigs, right out of a Brothers Grimm fairy tale. When he raised his camera to capture the scene, his view was suddenly blocked by a hand over his lens. When he looked up he saw a middle-aged man wearing a trench coat, a hat, and a very stern expression.

"No" was all he said. Berenson put his camera down and that was that, but it sent a chilling message: the man, apparently assigned to tail Berenson wherever he went, had been following him all day.

Some of the players and all the reporters had brought little cassette tape recorders. Yet one day, "none of them are working," Berenson recalls. "*None* of them. How does that happen? That was the Cold War."

The Canadians found themselves in the odd position of being less comfortable in both countries than their opponents were. While the Canadian players were getting booed by their own fans, the trip to Canada was the highlight of the Soviets' year. In Moscow, the Russian players were at home, with their own language and lifestyle, while the Canadians felt like they'd just landed behind enemy lines.

It wasn't for nothing that Frank Mahovlich suggested they should stay in tents to avoid being bugged and bothered. As they say, "Just because you're paranoid doesn't mean they're not out to get you." And they were.

Outside of Sinden and Eagleson, no one in the Canadian party expected anyone to call them in Moscow. Yet the players' phones started ringing each day during their afternoon naps—a revered ritual among pro hockey players—and in the middle of the night.

"The night before the first game it starts ringing, and it scared the hell out of us!" Gerry Park remembers. "You're sound asleep and the phone blares and you pick it up—and it's still ringing! Same thing the night before the next game, even after you took it off the hook. You had to put the receiver inside a drawer and pile all your clothes into the drawer, just to get some sleep."

One night, after being awakened by one of the phantom calls, Phil Esposito, not known for suffering fools gladly, ripped the cord out of the wall—then received a knock at the door from a repairman sent to fix it. Suffice it to say, Esposito responded in a manner consistent with his mood.

When the phones weren't ringing, the babushkas would knock at the door in the middle of their naps, or music would suddenly start blasting through speakers in the middle of the night. When the team was invited to a reception at the Canadian embassy, a large, old house with high ceilings, the Canadian ambassador waved everyone into the centre of the room, where they huddled around him.

"This is how we have our meetings so they can't hear," he told them. He added that their hotel rooms were surely bugged, and yes, they were being watched wherever they went. "Every week I have the bugs taken out, and there are still more."

"And this is the *Canadian* embassy," Berenson says. "Imagine what they were dealing with at the *U.S.* embassy!"

Clarke paid it all no heed. "A lot of the guys thought that the Russians were listening to us, or stealing our beer or our steaks. Maybe they were, but why would I care? I was just there to play hockey."

Savard was squarely in Clarke's camp. "All this stuff about bugging my phone, who fucking cares?" he says. "It's not like we're talking about state secrets. We're talking about our teammates and the shitty food! Why worry about that other stuff?"

"You knew what they were doing," Pete Mahovlich says. "They were putting up a front. The streets were empty—only government-issued cars. Everyone travelled by bus and subway. So you saw these huge boulevards with no cars. It didn't play on my mind because it was right in front of you."

Once they saw Moscow for themselves, the players knew the Vancouver teenagers who yelled to Esposito, "Communism is better!" didn't have any idea what they were talking about. If Team Canada had to win a hockey series to defend their way of life, at least they had no doubt they were defending the right one.

Living in Communist Russia for a week came with a silver lining: the state-controlled media effectively kept the players in the dark about the big stories swirling around the globe, including the bashing they were taking back home.

"There were no newspapers to follow in Moscow—no TV!" Park says. "We were in our own little world, which was probably a good thing. We were not talking about world events, but we were talking about each other, and that helped."

As they endured each inconvenience and insult, they could tell themselves that at least each night they would be enjoying some good Canadian steaks and cold Labatts. But they soon learned that much of their eagerly anticipated Canadian comfort food, which they'd had shipped over the previous week, had been purloined. At least 100 of their 300 steaks, and the entire supply of Labatts, were gone, probably sold on the black market, where it would fetch good money.

"Somehow half our steaks disappeared," Sinden recalls. "The hotel staff probably had a feast and made a fortune. The food we ate was horrible. They gave us peaches that were about as big as a marble. It was no way to get ready for some of the biggest games ever played."

The two things most sacred to a professional hockey player on the road—the afternoon nap and a good pregame meal—had been threatened. You couldn't leave your room without being bothered, and you couldn't stay in, either. Nothing seemed easy. They were on enemy territory now, and were reminded of it every hour.

Desperation grew. Some players, anticipating the shortages they were sure to face, had packed extra suitcases full of Coca-Cola—much to the chagrin of Dryden, who failed to prepare and pined for just one ice-cold Coke. Phil Esposito grew so hungry that he bribed a clerk to give him a key to Eagleson's room, and then broke in to get his hands on some real food.

"I remember stealing a turkey out of Eagleson's room," Esposito recalls, "and taking it back to our room with my brother, Parkie, Pete, Dennis, and Cash—who couldn't eat, because of his tongue!—and we *devoured* it. No idea how Eagleson got it. Who cares?! We were starving!"

Their weakness for food made them easy marks for a good prank.

"Another night, Whitey [Pat Stapleton] sent me and three or four other guys around the block for Chinese food," Esposito recounts. "Said it was great. Well, that sounded good to us! We went around and around the block, three or four times, and we couldn't find the damn place. Well, there *was* no Chinese restaurant! We came back and they're dying! Those bastards!"

"Pat Stapleton and Bill White had everyone believing them," Dale Tallon recalls. "They were terrific. I liked Whitey's pranks so much, I pulled that same trick eight years later at the Izvestia tournament in Moscow on Randy Gregg and some guys, telling them they've just got to go to a great Chinese restaurant that wasn't there. And it worked again!

"The Summit Series was a once-in-a-lifetime experience, and some of the fondest memories I'll ever have. Those guys were great."

NOTHING made Harry Sinden more paranoid than contemplating the referees they were about to face—again. Sinden had plenty of support for his suspicions, starting with five decades of international referees sending Canadian players to the penalty box for infractions that would never be called in Canada. Sinden, Berenson, Seiling, and Dryden had already seen it themselves playing for Canada overseas.

Part of the problem couldn't be fixed: the two continents played fundamentally different styles of hockey, which made it a challenge for any crew of officials to call a game between them fairly. But it didn't help that Sinden took a particularly aggressive approach to the game. His Bruins had held the title as the most hated team in the league until the Broad Street Bullies took it over, and Sinden was more prone than most to argue with referees during games. Adding John Ferguson on the bench did nothing to temper those tendencies.

Beyond these differences, Sinden was particularly worried about the two West German officials who would be taking the ice in Moscow, Baader and Kompalla. They had called the games in Sweden, where they impressed Sinden as the worst he'd ever seen—a judgment echoed by virtually every player on the team.

In addition to these subjective issues, Team Canada would be affected by the objective differences in the international system of officiating. While the NHL used one official to call penalties and two linesmen to call offsides and icing, the international system used only two officials, of equal power, who were both required to call everything. That often meant that, while struggling to keep up with the play, they would miss most of what the players behind them were doing—a blind spot that the Swedes had exploited. Sinden also believed it fostered one-upmanship, with both refs trying to assert control over the game by calling more penalties than the other.

Add to all that the fact that the 1973 World Championship would be played in Moscow, with Andrei Starovoitov, the head of Soviet hockey, serving as the IIHF's director of officials, responsible for picking the refs for the most prestigious honour an international referee could receive. It was not hard to fathom Starovoitov exerting undue influence on the refs for the Summit Series' remaining four games, with the promise of an invitation to the 1973 Worlds as bait.

This sinister scenario became easier to imagine after Sinden observed Starovoitov's conduct in Canada during the first four games.

When Sinden, Ferguson, and Eagleson had travelled to Moscow back in July, the two sides agreed that four American officials would work the four games in Canada, and four European refs would handle the games in Moscow. But because the Canadians still assumed they would be blowing out the Soviets, they not only gave little thought to accepting international referees, they let the Soviets pick all eight.

As a safeguard, the Canadians and Soviets set up a system: after the first two games in Canada, when they'd had a chance to see both American pairs work, the Canadians would pick the pair for Game Three and the Soviets for Game Four.

But that's not how it went down. After the Canadians beat

the Soviets, 4–1, in Toronto, "Starovoitov raced into the officials' room and flew into a rage," Sinden wrote, although he didn't learn about the tantrum until they arrived in Vancouver three days later—when it was too late. Although the Soviets were supposed to let the Canadians pick the refs for Game Three, the Soviets instead asked for their two favourite Americans for both Game Three and Four.

"The Russians reneged and we let them get away with it," Sinden wrote. "We let them have their way because they kept telling us in a nice way that if we truly wanted to play this series in the spirit of sportsmanship and friendship, then we should play the part of the perfect hosts and consent to their wishes."

The Canadians did so, and they soon regretted it—but not nearly as much as they would regret the referee selections in Moscow.

"I know one thing right now," Sinden recorded before Game Five. "The West Germans [Baader and Kompalla] are going to be used very little in this half of the series. I'm going to insist on it . . . I learned first-hand how incompetent the Germans are in Sweden and I'm not especially looking forward to seeing them again."

Sinden still believed he would have substantial control over the decisions.

24

ADDITION BY SUBTRACTION

On Thursday, September 21, the Canadians boarded the bus to the rink where they'd be spending much of the coming week. By Soviet standards, the arena—originally called the Palace of Sports of the Central Lenin Stadium, and later renamed the Luzhniki Palace of Sport—wasn't half-bad. Built in 1956, the big, hulking box of a building was entirely functional, but almost completely devoid of charm, like the hotel. The Canadians weren't any more comfortable at the Luzhniki Ice Palace—except for one very pleasant surprise.

Luzhniki had odd dimensions even by international standards: a reported 220 feet long and 95 feet wide (67 metres by 29)—20 feet longer and 10 feet wider (or 23 percent more surface area to cover) than an NHL rink.

The 13,700 seats had sharp corners, forcing the fans in those seats to crane their necks to see the action. The first row of seats sat between 15 and 100 feet (4.5–30 metres) from the boards, leaving a huge gap between the fans and the action. The seats were not centred around the rink, either, but weighted toward one end zone so that about 40 percent of the seats sat behind one of the goal lines—a perfect example of the limits of central planning.

This might answer a puzzling question: Why host all four games in Moscow?

"I think the Soviets were very self-conscious about everything they had, and how it compared to what we had in Canada," Rod Seiling surmises. "You've got to remember, they were always telling us everything they had was 'the best!' The best cars, the best hotel, the best everything—and they expected you to believe it."

The Canadians, Mark Mulvoy wrote, "were subject to a good deal of bragging by the Russians, who have, among other things, a government Department of Sports Propaganda. The Russians were still gloating over the remarkable showing of the Communist bloc at Munich. As every Canadian read or heard several times, the athletes of 11 Socialist countries accounted for only 10 percent of all participants in the Olympic Games yet won 285 medals—47.5 percent."

Each tour guide, no matter where they were taking the Canadians, invariably pointed out that the workers paid only $10 a month for housing.

"Yes," Joy Berenson says, "but when you see that four families have to share one living room, one kitchen and one bathroom, that's how come it's $10!"

Given the Soviets' ceaseless self-consciousness, it's no surprise that self-regard seemed to seep into every decision they made.

"Staying in one place for four games," Seiling continues, "you never really thought about it, but my guess is they had ulterior motives for that, like they did most things. If that's your best rink—with wire mesh instead of glass and the strange seating—well, they probably didn't want us to see their fourth-best rink and have that broadcast back to Canada."

If the Luzhniki Ice Palace wasn't exactly the Montreal Forum or Maple Leaf Gardens, it offered some advantages. Playing in one arena meant the Canadians had to learn the quirks of one rink instead of four, and it allowed them and their wives to stay in one hotel instead of packing every two days, which would have been made worse given the inefficiency of travel in the Soviet Union. All things considered, playing all four games in Moscow might have given a small edge to the Canadians. After the players had looked around the arena, they headed to their assigned locker room—or really, three, since the players would dress in two small locker rooms and the coaches in a third.

"That was the Luzhniki," Ron Ellis recalls. "We couldn't all fit into one locker room. It's the way it was. Half would get dressed in one room, half in the other, and then we'd get together in one room before we went on the ice."

When they walked to their locker rooms for the first time, they were stunned to see hundreds of telegrams from fans back home taped to the hallway walls—a considerable contrast to the nasty telegrams Harry Sinden had been receiving since their opening night loss exactly 19 days earlier.

"So, that was a long, 'Hooollly cow!'" Ellis says. "Oh my God!' Every inch was covered with telegrams. And postcards and Canadian flags and Bank of Nova Scotia posters. People said that Phil's speech was the catalyst. It had to be!"

"Even when Phil said that about the fans in Vancouver," Yvan Cournoyer says. "It was unbelievable how the fans backed us up. There were hundreds of telegrams on the walls. Hundreds!"

They came from towns of 200, with everyone signing it, and seemingly every school in Canada.

"People had to take the time to do all that," Pete Mahovlich says, "and they did it for a reason."

"I will *never* forget all the telegrams," Phil Esposito says.

Team Canada had felt besieged in Sweden—"50 of us against the world"—but the telegrams showed that they were now fighting for everyone back home.

When the players took the ice, they were in for a couple more surprises. The Soviets kept the ice three inches thick, four times the thickness of standard NHL ice, which caused it to chip, flake, and get a little bumpy. Behind each net, the goal lights were bigger than basketballs, more suitable for signalling a subway stop than a goal, and the rink was surrounded with mesh fencing.

"When I saw the fencing, and how the puck bounced off it," Pete Mahovlich recalls, "I said, 'Holy smokes, that's bound to come into play. It's going to cost someone. You just watch!'"

While they were getting used to their new hockey home, John Ferguson went up to Paul Henderson and said, "Henny, we're really counting on you. I want you firing that puck every chance you have. If we're going to pull this off, we need you."

"I could barely believe what I was hearing," Henderson says today. "I'm a good player, but I'm not fooling myself. I didn't have a Hall of Fame career. But I don't give a damn who you are: just a little bit of encouragement at the right time, just that little thing—'We're really counting on you.' Man, you'd have to be made of steel for that not to affect you. You look back on it, and it took a lot of guts for Harry and Fergie to put me in that position."

At the other end of the confidence spectrum sat Ken Dryden. On the flight to Moscow, Dryden thought that he'd played himself out of contention.

"I've resigned myself to the fact that I probably won't be playing in Moscow," he wrote. "Tony played very well the first game in Stockholm, and Eddie was superb in the second game. Now I'll have to think about getting myself ready for the start of the NHL season. We still have a whole season to play."

The 35-man roster was supposed to give more players the chance to play a few games during the expected whitewash of the Russians. When the opposite happened, the extra players seemed like less of a blessing than a burden. It was impossible to keep 35 All-Stars content with playing a game or two as a spare forward.

"When you point out the problems the 35-man roster created, people think you're pointing fingers or making excuses," Sinden says. "I tried to live up to my promise. But when Berenson told me, 'Harry, you can't keep everyone happy,' he was right. After that game [in Vancouver], there was no way I was going to live up to that anymore. We couldn't, and I think everyone knew that."

Most if not all the players recognized that Sinden couldn't keep changing the lineup every game and beat the Soviets. Further, there is a difference between practice shape and game shape. At some point, he would have to stick with the players who had played the most games, because they were in the best condition.

But that approach would create some tough decisions and hurt feelings.

AFTER warm-ups, Sinden gathered all the players at centre ice, then gave the lineup for practice, which they would be using the next night for Game Five.

On defence, Sinden announced that the Park-Bergman and White-Stapleton pairs would dress, along with Guy Lapointe and Rod Seiling, assuming Serge Savard's ankle wasn't ready. On offence, Sinden kept the Clarke line intact for its fifth game of the Summit Series, then replaced right winger Wayne Cashman, out with a cut tongue, with Rod Gilbert, on a line with Phil Esposito and J.P. Parisé.

And then came the most controversial announcement: because Sinden didn't feel the GAG Line in general, and Vic Hadfield in particular, had played very well in their two games against the Swedes, and Frank Mahovlich had looked good in the team's two practices right afterward, he kept Frank with Cournoyer and Jean Ratelle, and dressed Pete Mahovlich and Gilbert Perreault as the extras.

That left 16 players in the stands. The level of their unhappiness varied widely. Some, like Dale Tallon and Brian Glennie, were simply thrilled to be part of the series. But others were getting frustrated, including Rick Martin, who had scored 44 goals in his rookie season playing alongside Perreault in Buffalo.

Easily Sinden's unhappiest player, however, was no rookie but an established star: Hadfield, almost 32, who had just scored 50 goals the previous season, more than double his previous output, on the famed Goal-a-Game Line.

Particularly galling to Hadfield was seeing fellow left winger Frank Mahovlich stay home when they left for Sweden, then rejoin the squad in Stockholm for the last two practices without penalty. Some of Mahovlich's teammates thought he was going to skip the second half of the series.

"I never debated going to Moscow," Frank says. "I was going to play."

"Frank was more aware of what was going on than any of us," his brother Pete says. "He said to me privately that they're going to do everything they can to cheat—and not just on the ice, either—and that was true, of course."

"We go to Sweden," Brad Park recalls, "and Frank didn't come, but at the last minute he flies back and Vic gets pulled out of the lineup. Vic never went public with it, but that's what upset him."

Adding insult to injury, minutes after he announced the lineup at practice, Sinden unwittingly forgot to put Hadfield on a reserve line. While the other Black Aces rotated into the drills, Hadfield stood along the boards with nothing to do.

"For some dumb reason," Sinden wrote, "and it was an oversight on my part, I didn't put Vic Hadfield on any line. I must be getting a little senile because I did the same thing to Dale Tallon the other day."

When Ferguson pointed out the mistake, Sinden asked him to tell Hadfield to rotate in with the other reserve left wingers. When Ferguson went over to talk with Hadfield, Sinden didn't need a lip reader to see that Hadfield was seething. Ferguson skated back to Sinden and said, "He doesn't want to take part. He says he doesn't have to take this crap."

Sinden watched Hadfield retire to the bench, where he picked up a newspaper and started reading. Sinden went directly to Hadfield and said, "I think you should be out there practising. Your sitting there like that seems kind of silly."

"I'm not going to," Hadfield replied.

"Then you might as well take your stuff off," Sinden replied. "There's no point in you just sitting there and making all of us look foolish."

"Why did you bring me here?" Hadfield asked.

"Like everyone else, I brought you to play hockey. Like everyone else, Vic, the players decide who plays on this team."

"You mean the players voted or something?" Hadfield asked.

"No. I mean a player determines who plays by the way he plays."

They hadn't raised their voices, or even argued in the conventional sense, but the tension was thick.

A few minutes later, Eagleson waved Sinden over.

"I just talked to Hadfield and he's going home," Eagleson said.

"Fine," Sinden said. "Get him on the first plane out of here."

Sinden briefly considered talking to Hadfield again, then thought better of it. He felt he shouldn't have to beg anyone to play for Canada, and if he did, it would disrupt team chemistry even more.

While this melodrama played out, the rest of the players put in a particularly good practice.

"Our guys who weren't dressing [for the games] imitated the Russians in practice, and they did a good job," Gilbert recalled.

"The guys on the roster, whether they played or not, were all equal teammates—and still are," Park says. "They all sacrificed the time, the effort. If they didn't play, it's irrelevant. Wasn't their choice they weren't in. I can't think of one guy who wasn't a quality player."

The Soviet players watched all this from the stands—Sinden

couldn't do anything to stop them in Moscow—with the same insouciance the Canadians had displayed when taking in the Soviets' first practice in Montreal. The Canadians now lacked the power to strike fear into the Soviets, who seemed to feel they'd already learned all they could from their counterparts.

"Our scouting on the Russians was way off," Seiling says. "But the Russians scouted us wrong, too. From the games in Canada, they figured that's all we had—that we wouldn't get in better shape, we wouldn't come together, we wouldn't adapt to what they were doing. And they were wrong about all of it."

═

INSTEAD of going back to the locker room, Hadfield returned to the ice and finished the practice, including the rigorous skating drills at the end. This made Sinden think Hadfield had changed his mind, but not another word was spoken between the two. After practice, Hadfield left the rink for the last time.

He was soon joined by Rick Martin, who approached Sinden right after practice. As Sinden remembers it, Martin "gave me this line: 'I think I'd be better off back in Buffalo. I'm not going to play here, I'm not getting in shape, and I want to get back to the Sabres' training camp. I want you to know there are no hard feelings.'"

Martin was speaking for himself.

"We'll have you on the first plane out of here," Sinden said. That ended their conversation—but not the exodus.

Jocelyn Guèvremont says that when his wife got sick on her second day in Moscow and couldn't keep food down, he asked if she could see the team doctor. When he was told the doctors were for players only, they decided to go home.

Sinden makes no mention of such an exchange in his contemporaneous account, nor does he recall it today. In his book, he wrote that on the bus back to the hotel, Ferguson let him know Guèvremont also wanted out; Sinden replied that if that was the case, the young defenceman could talk to Sinden himself. Back at the hotel, Sinden wrote, Guèvremont told him he was "worried he might not be able to make it with Vancouver unless he had a good camp."

If true, it's hard to believe a player who had been picked third overall, who scored 51 points in his first season and was one of the best players the expansion Canucks had, needed to worry about making the squad. Sinden, for one, didn't.

"I'd be happy if you get out of here as quickly as you can," he replied. No sooner had Sinden dispatched Guèvremont than Eagleson told him Rick Martin was considering "hanging around for two more games to see if he would play or not," as Sinden recorded it.

Sinden was having none of it. He told Eagleson, "Unless he's with us all the way I don't want him around here. The same goes for Hadfield and Guèvremont."

It's often been reported that Buffalo (and former Toronto) general manager Punch Imlach—who, like NHL president Clarence Campbell and IIHF president Bunny Ahearne, was not in the habit of doing Harry Sinden any favours—urged Perreault and Martin to bail on the team and return to the Sabres' training camp.

"I don't buy it," Eagleson says. "I don't think Punch ever told them they had to come back. The players made up their own minds."

At the time, Sinden said into his tape recorder, "I don't have time for quitters. Everyone who doesn't want to be part of the team should be out of here. The worst thing a coach can do is keep trouble on his team. And right now these guys are a potentially fatal disease which could spread through the whole squad if I let them stay around . . . As far as I'm concerned, the less I see of these guys, the better."

He added that Hadfield had still not told him to his face that he was leaving, and the claim that they needed to return to their teams to get in shape "is a joke. They've been practising twice as long as any player back in Canada and will be in twice the shape of any guy on their team when they get back." Further, if you wanted to go against the best NHL players every day in practice, they were in Moscow.

"These players just can't see any sun on the horizon," Sinden wrote. "They want to get out before they become a part of the downfall of hockey in Canada, and the 'not being in shape' alibi is simply a cop-out. What else can they say? They aren't man enough to stand up and say they wanted out on the moral commitment they made to Team Canada because things looked gloomy."

Sinden wasn't finished.

"I'd like to make them walk back to Canada myself. What really frosts me is that we have to come up with something like $3,000 cash to get [each player and his wife or girlfriend] out of here in the morning. Fergie and Eagleson are going to have to take the money out of their own pockets to do it. The Russians don't believe in credit cards.

"But I don't care if it costs $10,000. I want them out of here."

THE other players suspected something was bubbling, but the exchanges between Sinden and the departing players were all so quick, quiet, and final that the rest of the team wasn't sure what was happening. Since the three players couldn't leave until the next morning, the rumours buzzed throughout the team all day long.

That night the Soviets rolled out the red carpet for the players and their wives, though probably less to please them than to impress them. The Canadian contingent would tour the 411-year-old St. Basil's Cathedral, the famous onion-topped building in Red Square; the nearby GUM state-run department store, rising three floors and spanning three city blocks; and the world-famous Moscow Circus.

But before they could get started, the Soviets stirred up trouble again.

"We were on the bus with our wives," Brad Park recalls, "and then the officials get on the bus to tell us our wives have to go on a different bus. So all the wives get off, but then we *all* get off, the men right behind them.

"They say, 'What are you doing?'

"'We're not going.' Finally they backed off, and our wives came with us."

"They just tried to push your buttons on every single thing," Gerry Park says. "They put up all these roadblocks, just for the sake of it, it seemed: 'Stand here. Now stand over there. No, you can't go here. No, you can't go there.' I will say it was one of the greatest experiences of my life, it really and truly was, and I even loved the people. But they were always trying to make everything so difficult for everybody."

"I joke about it but it's true: the worst thing the Soviets did was upset our wives," Brad says. "Giving them bad food, soup with fish heads in it, always threatening to move them or take them off the team bus. That was the biggest mistake they made, because when you piss off the wife of a Canadian hockey player, she's going to make sure her *husband* is pissed off. And that's the last thing you want to do, because now you've got a battle!"

The Canadians' countermove worked, which seemed to do more for their spirits than the size of the skirmish would suggest. They were standing up for each other.

When the tour finally started, they were in for some surprises.

"They took us to a 'dollar store,'" Joy Berenson remembers. "But not like ours. It's where we could use our Canadian dollars, which they wanted. We all bought chess sets," a nod to the recent Fischer–Spassky duel.

"The body odour was like nothing you've ever encountered," Gerry Park recalls, "and I'm a hockey wife and mom! Honestly, the smell at the GUM department store, this enormous flea market with so many people and the garlic and the onion, it was all so overwhelming, I couldn't even walk through there."

But the Moscow Circus was as good as advertised, complete with trained bears.

"They had a guy juggling big steel balls," Pete Mahovlich recalls, "bigger than bowling balls. Juggling them!"

"The highlight," Dryden wrote at the time, "was an incredible aerial act climaxed by a death-defying leap from nowhere into a long, thin, hardly visible net."

"If we were in Paris, everyone would have been going their own way," Berenson says. "In Moscow, I don't think anyone dared to go off on their own, but in fairness, we didn't have much reason to. The Russians showed us their best, and the circus was spectacular. Yet there was a cloud over us, and you couldn't get your mind off it very long. And now everyone was talking about who might be leaving."

"The circus was unbelievable," Henderson says, "but I probably didn't enjoy it enough. I'm generally pretty comfortable in my own skin, but Eleanor said she's never seen me more on edge—and your wife knows you better than you know yourself. 'Paul, enjoy yourself!' I didn't know I was so wound up, but she could see it."

Clarke took another approach. "We went to the circus. My wife was with me, so I had to. Saw Red Square and all that. But I wasn't going to the fucking Russian ballet. I was only there to play hockey."

When they returned to the hotel after the Moscow Circus, the word was out: Hadfield, Martin, and Guèvremont would be leaving in the morning.

"Rod and I went to Vic's room and tried to talk him out of it," Park recalls, "and he said, 'Hey, the other guys—Martin and Guèvremont—they're going, too.' But we said, 'Vic, you're the big name. You're not a rookie. No one's going to be talking about those guys. You're the one who's going to take the heat.' But he wasn't budging. He was gone."

The reaction of Hadfield's teammates, then and now, runs a range.

"Thinking about it, I don't understand how a player can leave," Dryden said at the time. "Sure, I'm certain some people are hurt and disappointed that they have not been playing, but at the same time what can they gain by going home? We are all part of a team and presumably should have some interest in how things are going around here."

Some, like Savard, feel the departures speak for themselves.

"Yes, you scored 50 goals, but it's not your decision," Savard says today. "You shouldn't challenge the coach. But I really think we became a team when those guys left. We had too many prima donnas, and you can't win a tough series with that."

Many feel the same way, even if they are less likely to say so publicly, while others understand Hadfield's position.

"If I wasn't playing, and I'm in Russia, I wouldn't have stayed," Phil Esposito admits. "No chance. So I can't begrudge those guys."

Of course, both positions can be true, but everyone agrees on two things: Sinden made the right decision to cut the cord, and the departures helped the team come together.

"Do I blame Vic for leaving?" Pete Mahovlich told me. "No. But did he think it was going to be easy, or that he was going to play every game with 35 players on the roster? I don't know. I didn't! Maybe he became a good team person by going back, and not being a distraction."

"You've got to give Harry a lot of credit for keeping that group together," Berenson says. "He gave us a sense of direction and made us feel important. We all felt uncomfortable about the guys leaving, but I don't think anyone quit on Harry Sinden. A few quit on the *team*, but not Harry. None of that 'Harry's an asshole' stuff.

"I don't think we were mad at those guys for leaving. It wasn't hard to understand. But it added more adversity when those guys were pissed off. So the guys who stayed, we backed into a corner together, and the good Canadian spirit came out.

"We became a better team."

PART IV

Against All Odds

25

GAME 5: DARKEST BEFORE DAWN

September 22, 1972

Early Friday evening, September 22, Team Canada's bus pulled up to the Luzhniki Ice Palace for Game Five, which millions of Canadians would watch in the early afternoon by skipping school, work, or whatever had to be done that day. The viewers included Mark Messier, an 11-year-old student in St. Albert, Alberta, who ran home each afternoon to see the Moscow games, which played at 2:30 Alberta time.

It was trickier for 11-year-old Wayne Gretzky, who lived in Brantford, Ontario. "The last four games in Moscow started at 12:30 in the afternoon," he recalls. "Well, that's school time, of course—but this is Canada, so at our school they gathered all the kids in the gymnasium and rolled in a TV to watch it. But it was a regular-sized black-and-white TV on a high stand. I remember telling my dad, 'It's horrible. I can't see what's happening!'

"So the next day, my dad told me, 'You get out of school at noon for lunch, and you get an hour to go home. So you can come home and watch the next three games.' Then he even let me go next door to the Rizzettos', because they had a colour TV! Better than Christmas.

"Mrs. Rizzetto and I would watch the games together, which was awfully nice of her because she wasn't really a hockey fan. She was doing it more for me. My mom would pop in once in a while to make sure I wasn't bothering Mrs. Rizzetto, but I was just intent on watching every shift like it was life or death—because it was to me!

"I really don't know what they were saying about me missing school, but I bet they figured out where I was. And it wasn't like I was really missing school, because they weren't in math class, either. They were all in the gymnasium, watching the game. I was just watching on a better TV. No snacks. No interruptions. Just the greatest hockey I've ever seen. I loved every minute of it."

Whenever the Canadians got off the bus at Luzhniki, the Russian kids would run up to swap souvenir pins for something as simple as a stick of Wrigley's gum, an exotic treat for those kids.

The two weeks between Games Four and Five had worked their magic. The players who wanted in had bonded with remarkable speed, and the three players who wanted out were all well beyond Soviet airspace before warm-ups. For all the ups and downs, the Canadians felt ready. They had whipped themselves into something close to game shape and started figuring out the Soviets' style and the Olympic-sized sheet. They were no longer taking anything for granted.

This naturally started with the team's unofficial captain, Phil Esposito, who was famously fastidious about his pregame routine.

"He goes at it like a bride preparing for her wedding," Harry Sinden wrote. "He puts his gloves and stick in front of him, and they're not to be moved. He also makes sure that his sticks are crossed, for some reason. And when he puts on his equipment everything has to go on in sequence, always following the same pattern.

"When Phil's bitchy, he's ready."

Phil Esposito was ready for Game Five.

Sinden felt his players were as jacked up for that night's game as they had been for Game One, even confident enough to joke around a bit before the game. Ken Dryden overheard J.P. Parisé, who would be playing on an odd line with Esposito and Rod Gilbert, make a crack at his own expense. "If you want to see a guy panic, just give me the puck in front of the net."

They got another shot of adrenalin when they took the ice for warm-ups and saw some 3,000 Canadians cheering them on with horns, whistles, Canadian flags, and signs saying "Mission Possible" and "Sarnia's Here, Whitey."

A champion water skier from Montreal named Pierre Plouffe, who had just competed in the Munich Olympics—where water skiing was a demonstration sport, and he finished 10th in jumping, 14th in the slalom, and 11th in tricks—travelled to Moscow with his bugle, which he brought to Luzhniki to pump up the Canadians. When the Soviet authorities tried to confiscate it, for no good reason except that it was fun, Plouffe handed the horn to the fans, who passed it down the line so the guards couldn't get it.

"On the Canadian side of the arena," Joy Berenson recalls, "it was all drunken Canadians in bright colours getting loud and having fun. On the other side it was Russians wearing black and brown and not having any fun at all."

While the fans got loud, Serge Savard went out for warm-ups to see what his ankle could do.

"That's when I made one of the biggest mistakes of my life," he says. "Before warm-ups, Harry asked me, 'How do you feel?' I tell him the truth. I said, 'I'm not 100 percent, but I'm ready.'"

That was enough for Sinden to keep Savard out and put Rod Seiling in.

"After the warm-up, I knew I was okay, but now I'm out of the lineup. I should have said, 'I'm 100 percent!'"

When the players returned to their locker rooms after

warm-ups, Sinden summoned them to the coaches' office. As Henderson remembers it, the coach tried to keep their mission simple: "We're not playing four games tonight, just one. So let's just focus on winning Game Five tonight, and the rest will take care of themselves."

Before the player introductions, in front of Leonid Brezhnev and other top Soviet officials, a Soviet figure skater dressed in traditional garb presented Jean Ratelle with a big loaf of bread, Russia's customary show of hospitality. When he bent down to kiss her on the cheek, the home crowd loved it.

Then 44 Soviet kids, ages six though 15, skated onto the ice, carrying bouquets for each player—but one of them dropped a leaf, unseen by the crowd, right before the announcer started introducing each Canadian player in numerical order. When he got to number seven, Phil Esposito skated out, slipped on the leaf, and fell right on his backside, skates pointing up to the sky.

Everyone roared with laughter, the only time most of the Canadians had seen the Soviet players so much as smile, and gave Esposito a warm ovation. Most players would have scrambled to their feet, mortified, but Esposito milked it for all it was worth. He got up on one knee, cradling his stick like a sceptre, then swept his right hand across his body as if bowing to the king.

"It is simply impossible to prepare for that moment," Henderson says, in admiration. "Anyone else would have just turned red, but Espo knew just what to do. I was laughing like crazy. A born leader—just a born leader."

Esposito's reaction made a big impression on young Mark Messier. "I remember him absorbing that moment with such grace. Shit happens to everyone. It's what you do with it that counts. He instantly brought levity and poise. You have to have confidence, *real* confidence, to play that off the way he did."

═

WHEN Game One started, the Canadians were surprised by the Soviet players. When Game Five started, they were surprised by the Soviet *fans*, who appeared bored. If an opponent got too rough, they would snap out of their slumber and start whistling in disapproval the way the Swedish fans had. But otherwise, they made little noise—the opposite of the raucous Canadian fans, who, though outnumbered four to one, outcheered their Soviet counterparts from start to finish.

The first few minutes featured a vigorous back-and-forth from two teams eager to get at it. With 4:30 left in the first period, Gilbert Perreault, making his second appearance of the series, started behind the Canadian net and went through the Soviet lineup, becoming the first Canadian to beat the great Vladimir Lutchenko. Despite Parisé's pregame joke, when Perreault gave Parisé the puck right in front of the net, he didn't panic, but banged it home.

The Canadians returned to their locker rooms with a 1–0 lead and a 12–9 shot advantage, suggesting they really were ready to win on Soviet soil.

At 2:36 of the second period, Bobby Clarke skated out from behind the net to stuff one between Tretiak's pads for a 2–0 lead. Six minutes later, Henderson used his quick trigger to put Canada ahead by three. With Tony Esposito knocking back all 22 Soviet shots in the first two periods, when the Canadians returned to their locker rooms for the second intermission, their 3-0 lead seemed insurmountable.

"I did think we were okay," Ratelle recalls. "They weren't fluky goals. We were playing well."

Just before the period ended, however, a Soviet player had tripped Henderson, sending him headfirst into the boards. His wife, Eleanor, pleaded with him from the stands, "Get up, Paul—get up! If you go to the hospital, I can't be all by myself in that hotel room!"

He got up, but between periods he complained of a pounding headache, which Dr. Jim Murray quickly diagnosed as a concussion. Today, Henderson would be out, perhaps for more than one game. But in 1972 he could turn to Sinden and say, "Please, please don't do this. Don't make me take my stuff off. I've gotta play."

Sinden paused, then said, "Paul, we sure as hell need you, and if you want to play, I would never stop you."

If Team Canada could simply hold a three-goal lead for 20 minutes, the series would be tied, reducing eight games to a best-of-three series. Sinden told his players they had played their best period since Game Two in Toronto, then admonished them *not* to try to protect their lead, but to go on the attack.

"And then," Ratelle says, shaking his head, "it came . . ."

Three minutes into the third period the Soviets broke the shutout, but just 1:22 later Clarke passed to Henderson, who scored his third goal of the series for a 4–1 lead. Henderson would finish with a team-high plus-6 in even-strength scoring chances, with Frank Mahovlich next at plus-4, justifying Sinden's decision to play him ahead of Hadfield.

Surely this three-goal lead would hold up, especially after the Canadians had learned their lesson in Games Three and Four. As the clock ticked toward the 12-minute mark, it certainly looked that way. But then, as Pat Stapleton recalled, "I don't know how the hell it fell apart—but it did, and in dramatic fashion."

Vyacheslav Anisin, the centre of their Kid Line, scored with 11:55 remaining to cut Canada's lead to 4–2. Just eight seconds later, Anisin set up Vladimir Shadrin to cut the lead to 4–3 and tighten Canada's collars.

"I don't think I ever saw a good team like ours so completely outplayed as we were in the next five minutes," Sinden said into his tape recorder that night. It was as if all 17 Canadian skaters were running a marathon, and they'd all hit the proverbial wall at the exact same time and suddenly had nothing left to give.

The Soviets struck again with 8:19 left to tie the game at four. Just three minutes later, Valeri Kharlamov set up Vladimir Vikulov on a two-on-one to put the Soviets ahead, 5–4. The normally staid Soviet crowd erupted like Canadians, and they yelled even louder when the horn sealed the Soviets' third, and least likely, victory.

Despite outshooting the Soviets in the third period, 13–11, the Canadians couldn't get anything to go in, while the Soviets scored five goals on 11 shots. But Tony Esposito's play was more a symptom of the Canadians' demise than the cause.

"Look, this one wasn't that complicated," Clarke says. "All-Star teams aren't made up of backchecking specialists. They're filled with goal-scoring attack players like Espo, Yvan, and most of our forwards. Great players, but defence is not their strength. So you're backed up in your own end the entire third period, and you can't get it out. A game like that is when you don't have enough Ron Ellises.

"And that's how you lose a game like that."

Sinden felt so angry, confused, and frustrated that he didn't trust himself even to be in the same room as his players, fearful that he would say something he couldn't take back. Instead, he and Ferguson stayed in the coaches' room, "stalking up and down," Sinden said, "cursing out loud until we were sure all the players had left. I didn't want to see any players. I would have said the wrong thing. There wasn't any right thing to say after this. I've said all I could for six weeks. They've listened to me enough. Now they've got to come up with their own answers."

Outside the locker room, Sinden told *Sports Illustrated*'s Mark Mulvoy—who described the loss as "especially humiliating"—"We can't put two good periods together, but [the Soviets] could play the same way 24 hours a day until midnight of the third Thursday next February."

Then Sinden concluded, "Maybe I should have stuck to building houses."

In Sinden's journal that night, he was equally unsparing. "We're just not destined to win this thing. No matter what we do, these people beat us. I've never felt so helpless in my life as I did tonight in the third period when the Russians scored five goals on us. Five goals against the 'greatest' players in the world!

"Why the hell do 17 of 18 guys all of a sudden stop skating? I could see it happening to one guy, or even a line. But a whole team? Explain it logically to me so that the next time it happens I'll know how to handle it."

Sinden probably made a wise decision not to address his players, partly for reasons he couldn't have known. The gloom in the players' rooms should have been as heavy as the cloud over Sinden's. After all, there are only two ways to win a hockey game—hold a lead or catch up—and Games One and Four had shown the Canadians couldn't catch up against the Soviets, while Games Three and Five showed they couldn't hold a lead, either. Game Two was starting to look like a fluke.

"When [Boston] played the Rangers, they couldn't beat us," Phil Esposito recalls. "When we played Montreal, we couldn't beat *them*. And the Rangers *could* beat Montreal. How do you figure all that? Well, that's hockey. Sometimes a team just has your number, and you can't figure out why."

That's what it looked like in Moscow. Team Canada now had to win three straight games there, after winning only one game out of four at home. Only a delusional optimist would expect the Canadians to pull off that miracle—and there weren't any of those in the press box. Mere minutes after Game Five ended, the Canadian reporters finished their eulogies.

"No way now," the *Winnipeg Free Press*'s Maurice Smith wrote, "that Canada's National Hockey League stars are going to win their series with the puckchasers from the Soviet Union."

And yet.

While Sinden paced back and forth, muttering to himself,

the reaction from the fans and players was virtually the opposite. Anything Sinden might have said could have squashed the optimism just beginning to bubble up around him.

After suffering another heartbreaking loss—each one worse than the last—and blowing their biggest lead of the series, the players never imagined they'd hear anything but boos. But the Canadian fans stood up in the stands and serenaded them with a heartfelt rendition of "O Canada," one of the world's most beautiful anthems. Every player still remembers it.

"Horrible loss," recalls Savard. "And then everyone is singing 'O Canada'! You do not forget this."

"I'm not that emotional when it comes to things like that," Phil Esposito says, almost a half-century later. "But I'm getting chills just thinking about it. The serenade was *emotional* for me, because I walked right through there."

"If you've got any emotion at all," Clarke says, "if you've got any caring inside you, it has to get to you. Has to. That really helped. Without even knowing *how* it helps, exactly, it helps. It was like the telegrams, the same kind of feeling. Players have to know that you care about them. You see the telegrams, you hear the song, and you know: we are cared about back home."

"Americans are proud to be Americans," Pete Mahovlich says. "They fly their flags wherever you go in the States. You see it everywhere. But Canadians are a lot quieter about it—and maybe because we don't always see ourselves as Canadians. We see ourselves as English or French or Maritimers or Westerners. But the emotion of wearing that Team Canada sweater—it got to me. I think all the guys felt that way. And after Sweden, we weren't Red Wings or Rangers or Bruins anymore. We were *Canadians*. And we felt that way—and I think we played that way.

"Then we lost Game Five, and it was very, very tough. But then all of a sudden you've got 3,000 people, representing a microcosm of the 22 million people back home, waiting for us. Boy, after

Vancouver, we were not expecting that! To come off the ice and see that—what a proud moment that was."

Five decades after the fact, Mahovlich pauses to collect himself, as if experiencing it for the first time. "And they start singing 'O Canada' . . ."

At this, the six-foot-five Mahovlich, a big, tough player, started squeezing out some tears and grabbed a napkin to mop them up—all through a stubborn smile.

"My eyes are starting to water. That's how much it meant to me. Just tells you how emotional it was. A *proud* moment."

The players could only guess the reaction back in Canada, but they assumed the worst. But the Canadians who made the trip to Moscow were completely behind this team, win or lose—and that's what mattered now.

IN the locker room, Eagleson recalls, "I was sitting next to Tony Esposito, who was apologizing for the third period. And in comes Red Berenson, his eyes lit up."

Berenson would never be described as a naive utopian, but watching from the stands that night, he saw something he hadn't seen before, and he rushed down to tell his teammates.

"In the third period, we backed off—big mistake," he says. "But I felt *good* about this game. We were a better team when we got to Moscow, and we showed it in the first two periods. We're getting going now, we're a different team, in better shape, getting closer. I felt more like a coach than a player that night. I don't remember yelling or shouting, just talking to the guys individually and in small groups. I told them, 'That's the best we've played. We're playing *better* than they are. We proved it for two periods. We had the lead! We were *outplaying* them. *We can beat these guys!*'

"Losing, and losing like that especially, should have crushed us. But we weren't down. We saw for the first time that we could outplay them after all, and on their ice."

"Normally, [when] a guy who hadn't played comes in and gives a pep talk, they say, 'Fuck off, dimwit!'" Alan Eagleson says. "But Red, they all respected him and took him seriously. They knew he wasn't talking to hear himself talk. When he comes in and says, 'I'm telling you, we can beat these guys!' everybody listened. He was so in sync with everybody."

"I only played in two games," Berenson says, "so I guess that was my claim to fame. There had to be some belief in there."

"We *all* felt that way," Gilbert said. "There were phases of the game we totally dominated, like we finally knew exactly what we were doing. We felt a lot of encouragement, even from the guys who were not playing. And that meant a lot to us, too."

"After Game Five, I wasn't upset," Park says. "It was the first time we were dominating for three, four, five minutes at a time, then for one or two minutes we weren't, then we were again. I was not thinking about the task ahead—no. I was just thinking, 'We lost, but we're on an even footing now.'"

When they returned to the hotel their fans were waiting for them, some standing on tables, Savard recalls, "and they were still singing, and the guy with the trumpet started playing!"

"There were at least a *thousand* of them," Henderson says. "And I know most of them were hammered, but I would suggest to you that the Canadian national anthem has never been sung with more fervour. If it didn't get to you, you were made of stone."

At least one player found even more motivation.

"They'd stolen our beer and our steaks," Gilbert recalled, "and then to make it worse, when we go back to the hotel after the game, they give us this Russian beer—the warm, skunky shit, and not the good, cold Labatts our sponsor sent. I remember thinking, '*These* pricks will never beat us again! They are not going to win another fucking game.' I swear in my heart I felt that way.

"I remember going to my room, trying to unwind—and then thinking, 'All this other stuff, we can deal with. But *they stole our fucking beer*!'"

Rod Gilbert made up his mind, right then and there, that the Soviets would pay for it.

26

THE LAST TO LEAVE

Since Team Canada's opening loss in Montreal, NHL president Clarence Campbell had seemed to gloat publicly over the team's failure, second-guessing everything Harry Sinden did.

So Canadian fans were surprised to see him at the Intourist Hotel bar after Game Five, having a drink. When a fan started questioning Campbell's hockey knowledge, *Sports Illustrated* reported, he predictably took the bait.

"I know more about hockey than anyone in it," he retorted.

"Ah, you mean you know more than Tarasov and Bobrov?" the fan countered.

Campbell paused, then said, "I was speaking about North America."

TEAM Canada had problems of its own. But before they could start sizing up the herculean task at hand, they had to contend with more self-inflicted distractions.

As soon as Sinden got his team back on the ice Saturday morning, September 23, for one of their three remaining full practices, Gilbert Perreault told Sinden he wanted to leave. It was particularly surprising since Perreault had played his second game the night before, earning an assist on his end-to-end run.

"He gave me the same party line as Martin and Guèvremont," Sinden wrote. "He had to get back to his own team; he wasn't in shape. His excuse, like that of the other two, was not true."

After dealing with the first three players who wanted out two days earlier, Sinden had his protocol down cold. When Perreault asked Sinden "not to make him look bad with the press," Sinden snapped, "Don't worry. I'll have you out of here as fast as possible. There's a flight leaving soon and you'll be on it."

Sinden had lost all patience with such attitudes and didn't care who knew it. Calling Perreault the team's "fourth defector," Sinden said into his tape recorder, "This is the reaction of a kid, a baby. When things don't go your way, go in the corner and sulk. Or, in the case of these three, go back to your team where you'll be the star and everyone can fawn over you and make you feel wanted."

Sinden was just as frank with *Sports Illustrated*. "Look at it this way," he said. "The best product of the Canadian teaching system the past few years probably has been Gilbert Perreault. He is a magnificent individual performer, but he has no real idea how to use the other four players on the ice with him. It's not his fault. No one has taken the time to teach him. It's that simple.

"The ironic thing is that our best players in this series," he added, "have been the so-called non-stars—people like Bobby Clarke and Paul Henderson and Gary Bergman, to mention a few."

When Mulvoy asked why J.P. Parisé was still in the lineup while fellow left winger Vic Hadfield was already back in Canada, Sinden said, "Parisé came here and worked. Hadfield didn't. You look at what the two of them did for five or six weeks, and it makes you wonder about all this star business.

"I don't understand it. Twelve and 15 years ago, Canada beat the Russians with guys who hauled lunch buckets all week. Guys who delivered milk. Guys who tended bar. Why can't these guys we have here—the highest-paid players in the world—beat them?"

This revealed an irony: it's often been said that carrying 35 players was a burden, yet if they had invited only the top 20 players available at the time, they probably wouldn't have had Clarke, Henderson, Ellis, Parisé, Dennis Hull, Pete Mahovlich, Bill White, Pat Stapleton, or Serge Savard—half their final lineup.

The remaining players seemed less upset than amused by Perreault's departure. Because the money the players made from the six exhibition games—three intrasquad scrimmages, plus the games with Sweden and Czechoslovakia—was to go into a fund to be divided equally at the end of the tour, Eddie Johnston was quick with a joke on the bus ride back to the hotel: "Does anyone else want to go home? If we can get rid of a few more, the pot will get bigger for the rest of us."

The players' unbridled laughter told Sinden all he needed to know. Because the remaining players' commitment was absolute, the departures were not a problem but a solution.

"Look, it helped the team when Vic and those guys left," Clarke says. "I'm not trying to put anyone down, but it's true. And I think everyone on the team would tell you that. The guys who left had become a burden, and you don't need that. The guy who sits and bitches is only here to bring you down, and it can spread.

"By the time Perreault left, everyone still there was in, full-hearted. And the proof is the other guys, guys like Marcel [Dionne] and Brian Glennie and Dale Tallon—those guys were good players, even then, who didn't play in the games but were an *asset* in practice. They took their roles seriously, they helped us, and they never complained. *Never.* No questions about any of those guys. They were thrilled they were part of the team, an important part, and we needed them."

"Vic was a teammate in New York," says Rod Seiling. "I don't disparage the guys who went home. There were a lot of politics at play, everyone reacts differently to that, and everyone's pride responds differently. I understand what was going on. I'll leave it at that."

Although Seiling learned at practice that same day that he would not be dressing for Game Six, he wasn't waffling.

"I was ready to play, but Harry made a decision, and I was prepared to live with it," he says today. "Was I happy about it? No, of course not. Players want to play and competitors want to compete. I would have liked to play all eight games, but what is, is. I was part of a team and I wanted us to win. It was a privilege to be there, and it was a thrill. I never considered leaving. Never. Never. Never crossed my mind.

"When the other guys left, it didn't affect the team as a whole—and in fact, one could argue it only made us stronger."

Dale Tallon had played only one game, in Sweden, but he was on board with both feet. "It was great fun in Sweden," he recalls. "We had a luxury hotel, good meals, a good time. But in Russia, it was crappy rooms, crappy food, crappy service. They screwed up cooking our eggs. Burnt them! How do you even *do* that? The food was so bad, I usually ended up eating borscht and drinking tea and beer. A good place to lose weight—and I lost eight pounds! You had to wipe your ass with what they wrap the chicken with. I swear to God that was 60 grit sandpaper. And the propaganda was endless. 'We have the biggest bell in the world, the biggest pool in the world, the biggest tower in the world'—but no goddamned toilet paper!

"But I was still enjoying the hell out of it, and I was learning a lot, and I was excited to be a part of it! I was an architecture buff, and I took Goldy's and Bergie's wives to the Moscow Circus and the Bolshoi. I took advantage of the whole deal, and I was having a blast.

"I was never going to leave Harry and Fergie—who'd put me on the team—and those guys in the room. I felt comfortable with everybody. I admired the hell out of Espo, Serge Savard, Guy

Lapointe, Parisé, Bergie, Ellis, Hendy—it goes on and on, just a *great* group of guys, guys I looked up to. And everybody knew their roles. And I'm rooming with *Rod Gilbert*—come on! An idol, a classy guy, who taught me a lot.

"For me, my decision was made. I was sticking. There just wasn't any question—and no reason to go home."

When the remaining players went beyond team chemistry and considered the defections' effect on the lineup itself, they still believed the team had improved.

"Perreault was an incredible hockey player," Henderson says, "but he liked to take the puck and go end to end—and that is not what's going to beat the Russians. He and [Rick] Martin didn't really work very hard, and no matter who they put with them in practice, it didn't work out. When Vic leaves, Dennis [Hull] moves up to his line. The last three games, all our lines worked together like a hand in glove. It clicked. When the guys left, I gotta say, it made things easier."

No player has yet disagreed with that statement.

"Hockey is a team effort," Yvan Cournoyer says. "Why are the playoffs different from the regular season? Because the first guy gets the same money as the guy killing penalties! That's why you see guys blocking shots. In the playoffs, you do your job. For a coach it's easier in the playoffs, because you just put the guy out there who will do the best. Nothing else matters. Well, when we get to Moscow, we are in the playoffs now. We just need to be together, to do our jobs. It's game by game from here."

Once Sinden told Perreault on Saturday, September 23, that he'd be on the next flight out of Moscow, the team finally completed the process of becoming a real team, once and for all.

BEFORE practice, Sinden and Ferguson had to decide on the lineup for the first of three do-or-die games—if they were lucky.

They wanted to pick a roster they could ride the rest of the way. All favours had been exhausted, all other considerations dismissed, save one: Team Canada absolutely had to win this game.

Given the largely positive results from Game Five—except for the final score—Sinden didn't want to start over the way he had after Game One. He figured they needed only to tweak the lineup that had worked so well for two periods.

Getting the forward lines and defensive pairs right can be as tricky as trying to pick the right rowers in an eight-man shell. With so many variables, it's hard to determine the constants. When a line isn't working, is it because of the left winger, the centre, or the right winger? Because logic only gets you so far, especially before analytics invaded the game, coaches ultimately had to rely on trial and error.

For example, logic would dictate that Esposito—accustomed to playing with big, tough guys like Wayne Cashman and Ken Hodge—would work well with a big man like Frank Mahovlich, who could clear out the corners and get the puck to the slot, and not with Cournoyer, the poster boy for the Flying Frenchmen, a super-fast, highly skilled, smaller player who was tough in his own way but no one's idea of a power forward. And yet the opposite proved true: Esposito and Cournoyer clicked.

"Yvan and I played a lot together in that series," Esposito says. "And we worked really well together. Frank and I, we had no chemistry. We lost Game Five. I had no goals, no assists—no points. First game without any. I told Harry, 'Get Frank away from me.'"

Sinden decided to take a chance and put Cournoyer on Esposito's line with Parisé, the grinder they couldn't take out of the lineup. Sinden wasn't about to fiddle with Clarke's line, which had accounted for six of the 10 points Team Canada had produced in Game Five.

That left Canada's third line. Sinden had to find a left winger to play with Jean Ratelle and Rod Gilbert. If Hadfield hadn't left,

Sinden would likely have put him in to reunite the GAG Line. Instead, he plugged in Dennis Hull to jump-start that line.

After Sinden announced the lineup before practice, Henderson told Hull, "Moses, you better come up big, because you've got to lead us out of the wilderness."

Sinden decided to stick with Pete Mahovlich as one of his "spare" forwards, often used for penalty killing, and put Red Berenson back in uniform. On defence, he kept intact his two best pairs, Park-Bergman and White-Stapleton, and made only one change: replacing Seiling with Savard, who was good to go, pairing him with his Canadiens teammate Lapointe.

Sinden had made only three changes—Savard for Seiling, Hull for Perreault, and Berenson for Frank Mahovlich—but just in case someone couldn't meet the moment, or fell to injury, Ferguson told defenceman Dale Tallon, "Be ready. You might play."

That left only goaltending. Esposito had suffered a terrible third period, but his series record still stood at 1–1–1, with a 3.33 GAA and .873 save percentage. Dryden had lost both his starts, letting in a total of 12 goals for a 6.00 GAA and an .803 save percentage, and he hadn't played since Game Four, 16 days earlier. Almost every coach in this situation would have gone with Esposito, by far the safer choice. But Sinden, showing his characteristic confidence in his people and his instincts, picked Dryden. Sinden had decided one man couldn't handle three straight games in hockey's worst pressure cooker. He would need them both.

The man most surprised by the decision seemed to be Dryden himself. When Ferguson skated over to the boards to get some water in the middle of practice, he asked Dryden, "How are you feeling, big guy?"

"Oh, all right, I guess," Dryden said. "But I'm still making stupid mistakes."

"Don't worry about them," Ferguson replied, "so long as you don't make them tomorrow night."

Dryden confessed in his journal that he was "bewildered . . .

It didn't make sense." Maybe not on paper. But on paper, the GAG Line should have been the best in the series, Seiling and Awrey should have been the top defence pair based on their training camp, and Vladislav Tretiak should have been the worst goalie they'd ever see—and of course, none of that had proven true once the puck dropped in this strange series.

To get the absolute best out of his team when nothing less would do, Sinden had to think on a different level. If Team Canada was going to have any chance of pulling off this miracle, he would have to disregard the odds, the statistics, the media, public opinion, players' feelings, and his own reputation, career, and future, to make all his decisions solely on the basis of what would give his team the best chance to pull off the greatest comeback in sports history.

"Harry gave us a chance to win," Clarke says, "because every decision he made on and off the ice was to help us win—nothing else. Oh God, I thought Sinden was outstanding."

By starting Dryden, Sinden ignored every external signal, and even Dryden's own feelings, to put his instincts above them all. If it backfired, Sinden, far more than Dryden, would be the national goat—and probably for the rest of his life. But Sinden obviously saw something in Dryden that no one else did—perhaps even Dryden himself, at least at that moment.

"To make those decisions, and trust your gut, in that situation—man, that's a tough thing to do!" Tallon says. "But that's the way it has to be, to be successful. Really, it was our only chance. We trusted him."

So that was it. Sinden had picked the players on whom he would bet Canada's reputation, and his own. He had just shoved all the chips in.

If they won Game Six, it only meant they'd live another day to do it all again.

AFTER three games and twice as many practices on the Olympic rinks in Sweden and Moscow, the Canadians were starting to figure out the big sheet.

For the forwards, the difference was either ignored or exploited.

"International ice?" Esposito asks. "Never noticed the difference. Never."

For speedy forwards like Cournoyer and Henderson, it was a blessing.

"It depends on your game," Henderson says. "If you were big and slow, it did you no favours. But if skating was a strength, you probably loved it. I told my wife that the big ice was made for me. By the time we got to Moscow, I felt very good about it."

Team Canada's defencemen were not so lucky.

"The bigger ice surface was much harder," says Park, who, like most of the Canadians, had never played on it before. "On our rinks, if their forward's got two strides on you by the boards, he's gone. You can't catch him. So you try to squeeze him at the blue line. But on their ice, if you tried to squeeze him at the blue line, he has too much room to move. You can't do it.

"But then you learned on the bigger ice that even with two strides on you, he's not around you yet. He has too far to go to the net, and you still have the better angle. So we had to discipline ourselves: don't overcommit. Be patient and you'll get him. We could adjust, because we weren't rookies.

"Same thing killing penalties. We learned to give 'em the perimeter instead of attacking them on the outside. We realized pretty quickly that the corners are so far away, you can't go there and get your guy and then get back to the slot in time. They'll burn you. We didn't realize that until Moscow."

Once the Canadians started to solve the big ice, some of the Soviets' strategic mystique faded, too.

"By the time we got to Moscow," Park adds, "all the Russian

criss-crossing never bothered me. It didn't matter if they changed their lanes, because we started blocking all their lanes. We had learned not to panic or overcommit, and to hold our ground."

Fortunately for Canada, they had more than one defenceman who could play the tight-hitting NHL game in compact rinks *and* also skate full speed with the Soviets on the big sheet.

"I like the big rink," Savard says. "It's not enough out there to be a big, tough guy. You have to be able to move. So, let's see who can."

—

WHEN not calling their rooms to interrupt their sleep, stealing their steaks or beer, turning off the lights during practice, or surrounding the rink during games with armed soldiers, the Soviets were wonderful hosts, inviting the players and their wives to see the Moscow Circus, the opera, and the world-famous Bolshoi Ballet. But everything came with a downside.

"For me it was great, really great," Berenson says, "but all I could think the whole time I was there was 'Get me out of here!' My desire to go home had nothing to do with my role on the team. I just found the whole place incredibly depressing."

"Being there was so shocking," Pat Stapleton's wife, Jackie, recalls. "Everything was so regimented. They toured us to death. I didn't have time to read Soviet history. I had five kids!"

The food was another issue, though it depended partly on your perspective. The wives would meet every day for lunch and dinner, with the meals predetermined by their hosts.

As Joy Berenson recalls, "I was one of the older women, and I'd grown up in Saskatchewan, where we canned everything for the winter—potatoes, beets, onions, carrots—so I was used to the food they were serving. Well, these girls were used to hamburgers and French fries. Before dinner they'd always serve us smoked salmon and caviar on toast points, but these girls wanted a sandwich, so I got it all to myself! Whatever we didn't eat would just come back the next day, so the soup never got any better. Might as well try to eat it the first time!"

The players strongly agreed that it was vital that their wives joined them, providing the players the only support they had outside the locker room. The wives even helped them to get to know each other better as people, not just hockey players.

"Frank [Mahovlich] spoke so highly of his wife," Jackie Stapleton says. "I had such respect for him after that. I took chocolate bars and gave them to Ken [Dryden]. He needed some energy. We took peanut butter, too, for protein. The bread was great, though."

In the era of Wonder bread, the Russians' fresh, flavourful bread was a rare treat. The tourists learned to enjoy the good stuff and ignore the rest.

27

GAME SIX: PLAYING A NEW GAME

September 24, 1972

Before Game Six, Harry Sinden admitted to himself: "I have three people I'm concerned with: the two German referees, and Ken Dryden."

For Game Five each team was allowed to name a referee. Sinden picked the Swede, Uwe Dahlberg, and the Soviets picked the Czech, Rudy Batja. They called the game well enough to go largely unnoticed, giving the Canadians five minor penalties and the Soviets six.

"By international standards," Sinden said, "they did a good job. By NHL standards they didn't." But, he said, he would have much preferred seeing those two again for Game Six than the West Germans, Franz Baader and Josef Kompalla, whom the Soviets picked to call Game Six.

"There's no choice at this point," he said. "We have to live with them. [But] I don't think I'm going to sleep too well with them on my mind."

Sinden might have been concerned about starting Dryden, too, but he had much more faith in him than the West German referees.

Sinden believed Dryden would come through—before Dryden did.

Every night in Moscow, Sinden, John Ferguson, and Alan Eagleson ate dinner together, sometimes with their wives, sometimes without. The conversation bounced around, Eagleson recalls, but included goaltending every single night. "I can tell you my biggest surprise was after Game Five," he recalls, "when Harry said he was putting Dryden back in. Tony had done a good job in Game Five—except for two minutes!" But those two minutes cost three goals, and the game.

When it came to personnel matters, Eagleson tried to stay out. "That was not my role. Kenny's a great goalie, everyone knows that. But I would have started Tony. Good thing I kept my mouth shut."

At six foot four, Dryden was an unusually big goalie, especially for his era. He had lightning reflexes, like all the greats, plus an uncanny ability to anticipate the play, due partly to being one of the most cerebral players ever to suit up. But when you talk to his Montreal teammates about him, they always come back to Dryden's real superpower, known almost exclusively to his teammates: his quiet confidence.

That calm, steadfast confidence is what allowed him to turn down Junior A to play American college hockey in the mid-'60s, when almost no serious prospects were doing that. It gave him the presence to calmly stare down the powerful Chicago Black Hawks in his preseason debut in Halifax in 1970, and do it again six months later, when the Canadiens faced Chicago again, this time in Game Seven of the Stanley Cup Final, for the Habs' 17th Stanley Cup.

It was Dryden's confidence in himself, so obvious to those who played with him, that made his coaches and teammates so confident in him. But his confidence, his rock-solid companion since he was a kid, had suddenly escaped him during the disaster in Montreal. It hadn't come back by Game Four, when he let in five goals in Vancouver, and it was still missing on September 23, when Ferguson told him he'd be starting Game Six the next day.

That left Dryden about 36 hours to find his confidence, screw his courage up, and act like he'd been there before—though nobody had. In the three games Dryden had played against the Soviets in his entire career, including the first in Vancouver in 1969, a 9–3 drubbing he suffered with the Canadian national team, he had let in 21 goals, or a staggering 7.00 goals-against average—the kind of stat that would earn a goalie a ticket to Chibougamau, Quebec.

In the fall of 1970, when Dryden faced the big, bad Black Hawks for the first time, he saw that, yes, that was Bobby Hull and Stan Mikita coming down on him, but the puck was the same, and so was the net, and it wasn't that different from what he'd already done before. But Game Six *was* different: different rules, different refs, a different rink with different dimensions, and, most important, a different opponent, playing a different style. To stop the Soviets, Dryden would have to master a new method of goaltending, staying back in his net and working laterally to shut down their backdoor shots. And he'd have to handle all of this in front of the world.

The morning of Game Six, he wrote, "Ever feel so nervous, so on edge that you almost can't stand up? That's the way I feel right now—and it's only quarter to nine in the morning, still 11 hours away from game time."

Later in the day, he added, "I wonder how the other players feel about Harry's decision to play me again. I'm sure they think Tony should be playing tonight, and I can't really blame them."

Yet he was able to muster three reasons why he might do his teammates proud in Moscow that night:

- He wasn't ready for Game One, but since then he had had two games and a month of practice.
- He had changed his style to counter the Soviets' offence.
- Team Canada was playing much better overall.

If you had to come up with some reasons to convince yourself that tonight's game was going to be different, those were as good as any. They also indicated that Dryden's superpower, his quiet confidence, was still flickering.

Dryden's teammates praised him so much during warm-ups, trying to pump him up, that it almost embarrassed him. But they knew what he knew: the man in net would have more impact on the outcome than any of them could.

═

ALMOST every player recalls Sinden's talk before Game Six.

"I remember Harry came into the locker room," Brad Park says, "and said, 'Boys, don't look ahead. Don't think we have three games left. We have one game tonight. That's all.

"'I don't want you guys thinking about Game Seven or Game Eight. I don't even want you thinking about the third period. The only thing I want you to concentrate on is your next shift—that's it. Just shift by shift. Shift by shift. Just win your shift, then get ready for the next one, and win that. That is your focus. What can you do in the next shift? That's all that matters.'

"That's a pretty good mindset, a good approach," Park says today. "We listened. I never looked ahead. I don't think anyone did. I was just focused on who's coming off, and now I'm going on. And that's how we played. By that time we knew the severity of the situation we were in, but we couldn't think about it. If you did, you're overwhelmed, worrying about failing and nothing will go right. You just can't play your best that way.

"That made it simple. We didn't want to think too much. So that's what we did: just focus on the next shift."

"You don't play three games in one night," Bob Clarke says. "You play one game, then you get two days off. So we just gotta win the next fucking game. And that means winning the next shift, then the next one. That's all we had to do."

The fact that so many players can recite Sinden's message years later suggests Park was right: it sank in.

"Very rarely will you ever hear a player come to tell you that was a great pregame talk," Sinden says. "But I prided myself on my talks. The two main elements of coaching boil down to what you said to them, and what you made them do. What else do you have? But that one, I know, they remember."

That night, Sinden recalls, he added a kicker: "I remember telling them, 'Guys, we're never going to lose to this team again. Just focus on your next shift, again and again, and we'll get there before you know it."

The Zen maxim is simple: "Be here now." But it's very hard to do. Our minds seem determined to dwell on past problems and imagine future ones, focusing on pretty much everything *but* the here and now. An already difficult task becomes that much harder when we're in high-pressure situations, and things are going badly.

But these players, under the toughest competitive circumstances, now had to do exactly that: focus solely on the present, without getting pulled down by the three games they'd already lost or daunted by the three games they still had to win, with zero margin for error. It is so rare in life that we truly do live in the moment, and almost unheard of for anyone to do so simultaneously with three dozen compatriots, and with the world watching. They were attempting to achieve not just one of the most difficult deeds in sports history, but one of the most elusive feats of human potential, in any field of endeavour: everybody exceeding their limits at once together.

That is why these games are burned into their memories so indelibly: not just what they did, but how they felt—and how they know they *all* felt.

═

THE Canadians had something else going for them, something entirely unexpected: a "home" crowd at the arena, thanks to the Soviets' mishandling of the 3,000 crazy Canadians.

The Soviets had given the best tickets not to hard-core Muscovite hockey fans but to top party leaders, who didn't know or care much about the sport—much the way the lower sections of North American arenas are often filled with high-rollers who leave with a period to play, while the passionate fans are stuck in the rafters, far from the action.

For Game Five the 11,000 Russian spectators were easily drowned out by the 3,000 Canadians. The Soviets found this so unnerving that for Game Six, they broke up the bloc of Canadian fans into smaller pockets scattered throughout the arena. But this backfired when the Canadian fans cheered even louder, creating the illusion that the rink was surrounded by Canadians, not Soviets.

"They always tried to break us up," Joy Berenson recalls, but the players' wives weren't having it. "We were determined to sit together, and we did. Oh yes, we did! There was always someone to pull you in."

"We'd all met just a few days before," Gerry Park says, "but we really bonded. Everything the Russians were trying to do to us made us a stronger, more cohesive unit. The 'us versus them' mentality, we got that right away."

When they played "O Canada," all 3,000 voices were put to full use—a moving display of patriotism from a people who rarely displayed it so openly.

"To hear those 3,000 Canadians singing the national anthem," announcer Brian Conacher told his audience, "is really an emotional experience!"

To which Foster Hewitt replied, "I've never heard anything like it."

For Yvan Cournoyer, it was simple. "When people were saying, 'The Russians are going to beat you,' that really scared me," he said in *Cold War*. "And when you're scared, you're a good player. I've always been afraid to lose. Maybe that's why I won so much."

"I didn't worry about the Russians," Phil Esposito says. "We knew what they were doing by then. There were no surprises left. The surprise was over! I worried about what *we* had to do. Quite frankly, we were better. I felt like if we played the way *we* were supposed to, they could not beat us."

There was nothing left to do but play the game and find out.

═

A focused Team Canada came out flying.

"This is going to be a different game!" Hewitt told the fans back home. "The Canadians are really hitting, right off the bat!"

But the Soviets weren't backing off, either, knowing just one more victory would seal the series—and their place atop the sport.

In the early minutes, Dryden said, "I made three really good saves. Each time I stopped the puck, I had a feeling of accomplishment. I also became more confident, more and more at home."

Sinden could tell from the start: "He had his confidence."

Dryden's trusty companion had returned, at just the right time. This, in turn, inspired his teammates to go full blast without undue fear of getting scored against. It was also clear early on that Sinden had made a lot of good personnel decisions. Serge Savard's ankle was holding up, and he looked strong.

"You could see how the three pairs [of defencemen] played together pretty quickly," Jean Ratelle says. "As a centre, I'd come back and pick up the second Russian coming in the zone, and then our D could get the puck carrier in the corner. You stop them like that, and then we're not playing in our end so much. Once we got in better shape, it became a more even game."

The Canadians were playing with a potent combination of confidence and urgency—and they would need plenty of both. Midway through the first period, the West German referees inserted themselves into the game, calling Gary Bergman for tripping and giving Phil Esposito an unheard-of double minor for charging.

The Canadians had to apply the lessons Park described: having the patience not to challenge the Soviets' potent power play at the perimeter, nor get sucked into the corners too far away, but to wait for them to come closer. The Canadians kept the Soviet power play at bay, giving up a total of only six shots on goal the entire period, while firing nine on Tretiak.

Team Canada also demonstrated it had begun to figure out this new game. The Canadian forwards took advantage of the Olympic ice, hitting the Soviet blue line with speed *and* numbers, often flying down the ice three on two, with their defencemen occasionally joining the rush, too. The fruits of their growth would not be harvested in the first period, however, with the teams returning to their locker rooms in a scoreless tie, and the tension on and off the ice rapidly rising.

A few years later John Ferguson said, "I've never played in a series that mattered when the going didn't get rough. My view on this: I don't care how we win, as long as we win."

Clarke recalled, "I remember John Ferguson giving the pep talk between the first and second period. He kept repeating that someone had to take care of Kharlamov. I looked around the room and realized he was talking to me."

Clarke got the message, loud and clear.

Just 1:12 into the second period, Yuri Liapkin took a low shot from the blue line that clipped a skate, then went straight toward the far corner of the net, just out of reach of Dryden's glove—1–0, Soviets. But the Canadians didn't panic, sticking with their new game plan.

Less than a minute later the referees called the Soviets' big, tough defenceman Alexander Ragulin for interference. But the Canadian power-play unit once again couldn't convert—the only chance it would get all night.

A minute after Ragulin returned to the ice, Rod Gilbert's rebound bounced out to Dennis Hull, who popped it over the fallen Tretiak to tie the score 1–1 with 14:47 left in the period.

"It was amazing how Dennis got used to us so fast," Ratelle says of Hadfield's replacement on the GAG Line. "He showed that he was a great player, he could skate, he could score—and the Soviets never scored on us. How the hell could Dennis do that? Well, you think about it. In Chicago, he plays with Pit Martin and Jim Pappin, two similar players. So it was a natural fit."

Hull provided the answer to a question that had been bothering Sinden for five games: Who can play with Gilbert and Ratelle? Like Clarke taking Norm Ullman's spot between Henderson and Ellis, when Hull replaced Hadfield, it clicked instantly.

"The only thing I can remember about that goal," Hull says, "was the picture of us skating back to centre ice, celebrating, and you couldn't tell who had scored from that picture. It looked like we'd *all* scored the goal. That's how we all felt."

Just 1:09 later, Berenson broke into the Soviet zone with all four teammates joining the rush—a new approach for the Canadians.

"I was having a good shift," Berenson recalls, "subbing for Parisé on Esposito's line with Yvan. He's a smart guy, and quick as the devil, so you knew he could get open. If I had played on his line [on a regular basis], I would just get him the puck—either in flight or when you knew he was about to take off—and I'd get a bushel of assists. He makes you look good."

After the puck came back to Pat Stapleton at the blue line, he blasted a shot on Tretiak, who redirected it behind the net. There, Berenson zipped it just as quickly out front, where he knew Cournoyer was crashing the net. Cournoyer knocked it in for a 2–1 lead.

"When I knew Yvan was in front, I threw out a no-look pass," Berenson says, "and he put it home, *bang*, just like that—so quick, Tretiak didn't have a chance."

A mere 15 seconds after that the Soviets tried to pass the puck out of their zone, but Henderson sensed an opportunity, stole the pass, and released an awkward but unexpected 40-foot (12-metre) shot that bounced its way under Tretiak's skate to give Team Canada a 3–1 lead.

After averaging just 3.6 goals per *game* through the first five contests, the rebuilt Team Canada managed to score three goals in 83 *seconds*.

With more than half the game left to play, the Canadians protected their lead with aggressive defence from Park, who probably played his best game of the series to date, and the penalty-killing unit of Savard, Stapleton, Bill White, and one forward, Peter Mahovlich, which one *Montreal Gazette* editor described as "brilliant."

WITH 11:31 left in the second period, and the two teams serving matching minors for roughing, Clarke committed what would become one of the most controversial acts in hockey history.

When Valeri Kharlamov came down the middle of the ice toward Park and Bergman, cut to the left at the blue line, and faked a shot, Clarke came rushing back behind him and delivered a quick two-hander, landing the heel of his stick directly on Kharlamov's left ankle.

Contrary to the legend that now surrounds the act, Kharlamov did not crumple to the ice, but kept his balance and battled for the puck in front of Dryden, who froze the puck. When the referees gave Clarke a delayed penalty, Kharlamov got inches from Clarke's face and gave him a light jab. The officials gave Clarke a two-minute minor for slashing and a 10-minute misconduct, which is probably what NHL refs would have given him.

Years later, it has become one of the most talked-about

moments from a series that doesn't lack for talking points. Kharlamov himself said, "I am convinced that Bobby Clarke was given the job of taking me out of the game. Sometimes, I thought it was his only goal . . . It had nothing to do with hockey."

But the comment that brought the incident back to life came from Clarke's linemate, Paul Henderson. In 2002, while Henderson was attending a hockey game, a reporter asked him what he thought of Clarke's slash in hindsight.

"It was the low point of the series," Henderson said, which sparked a public debate. Ten years later, in his book, Henderson stood by his comment but regretted giving it to a reporter, who had asked Henderson about sportsmanship in general and Clarke's slash in particular, then took Henderson's answers out of context and failed to include his mitigating remarks.

Clarke responded in the *Globe and Mail*, "I think it's improper to criticize a teammate 30 years later. If it was so offensive, why didn't he bother to say something after the game? I'm surprised at him, because we were a true team. Thirty years ago, we put forth the ultimate team performance. I thought it was foolish for him to say that. It doesn't hurt me, but I don't understand why he would bring it up now."

Ferguson seemed more offended than Clarke and came to his defence, unbidden. Before Ferguson had pushed to get Clarke on the team over Dave Keon, for eight seasons he had done whatever it took to protect the great Jean Béliveau. Béliveau was known as the ultimate gentleman, and Ferguson was not. No doubt Ferguson did plenty of things on the ice that Béliveau would never do, but he never judged Ferguson for doing them. Quite the opposite: he appreciated the fire Ferguson brought to the rink each night.

Likewise, it's safe to assume, as Stapleton often said, that Henderson would not have had as much room to work with if the Soviets hadn't feared Clarke's wrath—which helped Henderson play the best hockey of his life that month.

Ferguson told journalist Gare Joyce, "I remember that Kharlamov's ankle was hurting pretty bad. I called Clarke over to the bench, looked over at Kharlamov, and said, 'I think he needs a tap on the ankle.' I didn't think twice about it. It was us versus them. And Kharlamov was killing us. I mean, somebody had to do it."

"It's possible Fergie said that," Clarke says today, "but to be honest, I don't remember that. And that's not why I did it, in any case."

It says something that, given an alibi from a respected source, Clarke has declined it. Before that play, Clarke recalls, Kharlamov "gave me a little something, then he spun away." Later, when Clarke chased Kharlamov down the ice, "I went after him to get him. It wasn't an accident. But I didn't head down the ice thinking, 'I'm gonna bust his fucking ankle.' If he had lined up differently, I might have given him a cross-check. I was pissed, and I was getting even.

"Would I do anything differently?" He pauses, then says, "No, I don't think so. Some players react aggressively, and some don't. I do. Doesn't make me proud to have done it. But I'm not ashamed, either."

When Ferguson publicly defended him, Clarke recalls, "Fergie was trying to protect me. I talked to John and said, 'I appreciate what you're doing, but you don't have to.' Look, I did a lot of things I'm not proud of on the ice—but I never did anything just out of anger, or for effect. I was always playing to win. I can own what I did. I never thought anything about it after. [But] it became way bigger than it ever was at the time."

Since then, everyone who comments on the series feels compelled to address it. In his 2007 book, announcer Brian Conacher wrote that "from the broadcast booth I was shocked and disgusted when I saw Clarke viciously chop at Kharlamov's left ankle." Conacher noted that "emotionally these games had clearly gone beyond sport for Team Canada and had truly become unrestricted war on ice."

Esposito agrees with Conacher's last point but draws a different conclusion. "Don't you people get it?" he asks today. "This wasn't hockey! This was war! *This was war!* The only thing I regret is that Bobby didn't do it in the *first* game."

"I don't agree with what he did," Savard says today, echoing most of his teammates. "When we played the Flyers, I wore ankle guards. But one thing I always mention: Bobby didn't play any differently against the Russians than he did in the NHL. He didn't change his style for the series."

Characteristically, Cournoyer takes a lighter perspective. "You have to be good to do what Bobby did," he says with a grin. "You have to hit just the right spot. It's hard to do! How many times do guys try to chop your ankle, but nothing happens? That was not Bobby's first time!"

Years later, when Canadian journalist Dick Beddoes asked Clarke about it at a team reunion, calling it a "wicked two-hander," Clarke replied, "Dick, if I hadn't learned how to lay on a two-hander once in a while, I'd never have left Flin Flon."

Clarke was known from the start as an edgy player. When he played for the Flin Flon Bombers he scored 51 goals two years in a row and an impressive 305 total points in just 117 games—while being called for an equally impressive 271 penalty minutes. It's a wonder he was on the ice enough to score all those points.

When Sinden and Ferguson picked Clarke over Keon, they knew who they were getting. But through Game Five, Clarke had taken only three minor penalties, two for slashing, and would finish the series with four minor penalties, fewer than J.P. Parisé, Wayne Cashman, and Bergman, and the same number as his linemate Ron Ellis—and just two more total minutes than Kharlamov, who had already been called for high-sticking, slashing, holding, and a misconduct.

For all the attention the slash generated since, it's hard to believe it went virtually unremarked at the time. Conacher made no mention of it. Neither did Sinden or Dryden, both of whom recorded detailed accounts of the game hours later. Kharlamov was coming down on Brad Park, but, Park says, "I never even saw it, and I wasn't more than 10 feet away." That might be because it happened so quickly and didn't seem to amount to much. Kharlamov skated off under his own power and continued to play. Although he would sit out Game Seven, he played a regular shift in Game Eight, notching a crucial assist, though he was not at full strength. How much Clarke's slash actually affected the series is hard to say.

"I admired what Kharlamov could do on the ice, but in my mind I felt we could stop him," Park wrote years later. "I did not think we had to resort to that. There were a lot of other Soviet players that were dangerous as well. No one ever relies on just one guy. So I wouldn't say that it shortchanged our victory, but I am saddened that it happened anyway."

"For what it's worth," Park adds today, "the best player in the world wasn't Kharlamov, but a spectator in the stands named Bobby Orr."

Statistically at least, Alexander Yakushev would be the Soviets' best player, notching 11 points in eight games, with a plus-5. Vladimir Shadrin would finish second, with eight points and a plus-7. Through six games, Kharlamov had notched three goals and three assists for six points, and would add an assist in Game Eight to finish third on the Soviet team with seven points—and an even plus-minus rating, though he would play one fewer game than the other two. After Game One, thanks largely to Ellis's defensive work, with help from Henderson and Clarke, Kharlamov would score exactly once the rest of the series, a short-handed goal against Team Canada's power play, not Clarke's line.

As great as Kharlamov surely was, Park is probably right and Ferguson wrong: Kharlamov wasn't killing the Canadians. Clarke hurt Kharlamov, but he didn't knock him out of the series, either. Perhaps the one indisputable outcome of the slash is this: it eclipsed so much else that happened in the series.

"Clarkie's slash gets all the attention," Rod Seiling says today, "but it glosses over all the stuff that was unseen, and more importantly never got called by the referees. And what you saw there, I would submit, is this: when you keep getting hacked and whacked, but you're only getting a bunch of no-calls to show for it, well, eventually you take the game into your own hands. If the sheriff doesn't take over, it's no surprise when the vigilantes do. I'm not trying to make an excuse for it. Clarkie can speak for himself. But I'm stating what was a fact of life."

This was not a contest of angels. The attention the slash received also obscured the daily hassles the Soviets created for the Canadians.

"Oh, Christ," Gilbert said. "When we tried to take a nap, that big babushka knocked on the door, waking us up and yelling at us. When we have dinner before the games, they don't bring out our beautiful steaks. They bring out their shitty pork! They bug our rooms, spy on us around town, and even turn out the lights during our practice. Can you believe this shit? Anyone talk about *that*?"

This is not to excuse poor sportsmanship or dirty play, and Clarke's slash qualifies as both. But Clarke's slash did not occur in a vacuum. It was surrounded by shady antics that usually went unpunished and uncalled, and a long list of unsportsmanlike manoeuvres by government officials.

Given this complicated backdrop, as egregious as Clarke's two-hander was, to pull it out now as an isolated act seems disingenuous. If Clarke occasionally crossed the line, that was part of the package—and part of a much greater whole in the series itself. It wasn't always pretty, but it was all true.

Clarke's slash, however, was one thing that all the Soviet subterfuge was not: it was obvious. And that seems to be the main reason why it is still discussed today.

═

AFTER Clarke's slash the refs seemed to keep a sharper eye out for Canadian infractions. This in turn caused Sinden and Ferguson to bark at the refs even more, which didn't help.

Some of their players looked at the pair "as though we'd gone crazy," Sinden recalls. Dryden actually skated over to the bench and stared at Sinden, hoping he would regain his composure, while Berenson took the unusual step of telling the coach to calm down. Neither had any effect, with Sinden yelling at one of the players, "Get that damn Dryden back in the net!"

"Our lack of team discipline definitely made it easier for the referees to call us all night," Berenson says. "If the Russians wanted to play physical, they could, but they were sly. They wouldn't confront you directly. They'd kick your skates out from under you—and we knew they weren't going to call that, even if they saw it."

Seven minutes later, with 2:58 left in the period, the refs called Hull for slashing. Just nine seconds into the power play, Yakushev punched home the Soviets' second goal. Then he and his teammates skated back to the bench without so much as a smile.

"The bounces were not going our way," Park recalls. "I remember that shot bounced off Dryden, then off the pipe, then right back to Yakushev, no farther away than from me to that door. And he knocks it in. Easy." This narrowed the margin to 3–2 with 2:49 left in the second, more than enough time for the Soviets to tie the game—or score five more, as they had in the third period alone two nights earlier.

Thirty-five seconds later, Esposito's stick got Ragulin in the cheek, drawing blood, enough for the refs to call a high-sticking major. When Ferguson said a few choice words to one of the West German officials, the ref whipped around and gave Ferguson a bench minor. No one seems to recall what Ferguson said, though it probably wasn't praise for the official's good work. When

Ferguson expressed his objection by throwing towels on the ice, Canada was lucky the refs didn't tack on more.

All this gave the Soviets a five-on-three for two minutes, and a guaranteed five-on-four power play for three more minutes. If there was a time for Team Canada to collapse the way it had in Game Five, this was it.

Yet they did as Sinden had instructed, not daring to look any farther ahead than the next shift, conceding the perimeter to the Soviet power play and staying out of the deep corners. With Savard breaking up passing plays and Dryden kicking out whatever the Soviets were sending his way—often from the same high-percentage places from which they had scored 21 goals on him in his three previous games against them—the Canadians killed both penalties.

But Dryden believes the Canadians might have gotten a break in the last minute of the period. Still on a five-on-four power play, Yakushev, on Dryden's right, passed across the crease to Kharlamov, wide open on the back door—just the kind of play they had burned Dryden on in Games One and Four.

"I felt helpless as I moved over to try and stop Kharlamov's shot," Dryden wrote. "The puck hit my pad and caromed toward the net. What happened next I don't know. The puck could have hit the goalpost and flown back to me. Or it could have hit the mesh netting inside the net and flown back. All I knew was that the puck was in my glove and the referee was whistling the play dead."

A few seconds later, the horn blew, ending the second period with Canada still holding on to its 3–2 lead. Sinden and Ferguson chased after the refs on their way to the dressing room, screaming, while the Canadian players walked back to their rooms, urging each other to stay calm and stay out of the box.

═

BEFORE the third period Sinden engaged in some gamesmanship of his own, doing something he had never done before: he held his team back in the locker room to make the refs and the Soviets wait. He wanted to be sure his guys were ready to play, and it seemed to work.

Both teams stayed out of the box for the first 17 minutes of the last period. By now the Canadians could play five on five with the Soviets—if they gave themselves that chance.

With Dryden playing his best hockey that month, the Canadians remained vigilant and in control, determined not to suffer the same fate they had in Games Three and Five, when they repeatedly blew good leads. Despite nine shots from the Canadians and 13 from the Soviets, neither team could score. But with 2:21 left, the refs called Ron Ellis for a questionable holding penalty—not the kind of call NHL referees would make in that situation.

"Not a good call," Ellis says. "Sitting in that box, I felt horrible, and I was worried. But Phil [Esposito] and Pete [Mahovlich] skate by the box, and they both gave me a nod, as if to say, 'We know you got screwed, but we got this.' Not a word was spoken. They knew how I felt. That's when you know you're a team."

Esposito and Mahovlich didn't score a dramatic short-handed goal this time, as they had in Game Two, but with Dryden putting in his first stellar performance of the series with 27 saves, making four "miraculous saves" in *Sports Illustrated*'s account, Team Canada held on to win, 3–2.

"The last period was beautiful," Sinden wrote. "It was the first time in the series we finished stronger than they did."

"Almost perfect," Clarke says.

The win, Mark Mulvoy wrote, "made it possible, if unlikely, for the NHL All-Stars to take the entire eight-game series by winning the final two games in Moscow. Although nothing would remove the shock of the Canadian losses, Sunday's victory at least proved that Canada belongs on the same rink with the Russians."

The Canadians had not only played their best game of the series, they had started creating the first crude version of the hybrid style, taking the best from the East and West, that virtually all teams around the world play today. To do so in the middle of a high-pressure series was tantamount to performing an engine overhaul on a plane over the ocean—but that's what their desperate situation required.

Ultimately, however, the biggest difference probably wasn't systems, but the Canadians being in good enough shape to go hard into the dirty places, finish checks, block shots, and play competitive, hard-hitting, Canadian hockey.

Probably no one felt better than Dryden. "It sounds like a cliché," he wrote, "but I felt that the weight of the world had been lifted from my back."

He knew he probably hadn't been a popular choice to start that night, and Sinden had taken a big chance on him. After the game, Dryden's wife, Lynda, told him that a fan near her said Sinden was a "jerk" for "playing that idiot Dryden."

When you save 27 high-percentage shots and win, it's funny.

What they felt in their locker rooms that night was not joy. They were too far from the finish line to indulge that emotion. They didn't allow themselves much relief, either. But the game did fill them with confidence and determination, two qualities they would need again in spades in 48 hours.

In Sinden's postgame speech to his team, he picked up where he'd left off.

"Just worry about Game Seven now, and we'll tackle Game Eight when we get there."

They could afford to do nothing less.

28

A BRAND NEW DAY

A modern analysis of even-strength scoring chances in Game Six shows us Paul Henderson led the team with a plus-4, with Pete Mahovlich, Rod Gilbert, and Jean Ratelle all at plus-3—the latter two clearly benefiting from Dennis Hull replacing Vic Hadfield. This marked the first game that the team's three stalwarts, Phil Esposito, Yvan Cournoyer, and Frank Mahovlich, hadn't led Canada's offence by that measure. Thanks to better conditioning, better chemistry, and better strategy, other players were sharing the load.

On defence, with Sinden's three pairs finally locked in, not one defender notched a minus on even-strength scoring chances, and only two forwards came in at minus-1. In a tight, competitive game these were impressive results. "This indicates a strong effort up and down the lineup," analyst Evan Hall concludes, "with a team win the end result."

"I was happy with the changes I made," Sinden said hours after the game, and they had all worked, every one of them. "Seiling didn't like it and told Fergie he thought we were blaming him for the 5–4 loss Friday night. That wasn't the reason at all. Park and Bergman and White and Stapleton had been our best two defensive pairs. We felt Savard would work better with Lapointe and we were right."

But Red Berenson still had some misgivings. He had played well, making a nice pass on Cournoyer's goal and finishing with an impressive plus-2 on short-handed scoring chances—no small feat when Team Canada took a total of 31 penalty minutes to the Soviets' four. And yet he knew something was slightly off.

"I felt like I was still lacking a little bit of game conditioning, a little bit of timing," he says. "I wasn't quite getting in sync with my linemates."

All that is to be expected from someone who hadn't played the Soviets in 22 days, but Berenson decided that wouldn't be good enough for the remaining games.

"Now, if Harry had put my name on the roster for the next game," he says, "I would have been ready, I would have played, and I think I would have been okay. But I didn't think that was best for the team. So, after Game Six, I told Harry, 'You can't spot guys. You're gonna get the effort, but they're not going to be on top of their game. You gotta pick your players and stick with them the rest of the way.'"

"Red's a very intelligent person," Henderson says, "and that's what a team player does. Doesn't surprise me, by the way."

WHEN Sinden returned to his hotel room after Game Six, he said into his recorder, "The spell is wearing off. Whatever [the Soviets] had going for them isn't there anymore. We eliminated a big part of the Russian mystique tonight."

The Canadians kept chipping away at the seemingly insurmountable advantages the Soviets had in conditioning, strategy, and familiarity with the Olympic rink, until they had almost eliminated them—then discovered strengths they didn't realize they possessed until the cauldron of competition revealed them.

"We did have one advantage being in the NHL," Brad Park points out. "You would have no problem playing a seven-game series against the same team. You'd have no problem battling the same team, the same guys, night after night. You try to figure out what they're doing, and each game gets a little chippier. That's normal for us. But in the Olympics or the World Championship, the Soviets would play each team once, and that's it. They never played the same team in a long, tough series.

"So every night we keep coming and we keep coming and we keep coming. Mentally, we were more prepared for the long series than they were. Hey, we know it ain't over till the fat lady sings! So in the end, it's like that *Butch Cassidy and the Sundance Kid* scene, but now it was the *Russians* asking, 'Who are those guys?!'"

It took six games, but the Canadians had successfully flipped the script, overcoming their bewilderment and transferring it to the Soviets.

"When the series went on, you started to see the Russians only had one way to play," Gilbert added, "and if we broke that, they couldn't change their style. They couldn't adjust to us the way we adjusted to them."

"Rod's right," Park says. "They were like robots, and that was that. What you see in Game One is what you see in Game Six. Nothing changes. But we were more like jazz musicians. We could make things up on the fly. We could figure out how to stop them. And that distracted them. When we broke up one of their plays, you look over at their bench and you see them looking up at their coach like, 'What do we do now?' And the coach had no answer. They were lost."

The Russians could execute Anatoli Tarasov's timeless plan to perfection, and they possessed tremendous discipline. But once the Canadians caught on to it, the Soviets didn't have a Plan B, because they had never needed one.

One telling example: in the last two minutes of Game Six, with the Soviets trailing 3–2 on a power play, it never seemed to occur to coach Bobrov to pull Tretiak for an extra attacker, even though it would have given their potent power play a daunting 6–4 man advantage, and in the big international offensive zone, no less. Why he didn't make the move remains a mystery.

The Soviets agreed to the series, they claimed, to learn from the NHL, while the Canadians thought they had nothing to learn from anyone. Yet after Game Six the Soviets didn't seem to be learning anything from the Canadians, while the Canadians were changing their entire game, in an impressive display of hockey virtuosity. The survival of the fittest doesn't go to the biggest, the tallest, the fastest, or the strongest, after all. It goes to those who can adapt to a changing environment.

"The Russians just did the same thing over and over and over again," Dale Tallon says. "And they were good at it, really good at it, but later in the series, when we started catching on, that adaptability was the big thing. Same thing with communism versus capitalism. Communism doesn't adapt. It's why their jeans don't fit. But capitalism adjusts to the marketplace. Our jeans fit!"

Even the arrogance the Canadians had brought to the series was now on the other foot.

"When the Russians won that fifth game, they thought they've got this in the bag!" Berenson says. "I don't think Tretiak played as well in the series [after that], while our goalies started to play their best. We didn't go to Russia with the same overconfidence we had in the first game. Once we got over there, we were immune to the criticism. We had our own pride and our own challenges and our own togetherness that might not have been there in Canada. But we knew what we had to do. There was a focus we didn't have before."

The Canadians were also closing the chemistry gap. While the Soviets had played with each other most of their lives, the Canadians had to convert an NHL All-Star team into a real team, on and off the ice, in weeks. In the process, the Canadians found they had another advantage.

"The Russians never smile, never laugh, they don't even get mad, really," Ratelle says. "And not just the players, but wherever you go! But we have all the emotions all the time. That can hurt you, but that can help you too.

"By Game Six, we're all together now, all friends. If you didn't want to be there, you were already gone. In Moscow, we're playing as a team more and more. Our confidence is building up, playing with each other. We knew what the D were going to do in our end, in the other guy's end, and they know what we're going to do, too. Now, watch out!"

"After enough practices together," Park adds, "I learned where all our guys were going to be once I got the puck: Henderson was going to be over here, and Yvan was going to be flying up the wing, and so on. Once you get that knowledge of each other, things start happening pretty fast."

"One thing people don't seem to talk about," Bob Clarke points out, "Canadians all played the game the same way, with the same values and the same rules, even the same unwritten rules—no matter where you grew up playing. So a guy from Quebec played the same game as a guy from Toronto or western Canada. We all spoke the same hockey language—no translation needed. Maybe we didn't realize that until we were over there.

"So we were starting to be a hockey team, a real team. And we're starting to think, 'We're better than you.' And we're desperate, and we're dangerous, and we got fuck-all to lose.

"This is Canadian fucking hockey, boys—and we're coming right at you."

THE Canadians still respected the Soviets, but they no longer feared them.

They feared the refs.

Under ideal circumstances the chasm between the Canadian and European styles of play and officiating would have created problems—and by September 25, the circumstances were far from ideal.

"Yakushev, he was like Béliveau, pure class," Frank Mahovlich says. "But a few of those guys, like Mikhailov, were like Ted Lindsay with a stick! Man, they'd get you, and when you were least expecting it."

"In our culture, as Canadians," Park says, "we were taught if somebody cheap-shotted you, you grabbed him and you beat the piss out of him, and you both got five minutes: the bigger guy for beating him up, and the little guy for making him do it. In Canada we also have different levels of toughness. I was a level below the toughest guys, the enforcers. But whatever level you are, don't act like you're tougher than you are, or you get in trouble. Little guys weren't going to cheap-shot you in the NHL because if they did, they were going to get drilled.

"So when the Soviets did these little things to us, we didn't like it, so we did what we did in the NHL: we went after the guy. That's how we combatted those infractions. But now we couldn't do it, because the refs over there don't call the little things, and they don't let you fight, either. We could not retaliate. By the time we got to Game Six, we weren't physically trying to beat them up anymore, but that left us at the mercy of the refs—and that was a problem."

In Game Six alone, Team Canada received eight minor penalties, including a double minor to Phil Esposito for charging, one major penalty—also to Esposito, for high-sticking—and a 10-minute misconduct on Clarke for his two-hander on Valeri Kharlamov's ankle. All told, the Canadians received 31 minutes of penalties to the Soviets' four—a ratio that would be difficult for any competent official to justify.

After Game Six, Sinden described the two West German referees, Franz Baader and Josef Kompalla, to his recorder as "the most incompetent officials I've ever seen." His views were shared by almost all the Canadians, who nicknamed them "Baader and Worse." When I mentioned Kompalla's name to the former players in our interviews, no fewer than three Hall of Famers spat out the exact same phrase: "That little prick!"

Scotty Morrison, the NHL's referee-in-chief, held a clinic for all the Summit Series referees in Toronto during Team Canada's training camp. After Game Six he admitted, "I was especially disappointed with Kompalla because he impressed me [in camp]. I didn't expect much from Baader, but I liked Kompalla. But it looks now like the entire clinic was a waste of time."

Kompalla reffed about 75 games a year, earning $15 for a first-division game. "For me," he told *Globe and Mail* reporter Dan Proudfoot, "this refereeing is just a hobby. My job is as a manager of a discotheque. We're open from 5 p.m. to 3 a.m. I show people to their tables, you know?"

And yet the world had somehow conspired to put this man in charge of history's most important hockey game to date.

Dealing with incompetent officials presents two options: you can keep your mouth shut and hope that the penalties eventually even out, or you can put your foot on the boards, make a scene, and even throw a stool onto the ice (all of which Sinden would do), hoping to embarrass the officials into straightening things out.

The problem is, neither approach works.

Fair or not, the onus was ultimately on Team Canada. If the Canadians couldn't adapt to the situation, the officials weren't going to be declared the losers. The Canadians were.

"Our discipline was coming and going," Berenson says. "Looking back, that's the one thing we'd probably all say we were lacking. We had to learn how to handle the subtle interference, the spearing, the hooking, all the knick-knack things that were part of European hockey. We simply had to be more disciplined or we'd get blown out. Their power play was too good."

It was not for nothing that Sinden felt it was crucial they settle the referee assignments for the remaining two games as soon as possible.

AMONG Team Canada's 18 forwards who played against the Soviets, nine would be inducted into the Hockey Hall of Fame. Marcel Dionne, who didn't get into the series, would join them. To say that Canada's forward lines were loaded is a considerable understatement.

But it was the team's eight playing defencemen, three of whom are now in the Hall of Fame, who were the unsung heroes. After all, it wasn't the Soviet defence that had been driving the Canadians crazy. It was their innovative offence.

As Ken Dryden said after the team's first scrimmage in Toronto: early on, the defence is ragged, the offence dominates, and fatigue is the winner. But after almost six weeks of hard skating, Canada's defenders had met their moment.

"It might have been a no-name defence compared to the forwards," Berenson says, "but cripes, they played great. Our D were really good defensively, good with the puck, and smart. *All* our defencemen could handle the puck—Stapleton and White, Park and Bergman, who probably played the best hockey of his life, trying to keep up with Park—and then you've got the young Canadiens, Savard and Lapointe. They could all rush it."

"I consider Serge Savard one of the top five defencemen of all time," Phil Esposito says. "We don't agree about a lot of things, including politics, but I still respect him a *hell* of a lot. I think Serge had respect for me, too. Savard had this way about him, and still does—and his way is calmness. Calmness. I didn't realize in the beginning [of the series] how important that was, but in

Moscow everyone could see what Serge added, and how much we needed that."

"We had really good defencemen," Ratelle concurs. "That made such a difference in Moscow. It's a great thing to know you can make mistakes offensively and still be okay because they have you covered. We *had* to know that. You stop them at the blue line, then turn around and go the other way, and we have a chance."

"I really remember how hard our defence played," Gretzky says. "Pat Stapleton and Bill White, Serge Savard. Brad Park. Those guys competed every shift, every game. They just played their hearts out."

The forwards were also relieved to see that Sinden picked the right six to ride the last three games.

"When you skate into the faceoff circle you always look back to see who you've got on your blue line," Henderson says. "And sometimes, you think, 'Okay, I'll have to get back and help out.' But on this team, when you go out for a faceoff and you look back, you got Savard and Lapointe back there, as good as any in the league, then you've got Park and Bergman, then you've got Whitey and Stapleton. There's not a weak link anywhere in there, even against the Soviets. You see that, and you know you can be aggressive on offence—and we had to be."

By Game Seven, Team Canada's defencemen learned they not only *could* join the rush like the Soviets, but if they were going to beat them, they would have to.

AT practice on Monday morning, September 25, Sinden had to make arguably the toughest decision of his career—and perhaps the last one, if he guessed wrong: which goalie to start in Game Seven, and Game Eight?

"In August there wasn't any pressure at all," Sinden says. "It's going to be a walk in the park—right? We'd just play the games and go home. The guys had to wonder, 'Why are they ruining my summer?' But after we lost the first game, the press just turned on them, and the pressure had been rising with each game. It was enough for 17 skaters, but they could share it. The goaltender doesn't share it with anyone! I thought it was too much pressure on one goalie to play back-to-back games like that. So I wanted to make a decision, right then and there, and stick with it, no matter what happened.

"So I told the whole team, 'I've decided to go with Tony in Game Seven, and Dryden in Game Eight—regardless of the outcome of Game Seven.'"

And that was that.

"With two games left," Alan Eagleson recalls, "Tony had a 4.5 goals-against average—really, just one bad period—and Dryden had a 5.8. So why the hell would you put that guy in for Game Eight? What does that tell you? Statistics are not the be-all and end-all. You need a coach who could trust his instincts. Harry had that."

"Harry probably juggled the two goalies in his mind a long time before he made the decision for the last games," Savard says. "I don't think you can think about how your decision is going to look in the future. You can't, or you can't make good decisions. Harry made good decisions."

"That's one thing Harry is so good about," Ratelle says. "He comes out and says something that makes you say, 'He has confidence, and this is what we're going to do.' He was a fantastic coach and GM, too."

At one of the reunions years later, Stapleton recalled asking his teammates, "Does anyone remember Harry ever putting any doubt in anyone's head?" And Phil shook his head and said, 'I can't remember it.' No one could."

The players put in possibly their best practice since they started camp 41 days earlier—fast, quick, sharp, even fun. But this being Moscow, things could never be going well for very long. Team Canada had been scheduled to skate from 10:30 a.m. to 12:30 p.m. But at noon the Soviets' head coach, Bobrov, came to the boards to tell Sinden through an interpreter to get off the ice—another cheap intimidation tactic the fans and media would never see.

Sinden looked him right in the eye and said, "Drop dead," then skated off. It's a minor miracle he didn't give the interpreter more to translate.

When the players left the ice at 12:30, their already improved moods were enhanced when they saw thousands more telegrams and postcards, some addressed simply to "Palace of Sports, Moscow, USSR," being pasted on the walls. The flood of support from home showed no signs of letting up.

When Sinden and Ferguson returned to the coaches' room they asked Bob Haggart to bring in Alex Gresko, the Soviets' main negotiator, whom Sinden had already noticed at the rink that day. Gresko brought in another Soviet sports official by the name of Romansky.

"In quick order they admonished us for the night before," Sinden wrote. Romansky "went into a 15-minute sermon in which he lodged three official protests against our conduct the night before. First, he was upset by the way the Canadians acted toward the officials. Second, he was bothered by the way our players in street clothes were acting at the games. Third, they complained about the behaviour of Gary Bergman. Although I didn't know it, Gary had been needling coach Bobrov when he skated by the Soviet bench."

Neither Soviet official said anything about Clarke's two-hander on Kharlamov—another indication that it wasn't that newsworthy at the time.

"We let them get it all off their chests, because we really didn't give a damn," Sinden wrote. "When they were finished I told them: 'Look. None of this would have happened if you hadn't picked those West Germans [Baader and Kompalla] to work in this series. They are totally incompetent . . . If you guarantee me that the Germans won't officiate again in this series, then I will promise you there will be no further trouble from any Canadian player or official.

"They nodded and told us they agreed."

When the players learned of Sinden's deal with the Soviets, Dryden thought, "Poor Gary [Bergman]. Harry and Fergie may gag him."

From the exchange with the Soviets, Sinden jumped to this conclusion: "We got the monkey off our backs today. The Germans are definitely finished in this series . . . I could feel the relief pouring out of me."

Sinden actually believed it.

29

GAME SEVEN: DO OR DIE—AGAIN

September 26, 1972

The Soviets showed no sign of curtailing their gamesmanship. Just a few hours after Harry Sinden called Vsevolod Bobrov's bluff on his attempt to cut Canada's practice short, the Soviets took the players and their wives out for another cultural event. But the Soviets couldn't resist trying to pull the same stunt: telling the players' wives they had to get on a different bus.

"Same thing," Brad Park recalls. "But by now we're not thinking twice. We know what to do. We're in the habit of holding firm, sticking together, no matter what. We all get off. We're not going. Again, they back off."

The Canadian contingent had gotten better at responding to the Soviets' endless head games, but it was getting old—even if it was far from over.

The next morning, the day of Game Seven, the Canadians walked into Luzhniki for their morning skate to find officials at the arena, with no notice, telling them they had to go to a different rink because a kids' group was on the ice.

Alan Eagleson replied, "No fucking way!" then instructed

Dennis Hull to get his full gear on, get on the ice, and start firing slapshots.

"I always did what my coach told me," Hull says with a smile.

The schoolchildren quickly changed their plans and scampered off the ice.

Before the game that night, when the Canadian fans walked into Luzhniki, the Soviet soldiers confiscated their air horns. This only inspired the fans to yell even louder than they had for Game Six, and to get a little creative, too, chanting, *"Da, da, Canada!"* (Yes, yes, Canada!) and *"Nyet, nyet, Soviet!"* (No, no, Soviet!).

The Canadian fans were ready. Were the players?

Harry Sinden had been so pleased with the team's performance in Game Six, and so reluctant to disrupt the chemistry, that he made exactly one change to the lineup: replacing Red Berenson with Bill Goldsworthy at "extra forward." Sinden stood pat on all three defensive pairs and all three forward lines. He had his team.

"Our conditioning gets better every day, and our togetherness," Jean Ratelle recalls. "The last four games, that's how we operated it, and Harry reinforced that. We're playing our game now."

The Canadian locker rooms were filled with a calm determination, a group focused completely on the task at hand, saying very little.

"Some nights," Sinden recalls, "you read your team, and you tell them, 'You're that good.' Other times, when you're not sure, you say how great they are anyway, and you hope they respond. But that night I believed they were ready. I felt it."

Sinden didn't say much, and didn't have to. Nobody in those rooms needed to be reminded it was do or die, once again. Sinden repeated his simple command: no looking ahead to the next game, or even to the next period. Just focus on your next shift, win that shift, then get ready for your next shift. The players nodded.

"And that was it," Bob Clarke recalls. "Same thing: whatever we normally do to win, you do tonight."

═

WITH Sinden's preferred crew, Swede Uwe Dahlberg and Czechoslovakian Rudy Batja, calling the game, the penalties started just two minutes in, with three minors a side in the first period. But it was even, and Sinden could live with that.

The scoring started two minutes after the penalties, at 4:09. Paul Henderson passed to Ron Ellis in the corner. He found Phil Esposito in the low slot, where Esposito made a quick turnaround move for his fourth goal of the series. To the Canadian players, the 3,000 Canadian fans felt like the 16,000 fans who had packed Maple Leaf Gardens for Game Two.

The Soviets responded with a slapshot from Alexander Yakushev that found the five-hole on Tony Esposito, followed by a pretty deke by Vladimir Petrov on the power play. The 11,000 Russians cheered like Canadians—rare for them.

When the Soviets went on another power play, they threatened to break open a 3–1 first-period lead. Instead, the Canadian penalty killers once again attacked. J.P. Parisé passed to Serge Savard, who faked a slapshot, made his trademark spinarama move, drew three Soviets to him, then slipped a backhand to Esposito in the high slot. He fired a shot to the low corner to tie it up, 2–2.

Such was the fever pitch of the contest that Esposito—who, like his teammates, seems to remember almost everything about the series—cannot describe either of his first two goals. "I don't remember them!" he says today.

What the scoreless second period lacked in goals, it made up for in penalties: one for slashing, two for hooking, and five roughing calls—the kind you get in a hard-fought rivalry game. That the Soviets received three power plays to Canada's one makes it all the more impressive that Team Canada returned to their locker rooms for the second intermission still tied at two.

"We were setting ourselves up for bad calls, and it got ugly," says Berenson, who watched from the stands. "Bergman was playing like he was John Ferguson, bullying and intimidating.

Hell, *Jean Ratelle* took a run at a guy!" That Ratelle had just won the Lady Byng Trophy, awarded to the player who "best exhibits sportsmanship and gentlemanly conduct," shows just how the series was affecting normally rational men. "We got away from our game. It seemed like we had something to say about every call, and pretty soon we were worried more about the referees than the Russians. You can't do that. Whether we deserved the penalties or not, we made such a fuss that we'd talk our way into more penalties."

With the score tied, 2–2, the third period now stood as a 20-minute contest to determine whether Game Eight would matter or not.

Two minutes and 13 seconds into the all-important stanza, Dennis Hull, in Vic Hadfield's spot on the GAG Line, made a smart, quick no-look pass behind the Soviet net, knowing Rod Gilbert was there, all alone. Gilbert, who had earned the nickname "Mad Dog" from the Canadian columnists for his tenacious play that week, stepped out in front of Vladislav Tretiak and tucked a backhand between his pads for his first goal of the series, to give Canada a 3–2 lead.

A few minutes later, with Gary Bergman off for holding, the Soviets worked their power-play magic. Vladimir Lutchenko faked a slapshot and slipped the puck to Alexander Maltsev, who threaded a saucer pass through two Canadian defenders right to Yakushev, alone on the back door, who tapped in an easy goal.

"As much as I hated it at the time," Sinden wrote, "I have to praise them. This was something out of a hockey textbook, as close to perfection as you can come on the power play."

With the score tied at three and about 15 minutes left in the game, the clock was not the Canadians' friend. Ten minutes later, Boris Mikhailov and Bergman mixed it up behind Canada's net. Mikhailov grabbed Bergman and tried to pull him down, then Bergman did what NHL players do: he punched him, sparking the series' first genuine fight. Yvan Cournoyer, of all people, got in some good shots, while Esposito threw his arm around Yakushev's head to keep him out of it. Instead of returning Bergman's punch, Mikhailov worked to get him down on the ice, where he kicked him repeatedly—something NHLers never do—cutting through Bergman's shin pads to draw blood.

The refs, claiming they never saw Mikhailov's kicks, gave both players five-minute majors for roughing, ensuring that the game's last three minutes would be played four on four. If the West Germans had been reffing, it could have been worse.

The Canadians came after Tretiak with a vengeance, but he was at his best. With about three minutes left, Paul Henderson—whose line would finish the game plus-11 on even-strength scoring chances, by far the team's best—stewed on the bench, thinking, "'This might be my last shift, and we need a goal—desperately.' I had that sense, and kept repeating to myself, 'We need a goal, we need a goal.'"

He soon got his chance. When he crossed the blue line with the puck, he drew all four Soviet skaters within a stick length of him. With seemingly nowhere to go, Henderson pushed the puck between the two defencemen and faked as if he was going to follow, then cut around them to the left, causing them to bump into each other in confusion. Henderson retrieved the puck behind them and skated in on Tretiak until Gennadi Tsygankov, the far defenceman moving over to cover for the one Henderson had just undressed, desperately stuck his right leg out to trip him.

But while Henderson was going down, he kept his hands in front of him and his eyes on the net, then popped the puck over Tretiak's left shoulder. *Goal!*

Henderson's team-leading sixth goal of the series was as pretty as it was important, the one he would later say "gave me the most personal satisfaction" of his career. "I've been riding it for a lot of years," he says with a laugh. "I can remember it like it was yesterday. When it went in I was probably more surprised than anyone. The best goal of my career—no question."

Henderson jumped right up with defiant energy, giving a double fist pump before his teammates mobbed him.

Now ahead 4–3 with 2:06 left, in the final minutes Tony Esposito made another big save, his 26th of the game.

"Tony was really, really good in that game," Sinden recalls. "But then, he had to be. Nothing less would do."

Oddly, once again Vsevolod Bobrov didn't pull Tretiak for an extra attacker. Perhaps because they had trailed so rarely, they simply didn't know what to do.

When the game ended at 4–3, the Canadians had tied the series at 3–3–1, setting up an all-or-nothing Game Eight that nobody imagined when the series was conceived. The Canadian locker rooms sizzled with energy, but once again the players knew they couldn't let themselves fully enjoy it. Not yet.

Well, perhaps one player: Tony Esposito, who had just finished his work in the Summit Series with his second impressive victory, had done his part.

"He was extremely relieved not to be playing the eighth game," recalls Mark Mulvoy, who interviewed Tony that week. "The pressure to play the last two games really was too great for any one goalie to handle. Sinden was right."

Aside from the four players who had left early and were now presumably watching the games in North America, there was probably only one Canadian player who felt any ambivalence about the stirring victory: Ken Dryden.

In his journal he admitted, with refreshing honesty, "I had mixed emotions as I walked toward the dressing room. I was happy that we had won, of course, but now I realized that we had to win the final game. And I would be playing goal. Wouldn't it be nice to live without that pressure the next two days! I was shook up, nervous, yet all the other Canadians were jubilant. They were even singing 'Jingle Bells' because it was snowing outside. I could not share their jubilation at the time."

Before he congratulated his teammates, "one of the players said to me, 'You better be ready Thursday night, big guy.' He meant it as a joke, and we both laughed, but the reminder was there: I am going to be in a tough spot two days from now."

Compared with the outsized Game Eight looming ahead, Dryden's Game Six triumph, as big as it had seemed two days ago, now looked like a preseason contest.

Sinden kept it simple: "We won Game Seven. Now let's go for Eight."

He didn't have anything else to say to his team, but to the press, he put the cards on the table: "I think the last game will be the greatest ever in hockey."

"I meant it," he said in his journal that night. "The talent is here. The emotion is here. The drama is here. And both teams are getting their share of the luck. We got ours tonight, so maybe this superstitious stuff is working."

But no moment in Moscow was ever so great it could not be interrupted by the police state.

After the game, the fans' celebrations spilled into nearby bars. At one, Rod Gilbert recalled, Pierre Plouffe, the champion water skier who played the bugle, "tried to play it in a bar, and they throw him in a Moscow jail overnight. And we hear about this the next day, but they wouldn't tell us where he went. We said, 'We're not playing the game unless they release him!' The word was they tattooed his wrists so he wouldn't come back. Really? Who the fuck would want to come back *here*?!"

Then Gilbert repeated his rallying cry, as mad as he was the day it happened: "They stole our fucking beer!"

When Henderson returned to their hotel room, he recalls, "I told Eleanor, 'I will never score a bigger goal in my life! I can die a happy man now.'"

The Canadians brought many strengths to the series, but prognostication skills were not among them.

30

LIAR'S POKER

The stakes were simultaneously intangible—no title, trophy, or cup would go to the winner—and immense: whoever won would be the sport's new kings.

Harry Sinden's biggest decision of his career—who would start in net the last two games—he'd already made three days earlier, before Game Seven: Tony Esposito would start Game Seven, and Ken Dryden would start Game Eight. But the choices still came as a surprise to the fans and the media, who weren't in the room when Sinden told the team; and even the players, who already knew, but now gave it more thought as Game Eight approached.

"I don't think there was a guy on the team who thought Harry was going to start Dryden for the last game until he told us," Paul Henderson admits. "Tony was playing better." Esposito's strong play in Game Seven only bolstered that idea.

Even Dryden agreed. A few hours after Game Seven, when Dryden knew he'd be playing for all the marbles in two nights, he tossed and turned, unable to get a good night's sleep when he most needed one. At breakfast the next morning, "Phil Esposito walked by and said, 'Boy, you'd better be hot tomorrow night,'" Dryden wrote. "He meant it good-naturedly—I knew that—but it was there nonetheless. No one ever seems to go to a defenceman or a forward and say, 'You have to win it for us.' They come to the goaltender. If the goaltender doesn't contribute, his team usually loses. A forward or a defenceman can have a bad night, though, and the team might win because some other forward or defenceman had a big night."

Almost all the players felt more pressure heading into Game Eight than they ever had before—though not equally. How much depended on variables like playing time, their position, and if they played for a Canadian-based NHL team, which increased the heat. By all those measures, no one faced more pressure than Dryden—and he knew it, which probably didn't help. During practice that morning, a day before Game Eight, he didn't feel any better and couldn't seem to get comfortable.

"I assume that if we'd lost that series, players of my stature, we wouldn't have gotten much criticism," Bob Clarke says. Although Clarke had finished ninth in scoring the previous season, it was his first big year, leaving him a notch below the biggest names on Team Canada. "The great players would have taken the brunt of it—Dryden and Park and Espo. I would have deserved some, we all would have, but they had more pressure."

Park definitely felt it, but experience helped. "Eight days in Moscow, and each game had two days of anticipation before it," he says. "I knew from playing in seven-game series that the anticipation is worse than the participation. You had to learn how to handle it, and I think we had an advantage there. We'd all done it. I took Harry's word: don't think about the game two days away, or you'll go crazy. Just think about your next shift."

Phil Esposito's mindset occupied the other extreme. "After Game Seven, I couldn't *wait* to get to practice the next day," he recalls. "And I was *never* like that! I normally *hated* practice, but this time I couldn't wait. It was *so* boring in Moscow that if we did not practise, the boredom would have been devastating and we'd have nothing to do but think about the damn game. We practised for an hour, *hard*. Harry read us right. We wanted that. We did Harry's new neutral-zone thing again—blow the whistle and regroup. I dissected it, and that's the only way we could beat them."

By all accounts they practised better than they had the day before Game Seven, their previous best, and it couldn't have come at a better time.

But the Canadians' good feeling didn't last long. In Moscow, it never did. In Game Seven, Gary Bergman had hurt his back, and Pat Stapleton and Bill White had both injured an ankle. The practice confirmed that all three injuries weren't going away that quickly. Could they play the next night? In case not, Ferguson put Dale Tallon, who had played one game in Sweden, on full alert once again.

As soon as Sinden walked into the Intourist Hotel, he got pulled into another imbroglio over the referees—the very issue he thought they had put to bed two days earlier, when the Soviets assured him the West Germans, Franz Baader and Josef Kompalla, a.k.a. "Baader and Worse," would not officiate in the series again.

When Sinden took the call from Vsevolod Bobrov and Aleksander Gresko, he reiterated what he assumed to be the deal they'd agreed to for Game Eight. But they said no, they had said no such thing. This was a bald-faced lie, and everyone involved knew it. But the Soviets also knew the Canadians couldn't refute it with anything other than a weak "Yes, you did." The Canadians had nothing in writing, and no IIHF officials had been informed of the agreement. Besides, Sinden knew Bunny Ahearne would never come to the Canadians' defence, even if he could.

Sinden was screwed.

The Soviets then told him the two West Germans, Baader and Kompalla, would be officiating the next night—Sinden's worst nightmare.

"They lied to us," Sinden wrote, as outraged as he was surprised. "Can you believe that? Spirit of friendship, my ass. These guys would steal the fillings out of your teeth if you smiled long enough. Well, they're not going to get away with it. They think they've got us hanging by our thumbs, but we're not going to take anything from them."

Sinden fetched Alan Eagleson and hustled back over to the Palace of Sport to confront Bobrov and Gresko. The second the Canadians sat down, they made themselves crystal clear: if the Soviets didn't remove the West Germans, the Canadians weren't going to play. Period. They had made a deal, after all, and the Canadians had kept up their end of the bargain. In Game Seven, Bergman hadn't said a word to the Soviets all night, as promised, while Boris Mikhailov had been making the "crazy" hand gesture toward Ferguson until the Canadians sent a note to the Soviet bench to knock it off. Money also happened to be on the Canadians' side—lots of it. European TV had already given the Soviets $200,000 per game, and the Soviets did not seem too enthusiastic about returning the eighth cheque.

"They like dollars," Eagleson said. "I've found that a lot of times the Russians will let money make up their minds for them."

The Soviets told the Canadians they'd make their decision by six o'clock that evening, about 24 hours before they were scheduled to play Game Eight.

While the two sides clashed over the referees, *Globe and Mail* reporter Dan Proudfoot published an interview with Josef Kompalla himself, the West German discotheque manager and part-time hockey hobbyist, who spoke freely of his disdain for the Canadian players.

"They make a lot of noise about one faceoff, whether it should be a few feet away," he said. "They're very childish. They come and swear at us and call us blinkety-blank German referees who don't know anything. They're all bad. Ratelle is a very good and disciplined player, and the blonde defenceman No. 3 [Stapleton] also is very good."

Kompalla added that he believed Canada should have sent the New York Rangers or Boston Bruins instead of an All-Star team.

"The Canadian team is no team at all. They've spent four weeks together. The Russians have been getting together for four years. The Canadian players are hotshots, but Phil Esposito cannot play 60 minutes. The Canadians need 10 or 15 games to be in top condition. I do think they could win if they were in top condition."

Proudfoot added that Kompalla "professed to not worry about Team Canada criticism. 'I let it go in one ear, and out the other.'"

In North America, referees almost never talk to the media—they're often contractually prohibited from doing so—and Kompalla's interview showed why. It's possible Kompalla had assumed he would not be reffing the final game, and therefore could speak freely. But it's hard to imagine any reputable referee, with a gag order or not, delivering such direct and personal comments about players and teams whose last game he could still be officiating.

But then, if IIHF president Bunny Ahearne could blast Team Canada with an official statement after Game One, the example had been set from the top.

DURING their last free afternoon in Moscow, the Berensons went for a walk.

"One of our best experiences there had nothing to do with the scheduled events or even hockey," Berenson says. "Joy and I stumbled upon a sports store along the way. We walk in and see all these bikes, brand new, fresh off the truck. But they weren't like the rack of Schwinns you'd see in the stores at home, every colour you could name. These were all pea-green. No choices. No red bikes, no silver bikes. Just light green bikes, with no wheels, and grease all over them, literally lying on top of each other, like they'd all fallen over.

"And this kid and his dad come in and they want a bike, and the kid is thrilled to be there. So they finally get the sales guy, and he takes one to the back to clean it up and put the wheels on, and he brings it back out with shiny wheels and all the grease off. And the kid was ecstatic. I mean, just *beaming*. We'd seen all the big things—the circus, the ballet, Red Square—but that was the best thing I saw in Russia, the most human thing. Someone was happy in Russia!

"It was the rarest thing, too. I can still see that kid's face."

BY 6 p.m. the Soviets still had made no decision about the refs, but they told Sinden they would by 11 p.m. So he decided he'd be better off going with the team to see the Bolshoi Ballet perform its interpretation of Leo Tolstoy's *Anna Karenina* than sitting by the phone, waiting for a call that might never come.

Because some of the players had had their fill of culture, Tallon often escorted their wives to the events, but he left the ballet after the first act. "My God, the body odour and dandruff everywhere. I couldn't breathe!"

During the intermission, Sinden, Ferguson, and Eagleson discussed the issue of the referees.

"Harry," Eagleson said, "we can't make a threat to leave unless we're prepared to back it up."

Sinden agreed, but he considered the West German officials so bad, he wasn't bluffing. If the Soviets wanted to put them in, Sinden would not take the ice.

"Okay, that's our position," Eagleson said. "If they try to force those two refs on us, we're not playing. We all have to agree."

They made a pact: if the Soviets tried to bring the West Germans back, they were willing to walk. But just as they thought they had settled the issue, at least from their side of the table, a reporter noticed them and asked if they were serious about not playing Game Eight if the Soviets insisted on the West German referees.

Absolutely, they assured him.

Then why, he asked, did Arthur Laing—a newly minted senator from Vancouver who was also a member of the Trudeau cabinet and leader of the delegation representing the Canadian government in Moscow—just tell the Soviets that Sinden's stance "was just a ploy"?

"As luck would have it, who do I see at the theatre but Senator Laing," Eagleson recalls, "who's now trying to hide." Eagleson went directly for Laing and said, "Senator Laing, I tell you what: the entire team is sitting over there. You can go tell them yourself what you told the Soviets." The senator declined.

The trio was back at the Intourist Hotel before 11 p.m., but it came and went without any word from the Soviets.

The Canadians awoke on the morning of Thursday, September 28, with no idea who would be officiating their game that night, or even if they would play. While leaders from both sides continued their negotiations, the players went through their morning skate on the assumption that, somehow or other, the show would go on.

White's and Stapleton's ankles were still bothering them. A team doctor told Dale Tallon, "Be ready to play."

"I said, 'Wow! The biggest game in the history of hockey. Thanks a lot!'" Tallon recalls. "I was 21! I was nervous as hell. But I wanted to play—and make sure I didn't hurt the team."

When the skate ended, Sinden, Ferguson, Eagleson, and Aggie Kukulowicz—"Mr. Fantastic," the former hockey player turned Air Canada baggage handler who became "the Henry Kissinger of Hockey," often serving as Eagleson's translator—met at the rink with their now-familiar counterparts, Gresko, Romansky, and Andrei Starovoitov, the Soviets' director of hockey.

As Sinden and Eagleson recall, they sat down with a big crystal pitcher of ice water in the middle of the table. The negotiations were just as cold.

The Canadians opened the conversation by going over all the prior agreements, from the first negotiations in the spring and summer, to the discussions in Canada, to their conversation just two days earlier—all of which indicated it was the Canadians' turn to pick the referees for the last game. So, they concluded, they wanted the Swede, Uwe Dahlberg, and the Czechoslovakian, Rudolf Batja.

"You can't pick them," Gresko said. "The Germans will be the officials."

Sinden and Eagleson became outraged, and threats started flying back and forth. Ferguson sat silent, leaving the negotiations to Sinden and Eagleson.

"Okay, then," Sinden said, "I want you now to officially break your word. Tell me that we can't pick the officials for this game as we agreed last July."

What might have shamed a Canadian didn't make the Soviets blush. They didn't care, and they didn't budge. After more fruitless arguing, with neither side giving an inch, the Soviets had worn down the Canadians to the point where they were willing to accept a compromise: each team would pick one official. Better to take half a loaf, the Canadians figured, than nothing.

Not surprisingly, the Soviets picked Josef Kompalla, the part-time hockey official and full-time discotheque manager.

"It was at that point," Eagleson recalls, "we knew we were stuck with one of the fucking Germans."

The Canadians selected the Swede, but the Soviets were ready for that.

"We're sorry," they said, "but Dahlberg is sick."

This sparked more shouting. That's when Ferguson picked up the crystal pitcher filled with ice water and threw it like a shortstop against the wall, splashing water and shattering the glass into small pieces.

When things finally settled down, the Soviets claimed, "We happened by Dahlberg's hotel this morning and he doesn't feel well enough to work tonight."

Eagleson had known Dahlberg for five years and pounced. "I saw him at breakfast this morning! There's nothing wrong with him!"

Unfazed, the Soviets calmly claimed, "Well, he's sick *now*."

Eagleson immediately called Dahlberg from the office and confirmed that he was in perfect health. But what could the Canadians do? Given the remaining choices—the Czechoslovakian, Batja, and the other West German, Baader—the Canadians didn't hesitate to pick the former. But the upshot was still unsavoury: the Soviets had managed to replace Canada's preferred referee, Uwe Dahlberg, with Canada's least favourite official, Josef Kompalla.

When they departed, Sinden wrote, there were "hard feelings all around. We shook hands but it was the cold fish treatment."

But the game was on.

TEAM Canada's leaders didn't have much time to indulge their frustration. They had to hurry back to the Intourist Hotel to finalize plans to get their contingent—counting coaches, players, officials, wives, and girlfriends, almost 100 in all—out of Moscow. All but a few of the players would fly to Prague the next morning for the final exhibition game, against the Czechoslovakian national team, while the wives would remain two more days in Moscow before flying home. This prospect cheered everyone, as if they were planning their escape to freedom. No matter what happened that night, knowing the end was near was a prospect they savoured.

"The one thought that was all-encompassing, that everyone felt: we couldn't wait to go home," Joy Berenson says. "No one felt comfortable. We didn't feel safe and secure. It was like being in prison. The series wasn't over, and the game was important—but we couldn't wait to get it over with."

After the departure planning meeting, the players retired to their rooms for their ritual pregame nap. More than a few, including Dryden, couldn't calm their thoughts, knowing the biggest game of their lives was just a few hours away.

Tallon was still "on call" to replace White, Stapleton, or Bergman if their injuries proved too much. "Needless to say," Tallon says, "my afternoon nap wasn't much. My mind was on fire."

When the players gathered for their last dinner, they learned that, thanks to the black market wizards who'd stolen about half their 300 steaks, their remaining supply had run out. No steaks tonight.

"I hope they choke on it," Sinden said.

"Before the eighth game," Stapleton recalled, "the Russian chefs walked in to explain the meal—the potatoes, the birds, etc., describing all the courses—which is their custom. But no one cared about the damn presentation. Tony [Esposito] interrupted him. 'Stick that bird up your ass and let's eat.'"

His teammates agreed. They ate.

Next stop, for the last time: Luzhniki. In the locker rooms, some of the players were surprisingly loose, which leavened the atmosphere for those who weren't.

"I didn't think there was any pressure," Dennis Hull says. "We thought if the Russians lose, they'd go to Siberia. We didn't think if we lost anything bad was going to happen to us. But we're Canadians, and Canadians don't lose—not in hockey."

Phil Esposito felt the same way. "I still tell players, if you think they're gonna beat you, they will. Well, I didn't think they were gonna beat us! *I just wasn't going to let that happen.*"

"My philosophy my whole career was simple," Pete Mahovlich says. "If I give what I can, that's all I can do. There are too many other factors you don't control. But I never, ever played on a team that was good enough to win that *didn't* win."

Amazingly, he had never lost in the finals of any professional tournament, going a perfect two-for-two in the American Hockey League and four-for-four in the Stanley Cup Final. In 17 international games, he lost a grand total of two—both in the Summit Series: Games One and Five. Though not given to bold statements, prior to Game Eight, Mahovlich recalls, "I wasn't playing on a line. I was primarily killing penalties. But I always felt: just get me to the final game. *I don't lose*."

Unlike Pete Mahovlich, Henderson *was* given to bold statements before games, at least privately. Before Game Eight he turned to Ron Ellis and said, with complete conviction, "I think you're going to get the winner tonight."

Dale Tallon dressed for warm-ups in case one of the three injured defencemen couldn't play. "I was buzzing around the rink," he recalls. "Then I was told they were all ready to go. Well, what'd you expect? Those are some tough birds. By then I was ready to push the Zamboni around the ice. I was jacked! But I had nowhere to spend all that energy."

When Tallon returned to the locker room he took his equipment off. Instead of joining his fellow Black Aces in the stands, however, "I just stayed in the room after everyone went back out. I looked out toward the rink, then back to the room. No TVs. The rooms were really primitive. No stalls, just makeshift bars tied to the ceiling to hang your clothes on.

"I don't know why, but I was superstitious that night. That was the feeling I had. I thought maybe it would be good luck if I stayed there."

For the final pregame gift exchange, the Canadians had brought a totem pole at great cost and trouble. When a Soviet official suddenly claimed that there would be no time for that, due to TV coverage, Eagleson was having none of it.

"You get back and tell your people that we're going to take this totem pole and bring it to centre ice and they'll have to take it or skate around it the whole game." That Eagleson didn't suggest they find an alternative location for the totem pole might be considered a small victory for international diplomacy.

On the grand scale, the incident was pointless—but that *was* the point. For a solid month the Soviets had turned the most trivial issues—from practice times to bus rides to what they served for dinner—into international incidents that had to be fought over tooth and nail. The endless squabbles, broken promises, and underhanded dealings had pushed the Canadians to the edge.

Before the faceoff Eagleson saw Dahlberg, the Swedish official they had requested earlier that day but had been told by the Soviets was sick in bed, sitting in the stands, looking robust, preparing to watch the game. When Eagleson asked him what had happened, Dahlberg said the Soviets' director of hockey, Andrei Starovoitov, who also served as the IIHF's director of officials, told Dahlberg that if he officiated Game Eight, they'd never let him ref another game for the IIHF.

"So," Eagleson said, "he did what I would have done: played along."

It was dirty, but who exactly would hear the Canadians' complaint—Bunny Ahearne? They'd been had, but they were powerless to do anything about it.

By faceoff time, all the ill will generated by the Soviets' subterfuge over the previous month, on and off the ice, had removed any pretense of sportsmanship.

Esposito was right: this was war.

31

GAME EIGHT: THE BIGGEST GAME YOU NEVER SAW COMING

September 28, 1972

The Stanley Cup Final doesn't sneak up on anyone.

Once you get to training camp you already know when it's scheduled, and how much it's going to mean—if only you can get there.

But when the players signed up for the Summit Series, no one, not even the Soviets, anticipated the eight-game format—whose very design seemed to preclude any chance of a "winner take all" final contest—would come down to the mother of all hockey games.

But that's what it was: the biggest game any player on either team had ever faced—despite the fact that it was, essentially, a mere exhibition, sanctioned by no one, leading to nothing. Yet it was nothing less than the most important contest in hockey history—and in any sport in Canada or the Soviet Union.

Back in Canada, unbeknownst to the players, everybody had dropped what they were doing to watch the game, which started at 8 p.m. in Moscow and 1 p.m. in Montreal and Toronto. At

Montreal's Central Station, 5,000 fans gathered around a mere 10 TV sets—500 people per screen. There was no talk of separatism on this day. Thousands of schools brought TVs into classrooms and gyms. In Scarborough, Brad Park's hometown, his younger sisters Lori and Shelley, both in high school, watched the game with their classmates in the cafeteria. It's fair to assume very little work got done in Canada that day.

"Everyone understood that our national pride was on the line," Gretzky says. "This was our game, and we thought we were the best at it. Hockey was always big in Canada, but now we'd been challenged. Could we respond? You had to watch!"

All this created something between a national holiday and a moon-landing moment. And, it would turn out, more Canadians would watch Game Eight than had watched the moon landing just three years earlier. To say the stakes were high doesn't do the phrase justice. This was particularly true for the Canadians, who had everything to lose, while the Soviets had already far exceeded everyone's expectations, including their own, whether they won or lost the last game.

This was not the Stanley Cup Final, where there's always next year. This was a bet that had never been made before and would never be made again.

But if Team Canada lost this final game—or even tied it—then what? Not only would people around the globe conclude that the Soviet Union was now the world's greatest hockey power, but they'd have to start calculating just how long that had been the case. How far back did the Soviets' superiority actually go? Instead of Canada getting credit for sending its amateur teams all those years, even when they lost, it would now look as though it had been ducking real competition for a decade, hiding behind the facade of the NHL.

"Losing," Harry Sinden says today. "Certainly you *fear* it. I didn't try to dismiss that on any of the teams I coached, because

I think it was an asset: fearing the ramifications of losing, before a game, is one way to make sure you're ready. But Game Eight in Moscow, losing that was such an unbelievable fear, an overwhelming threat, that it was too big. You tried to *stop* them from thinking about it."

That was particularly so for the coach.

"These guys were All-Star NHL players," he continues. "They would take some heat if we lost, but no one would lose their jobs over it, or their place in the Hall of Fame. I wasn't an All-Star player. Just a coach, trying to get back in the game. The tendency is to give a coach more credit than he deserves when they win, and put a lot of the blame on the coach when they lose. My future was at stake. Theirs wasn't. If we lose Game Eight, would I be out of hockey? I think possibly. Probably."

Given this, it's worth underscoring the courage it took to make the decisions he made, from his new hybrid strategy to his roster. Unlike many modern coaches, Sinden seemed inured to the public criticism he had already taken since Game One, and he dismissed it when filling out the final score sheet.

For the first time, he made only one change in the entire lineup: Dryden in goal.

The tension in Luzhniki that night was unequalled—for better and for worse.

"For the last game," Gerry Park recalls, "it seemed like they'd brought in the entire Red Army. They had soldiers with guns lined all the way around the entire rink, and they tried to contain [the wives] in one little area. I don't ever in my life recall feeling so intimidated. The seats I had when the Rangers played in Boston, where loud drunks poured beer on you—that was bad, but nothing compared to this. This was very, very intimidating. This seemed serious."

═

THE final game started exactly as the Canadians had feared.

With the West German Josef Kompalla—the "Worse" of "Baader and Worse" fame—back on the ice, the parade of penalties started almost immediately. Just 2:25 into the contest, Kompalla made a dubious holding call on Bill White, who had averaged less than a minor penalty every three games the previous season. Thirty-six seconds later, he also called Pete Mahovlich for holding, giving the Soviets a five-on-three power play for a minute and 24 seconds.

Sure enough, 33 seconds later Alexander Yakushev knocked in a rebound to open the scoring at 1–0.

Just 10 seconds after that, the refs called Vladimir Petrov for hooking, setting up a four-on-four situation for the next minute and 17 seconds. Alexander Maltsev took a pass at his own blue line and tried to skate around J.P. Parisé, who put his stick out far enough to spin Maltsev around before he fell to the ice. Batja, the Czechoslovakian ref, was in perfect position, standing along the boards just a few feet away, and gave the "safe" sign, indicating a clean play. But Kompalla, positioned on the boards across the rink, whistled Parisé for interference, the third penalty called against Canada in the first 4:10, and the first of five interference calls made that period. The call was bad enough for both Phil Esposito and Serge Savard to appeal to the two referees in the semicircle by the scorer's box.

Parisé, holding his stick with one hand while skating away from Kompalla, hit it against the ice—a common reaction, and harmless. Kompalla immediately signalled Parisé for a 10-minute misconduct—something Parisé had never received in five full seasons with the North Stars.

"J.P. was not a hothead," Esposito attests. But when he saw Kompalla's misconduct call, he "exploded," Pat Stapleton recalled. "Just *erupted*."

Parisé turned on a dime and burst toward Kompalla, holding his stick with two hands by the handle like a baseball bat and motioning as though he might bring it down on Kompalla's head. Kompalla took the threat seriously and recoiled, but Parisé pulled back at the last split second. Guy Lapointe directed him away from Kompalla, and Parisé left the ice for good with a game misconduct.

"Bedlam now prevailed in the arena," Sinden said.

The Russian fans let loose their high-pitched whistles, while the Canadian fans screamed, "Let's go home! Let's go home!"

Sinden grabbed a small stool and threw it across the ice, shattering it—the most extreme act of his coaching career. He then tossed Ferguson's chair onto the ice, too, while others threw towels, sticks, gloves, and pucks. The Canadian players crowded the refs, the Canadian fans threw toilet paper, and the Red Army soldiers surrounding the rink stood at the ready, on full alert—a scene as tense as it can get in a hockey rink.

At the end of the 15 minutes of mayhem, Sinden saw Alexander Gresko, the Soviet official who helped finagle the referees that morning, standing just 15 feet (4.5 metres) away, hiding behind the Soviet bench. "This is all your fault!" Sinden screamed. "You asked for this. We told you this would happen if you put that German out there."

Sinden believed his tirade actually got to Gresko, who was "embarrassed. He knew I was right, and . . . just hung his head and looked at the ground."

The ejection had two lasting effects. First, with Parisé now off the Esposito-Cournoyer line, Esposito recalls, "I tell Harry, put *Peter* with me. I felt comfortable with Pete and Yvan."

This would mark the first time in the series that Pete Mahovlich, who had played in all but Game Four, skated on a regular line—but this small move would create large ripples. "One of the best moves Harry ever made," Dennis Hull says, "was putting Peter Mahovlich on that line."

The second consequence of Parisé's penalties and response, according to Pat Stapleton: "After J.P. went nuts, the refs stopped with the crazy calls. That made a big difference."

"J.P. wasn't flashy," Clarke says, "but he's a guy you wanted on your team. He was a passionate team guy who became so frustrated, he didn't know what to do. But that didn't hurt us—and it might have helped. It forced the referees to recognize how ridiculous things had gotten. I thought that there would be some kind of relief after that, and I think there was."

Trying to intimidate poor referees usually backfires, but not this time. Years later, the Czechoslovakian referee, Rudy Batja, told the *Edmonton Journal* that, amidst the chaos, he sought out Starovoitov, the Soviet director of hockey and the IIHF director of referees, "and persuaded him that no further penalties would be handed out [for the incident]. 'After that, Kompalla was so upset and absolutely down. I refereed the rest of the game. [Kompalla] was on the ice, but for nothing.'"

While they did call four more penalties that period—all for interference—they alternated calls against the Soviets and Canadians. And after calling 10 penalties in the first period, seven against Canada, they called only seven penalties the rest of the game, four of them offsetting, with one more on the Soviets than the Canadians. By that measure, Parisé could be said to have taken one for the team.

Eight seconds after Team Canada killed off Parisé's penalty, the refs called the Soviets' Gennadi Tsygankov for interference. Seventeen seconds later, Park fired a slapshot on Tretiak, who left the rebound right in front of him. Lutchenko inadvertently slid the puck back under Tretiak into the net, but Esposito would get credit for tying the game, 1–1—only Team Canada's second power-play goal of the series.

On the Soviets' next power play, Lutchenko wound up from the point with a good screen, firing it past Dryden to put the Soviets back up, 2–1. Then, at even strength, Park slipped a backhand pass to Jean Ratelle at the Soviet blue line. Ratelle sucked in the defenceman, then gave it back to Park, who cut in on net and snapped it past Tretiak on the far side. Although Park should have been credited with Canada's first goal, this one was officially the first in the series for any Canadian defenceman, tying the game at two.

Back at Park's old high school, his sisters were "absolutely mobbed by all the students," Shelley said. Lori "and I were lifted up on chairs in the cafeteria and paraded around the school while everyone began to chant, 'PARK! PARK! PARK!' It was scary, but at the same time I was very proud of him."

The off-ice drama never stopped for long. After the first period, the Soviet soldiers blocked the Canadians' path to their own locker rooms. What exactly this was supposed to achieve is not clear, but this time Sinden "wasn't going to be the nice guy and ask permission to get into my own dressing room. About 20 feet away from this solid wall of uniforms I took off and lowered my shoulder, blasting two of them out of the way with a block before strolling into the room."

When the players made it through the doors, they found Dale Tallon sitting there. "I never left. I didn't have a TV, but I could tell when each team scored. You could hear the Russians' deafening whistles and the Canadians shouting."

IN the second period the game settled down and so did the refs, issuing only two penalties: one to Stapleton for cross-checking, and another to Viktor Kuzkin for elbowing. But the scoring continued apace.

Just 21 seconds into the second stanza, Yakushev crossed the Canadian blue line and fired to the right of the net, and high—but the puck hit the fencing Pete Mahovlich had warned about during their first practice, then did exactly as Mahovlich had feared:

it caromed right past Dryden, who almost caught it on the way back, then took two bounces right to Vladimir Shadrin. Dryden got back into position remarkably fast, but so had a Soviet forward and a Canadian defenceman right in front of him. Shadrin shot it past all three to give the Soviets a 3–2 lead.

Ten minutes later Rod Gilbert held the puck near the boards in the Soviet zone, working back and forth while Bill White, stealing a page from the Soviets' book, left the blue line to sneak down to the back door. Gilbert faked a slapshot and snapped a pass right to White, who redirected it home.

"You won't see a more beautiful scoring play in hockey than this play," Conacher said on TV, followed by another joyous celebration. White's goal, the second for Canada's defencemen after Park's, tied the score at three.

Later in the period, Shadrin beat Esposito on a faceoff in the Canadian zone, got around him, and swept the puck with one hand on his stick toward the slot. The puck deflected off Park's skate, right to Yakushev in front, all alone. He outwaited Dryden before flicking it into the lower left corner.

It was now 4–3, Soviets—but you couldn't tell by their expressions, which looked exactly the same as they did after White's goal.

With 3:16 left in the second period, on a Soviet power play, Valeri Vasiliev tried to pass to Shadrin on the back door, but instead bounced it off Bill White's knee into the net for a daunting 5–3 lead.

AFTER the second period ended with the Soviets still ahead, 5–3, the Red Army did not attempt to block the Canadians' way to their own locker rooms, apparently deciding they'd seen enough of Harry Sinden's shoulder.

Sinden had managed to remain confident in his players at

every turn—but even he had his breaking point, and he reached it during this intermission.

"They had a table in the coaches' room about as big as my desk," Sinden says, "with a nice, big Russian coffee pot. And all of a sudden I shovelled everything off the table onto the floor. Big crash. Honestly, I don't know why I did that."

But anyone who'd followed Sinden would know why: if they lost, he would not only be out of hockey—at age 40—but he would be known as a national pariah in his homeland the rest of his life. With his company bankrupt, he would also need to find another line of work.

"But," he says, "I would never show the players that."

Because Sinden kept his angst to himself, the players could regroup.

"Between the second and third, we're down by two, 5–3," Ratelle says. "Yes, that was pressure. We know that. But we are confident, and we are not scared because we know we can beat them. Nobody was panicking. Our coaches reassured us we have to keep playing the same way—nothing different. Phil got up and said, 'We're gonna go out and we're gonna win this game!' And we believed him!"

"I think it was Yvan [Cournoyer]," Clarke says, "who was walking around saying, 'I'm gonna get one, guys. I'm gonna get one for ya!' He had that quality, whatever that was, that he'd put it on himself. That was Yvan. That was his way of getting ready."

Sinden still had to pick their strategy, and he had to be right.

"When you're already behind in the third period," Sinden says, "one of the most common things teams do is play too aggressive. It's difficult to correct as a coach, because no matter how much you talk about it, and how much everyone understands how futile and dangerous it is, you have to face it almost every time. It's understandable, but if you succumb to temptation you're cooked.

"Third period, I wasn't worried about them being aggressive

enough. I was trying to keep them from being too reckless and getting down by three. I said, 'Look, we've got to keep playing the way we're playing. We're doing well, but another goal against us and we're dead in the water. So let's make sure they don't score the first half of the period. We don't have to let it all out until the last five minutes."

This naturally put even more weight on Dryden—as if he needed it. Although he had let in five goals on 22 shots through two periods, Dryden had actually played quite well. Of the five goals, three came off power plays, and he barely had a chance on four of them: a backdoor power-play goal; a screen; a bounce off the fence *plus* a screen; a nice deke move he might have stopped; and a power-play goal that bounced off White's knee. Dryden had stayed back in the net, maintained good angles, and defused a number of lateral plays—the best of his old and new styles.

"Had Dryden not been both lucky and good," *Sports Illustrated* said, the Soviets "might have led by 8–3."

"Dryden made some amazing saves," Eagleson says. "Could've been 10 goals."

Yet the math was still stubbornly obvious to all: Dryden simply couldn't let in one more goal, no matter what.

Unlike most of his teammates, Henderson admits he "was always saying something to someone. Guys like Ronnie Ellis never said a word to anyone. I'm the total opposite. I had enough self-confidence for both of us. After the second period, I'm revved up and I'm never gonna shut up.

"So I tell Dryden, 'You board this thing up, we'll be okay. We can get three. But you sure as hell better not let another goal in, or we're going to be in trouble.' I actually said that to him. I look back and wonder, 'What the hell was I thinking? How do you say that to the guy who already knows the whole thing is on his shoulders?' But in the heat of battle, you do what you feel you have to do."

What they had to do was shut the door on the Soviets and

score three goals themselves—something they had managed to do in exactly two periods out of the 23 played so far: the third period of Game Two and the second period of Game Six.

"Hey, if they can get five goals on me in one period," Tony Esposito said, referring to Game Five, "we can get three goals on Tretiak in one period."

But nothing was ever that simple in Moscow. While Park recalls them saying to each other, "Let's tie this thing up and get the hell out of Dodge," with about three minutes left in the intermission Eagleson walked in to inform them the Soviets had just told him that if the game ended in a tie, they would declare themselves the winners based on total goals, since they had a two-goal lead entering Game Eight.

"I just laughed," recalls Rod Seiling, who was in street clothes that night. "I thought, 'Man, you can say anything you want, no one's going to believe you.' It was a typical Soviet trick. They're always claiming, 'We've got the best of this and the best of that,' but they've got grandmothers with half a broom of twigs sweeping the streets. Give me a break. This is the armpit of the world! It was all about 'Our way of life is better than yours.' They had to declare themselves the winner of something."

Nonetheless, Park and others took the threat seriously. "We knew we couldn't sit back and let them declare victory. We had to go out and get three goals."

"We were behind, 5–3," Clarke recalls, "but we weren't down. No fear. After all the shit we've gone through, we know we just gotta win one period. One period. Save it for nothing. Let's go."

When the players headed back out, Tallon stayed behind again, by himself.

"I couldn't have sat in the crowd," he says. "And they weren't the most comfortable seats, either! Just wooden benches with curved seats. I had the option to sit on the bench, too, but I was too jacked up."

Looking around, he found a rabbit's foot hanging in front of Bob Clarke's spot and decided to camp out there for good luck.

"And then I prayed like hell, like a good altar boy!"

THE moment the Canadians returned to the ice, Mulvoy wrote, "their 3,000 fans inside the Sports Palace made enough noise to be heard in Saskatoon."

"I can't recall the details of every game," Gretzky says, "but Game Eight—oh, I can recite it goal by goal. That third period I watched like never before. The *tension*. Every shift a battle. Nobody saving anything. They knew there was no tomorrow. We were down, 5–3, but I wasn't scared. We were so good, and so inspired, I was convinced we could do it."

The players poured out everything they had, shift after shift.

"We started the period down, 5–3," recalls Pete Mahovlich, "but I don't think about those things. *Just go*."

Two minutes into the final period, Mahovlich took the puck behind Canada's net, then passed up the right side to Cournoyer, who gave it right back to Mahovlich, then joined him on the rush.

"We were flying down the ice," Mahovlich says. "I'm carrying it down the right side and end up chasing it into the corner. The Russian defenceman knew I was going to run him. But instead of barrelling through, I stop, I get the puck from him, and throw it out to Phil in front. But their D knocks it into the air . . ."

"This was the first and only time in my life where it all happened in slow motion," Esposito says. "Pete picks the puck up behind our net, steams up the right side, and I cut to the middle. He flips it into the corner, he gets it back, and he passes out to me. Their D tips it up. I grab it with my glove, drop it down, and whack at it, but I whiff. I whack it again, and *boom*! Goal!

"All in slow motion. That I absolutely recall.

"I remember talking to Joe Namath years later about winning

the Super Bowl. And he said the same thing: a lot of that was in slow motion for him."

Just 2:27 into the final period, the Canadians now trailed by just one goal.

"After all that, we scored in the first few minutes," Sinden recalls. "New game."

This goal was crucial to prevent the players from panicking, trying to do too much, and falling behind by three. At 5–4, they would have the confidence to stick to their game, be patient, and avoid getting sucked into taking bad chances.

"I hear the cheers," says Tallon, who was still sitting in Clarke's stall. "I know that's a Canadian goal. I run out and see the celebration. And now I'm not moving! I'm going right back to Clarkie's seat with the rabbit's foot and I'm staying there!"

Esposito's biggest play, in his estimation, occurred not too long after his second goal—at the other end of the rink.

"I had two goals and two assists in that game," Esposito says. "But the best play I made, no one remembers."

When Yuri Blinov deked Dryden, "Kenny was out of position," Esposito recalls, leaving Blinov an open net. "So I slid into his shot and blocked it from going into the net. That would've made it 6–4, and that might've been it."

Soon thereafter, "for some reason which I'll never really understand," Sinden wrote, "the Russians, for the first time in seven games, two periods, and 10 minutes, changed their game. They went to defence. Instead of pressing like they had without fail, they started to hang back and protect the lead. This opened it up and gave us better chances."

The Canadians battled shift after shift, never looking ahead, just as Sinden had told them to. They kept the puck in the Soviets' end, peppering Tretiak with shots, but they couldn't get anything to go in. Two minutes went by. Then four. Then six. Eight minutes of hard-nosed hockey, with nothing but shots to show for it.

Gilbert recalled, "We're losing, 5–4, with nine minutes to go, and we're facing off in their end. I got an idea, and I think this might pick up the team. I'm going against number 12, Mishakov, the strongest guy I'd ever seen. And their *stamina*! He'd been throwing me down like a piece of paper all month. On the faceoff I came up and smacked him right on his nose. But the problem is, he didn't go down!

"He looked at me. He wasn't happy with me. And now we're going."

Park recalls it just as clearly. "I skate over and Rod's going with this guy twice his size. All right—I'll grab a Russian here and another there, and I'll watch this for a little bit. And Rod's doing okay!"

"Bergie finally had to pull this gorilla off of me," Gilbert said. "I think this might inspire the guys. Now the ref's got me, pulling me away, but I sneak a fist around and go *boom*! I break his nose—blood is gushing—and he's looking at me like he's gonna kill me."

"I think that was the only fight Rod ever had in his whole career," Henderson says. "When Rod Gilbert starts fighting, you know things are getting serious—or crazy—or both. But it definitely got our attention."

Dennis Hull recalls, "I told Rod afterward, 'I played against you for 12 years and never saw you get in a fight.' He said, 'I never had to play against *Russians*!' I'm not a big fight fan, but I liked that fight. We didn't need any waking up, I'll tell ya, but it made everyone laugh to see Rod fight. And he got the guy!"

"You know," Pete Mahovlich says, "when we started camp, I thought Vic Hadfield would be the ultimate team guy and Rod Gilbert would be the least, a pretty boy who only wanted to score. Boy, was I completely wrong about both! What a *great* team player Rod is. Big heart. You could see it every game."

With a little more than seven minutes left, Esposito recalls, "We huddled on the ice. I told Parkie, 'Get it up to Yvan, and he'll go.' Same sort of play we did with Pete in Game Two—but now they were aware of it, and they had a guy back. If I'm not mistaken, it was Lutchenko."

So instead Park fired a pass across the ice to Esposito, open on the far right side, who carried it over the blue line. Thanks to the Soviets' defensive shell, they had four players surrounding him, yet he was still able to cut to the middle, around the defenceman, and get a clean shot off.

Tretiak stopped it with his blocker but couldn't control the rebound. Esposito whacked at the puck in mid-air and knocked it against the boards, then fetched it. Eventually he backhanded a short pass in front to Cournoyer, who popped a forehand off Tretiak's stick. When the rebound came right out to Cournoyer's backhand, he gathered it and launched it over the sprawling Tretiak—goal!—just like he'd promised his teammates during the intermission.

While Cournoyer, Esposito, Pete Mahovlich, Park, and Bergman celebrated in a group hug, four Soviet players were still in the crease, and another just outside it—three of them off their skates, literally collapsed around their net.

Cournoyer's goal tied the score at five, with 7:04 left in the series. This was it.

Or was it?

The players on the bench noticed that the huge red goal light, manned by Soviet official Victor Dombrowski, had not gone on. In a normal game, you wouldn't think twice about it. Cournoyer's goal couldn't have been more obvious, a simple backhand lofted into the netting, seen by everyone and signalled by the ref, with the puck still in the net.

But this game was anything but normal, played in a month that had already seen a chess match require the intervention of U.S. Secretary of State Henry Kissinger; an Olympic basketball game end three times before the Soviets were finally declared the winners; and a marathon whose winner thought he was being booed on his victory lap, unaware an imposter had snuck in before him. In September of 1972, absolutely anything could happen.

With the Canadians' paranoia now honed to a fine edge, they immediately suspected the Soviets were trying to claim the goal didn't count. Alan Eagleson, seated across the rink from Team Canada, hurriedly climbed past spectators and soldiers to get to the official scorer's booth.

"I wanted to go down and punch the damn goal judge," Eagleson said. "Here we had tied the most important hockey game ever played, and our 3,000 fans here and the 20 million people watching on television in Canada did not know what had happened."

The soldiers stopped Eagleson and attempted to carry him out of the rink, adding fuel to the fire. The confrontation created enough of a stir in the stands that the players started to notice. Within seconds, the TV cameras showed the backs of five, then 10, then 15 Canadian players leaning over the far boards, into the stands.

"I asked my brother, 'Where is he?'" Pete Mahovlich remembers.

"'Over by the penalty box!'" Frank recalls yelling. "Without looking or thinking—and these guys are armed, remember—Pete goes over there and lifts his stick as if to hit the soldier, and then he climbs over the boards to get Eagleson."

With the younger Mahovlich and Eagleson now surrounded by dozens of soldiers who quickly flooded the area, the other Canadian players waved their sticks to keep the soldiers off both of them.

"At the time, all I kept thinking to myself was that here we were, playing in the biggest game in hockey history," Park later wrote, "with the score tied in the final period—and instead of playing the game, we're swinging our sticks at the Soviet Red Army in the stands. It was unbelievable. It was late in the third period with the score tied and we weren't thinking hockey, but fighting the evil empire . . . They make movies about these things."

After the players came to Pete's and Eagleson's defence, "the soldier lets Eagle go," Frank recalls. "And on the way across the ice, Al gives the finger to Brezhnev."

"Hey, Eagle fought for us," Pete says. "We may have gotten screwed by him later, but we needed him in Moscow. Can't deny it."

After Sinden himself walked over and pulled Eagleson from the group of players, with Brad Park escorting the two men across the ice, the doors at both ends of the rink burst open and the Red Army marched onto the ice. Back on the bench, Bill Goldsworthy turned to Wayne Cashman, who was in street clothes, and asked, "Well, how do you feel about spending the rest of your life in Siberia?"

The goal light finally went back on, Cournoyer's goal held, the score was now officially tied, 5–5, and the next seven minutes would determine their fate.

It seemed preordained that, one way or the other, Phil Esposito would play a central role in the outcome.

"I wouldn't come off the ice," he says. "I had too much faith in myself. 'We will not lose. We will not lose.' I said it out loud, I said it to myself, I said it to everyone—constantly. 'Guys, we're going to get 'em. *We will not lose!*

"I was possessed! I wasn't going to lose! *I WASN'T GOING TO LOSE!* I just was not. Going. To lose. Not me. And I wasn't going to let anybody else lose, either. I wish I got that feeling more when I was playing in the NHL, but that was a once-in-a-lifetime feeling for me."

The Soviets repeated their threat to claim the series title if they tied.

"If the game ends in a tie," Alexander Gresko told Eagleson, wagging his finger, "we automatically win the series on total goals scored."

Sports Illustrated reported that "Eagleson yelled back at Gresko, and for once the Russian did not need his interpreter to get the drift."

"With three minutes to go," Esposito recalls, "I hear the Russian minister of sports tell Fergie, 'If we tie, we declare win.' Fergie says, 'Fuck off.' I looked at Fergie. He looked at me. No words spoken—but we knew: we gotta score."

While these crude dialogues continued, Clarke's line was on the ice. They came off with about two minutes left, and Esposito's line went back out.

"Harry says to us, 'If there's anything left,'" Henderson recalls, "'you guys got it. Be ready.'"

"The faceoff is in our end," Pete Mahovlich says. "Now we're up and down the ice, and we get a few chances."

Canada would outshoot the Soviets by a remarkable 14–5 in the final period.

"We were trying to get Pete off," Sinden recalls, "and Phil off, too, to get Clarke's line on one more time. But Phil stayed out as long as he wanted to on almost every shift that game."

Esposito wasn't coming off for anyone.

"No way!" he says. This was no longer about conditioning, or mere adrenalin, but something deeper driving him. "They should've known better by then!"

With Esposito staying out, Clarke would not get back on the ice. But Henderson had other ideas.

"I'm sitting there," he says, "and at about the one-minute mark, I did something I never did before in my entire 18-year career, and would never do again. I started yelling for another player to come off. You just didn't do that. No one did. I can't explain it to this day, but I kept saying to myself, 'I gotta get on the ice. I gotta get on the ice.' I cannot tell you what possessed me, except this feeling that came over me that I'd never felt before or since, that if I could just get out there again, I would score. *Complete certainty*."

"Think about this," Esposito says. "Paul was yelling at Pete to come off—'Pete! Pete! Pete!'—but he has no business calling him off."

"Frank [Mahovlich] was sitting beside me," Henderson recalls, "and he says, 'What the hell are you doing?' Imagine if I take Pete off, and they came down and scored. I'd be moving to Siberia!"

"So," Pete Mahovlich says, "with maybe 45 seconds to go, I come off. But Yvan and Espo stay on the ice."

Henderson jumped over the boards and chased after Esposito, who was carrying the puck down the ice. In the offensive zone, a Soviet defenceman tripped Henderson, sending him into the boards behind the Soviet net. Henderson recalls saying to himself, "I still got time!"

He got back up, watched Soviet defenceman Yuri Liapkin fumble the puck, then Henderson dashed to the slot on faith. Esposito, who seemed to be everywhere, didn't waste a second gathering the puck or regaining his footing—or even looking around for options. Still off-balance, he got what he could on the puck, flicking it on net.

"I'm just past the dot," Esposito says. "I don't know how I got anything on it. I'm one of the few guys who could get it on the net while twisting and turning. It wasn't a hard shot, it was an easy shot, but Tretiak—for some unexplained reason—he kicks it out right in the slot, and Paul's right there."

Henderson banged at it. "On my first shot, Tretiak fired his leg out and got it," he recalls, "but the rebound comes right back to me. I could see I had enough room inside the right pipe to squeeze it in."

Unlike Henderson's artistic game-winning goal in Game Seven, the best of his life, there was only one beautiful thing about this goal: it counted: 6–5, Canada.

"When Henderson scored with 34 seconds left," Esposito says, "I'd already been on the ice for two minutes. But I was so thrilled! Ecstatic! That was the closest I've ever come to kissing a man!"

"From the bench, I saw it going in the net," Clarke says. "You could just about feel it, the load actually coming off you. Is relief the right word? Something bigger. Then the excitement."

Henderson jumped up into Cournoyer's arms—creating one of the most iconic photographs in hockey history—and his teammates jumped over the boards to join the celebration. Even Dryden left his crease to skate the entire length of the ice—the only time in his career he would ever do that.

Foster Hewitt made the call: "Henderson has scored for Canada!"

Not just "scores," or even "scores for *Team* Canada." But for *Canada*, the country, and all its native sons and daughters. And they were all watching. When Gretzky and Messier constantly refer to Team Canada as "we," though they were just 11-year-old kids watching, that tells you what that team meant to the country. By Game Eight, Team Canada *was* the country.

"Everyone in Canada knows where they were when Paul scored," Tallon says. "You were invested. How could you not be? I still get this even now: 'Where were you when Henderson scored?'"

Dale Tallon might win the prize for the strangest place to be during Henderson's "shot heard 'round the world": still sitting in Clarke's seat, rubbing the rabbit's foot. He hadn't budged, and he wasn't about to leave that lucky spot with 34 seconds left. He didn't see the goal, but he knew instantly.

"When the puck went in," Berenson says, looking as if he's just been transported back to that moment 50 years earlier, "it was *magical*. Holy cow!"

"I always said Paul Henderson could score on Tretiak," Ratelle says. "He had his number. And Tretiak did not want Paul to shoot on him, because he didn't think he could stop him. No confidence by then.

"Man, that felt *so* good. Thirty-four seconds? I don't remember. Maybe I wasn't looking! I finally think we have a good chance to win! We've got to kill the last 34 seconds. Really good defencemen, Pat [Stapleton] and White, they're back."

"We get back to the bench, and Harry said, 'You guys finish it off,'" Henderson recalls. It made perfect sense, since Henderson had been on for only a few seconds, and Clarke and Ellis were fresh. Besides, they were the team's best defensive line, by design, from the start.

But just as suddenly as Henderson had jumped onto the ice, convinced it was his destiny to score the most famous goal in Canadian history, he knew that his magical powers, which had carried him for a month to a plateau of hockey he'd never seen before—and would never see again—had vanished into thin air, just like that. And he knew it, in his bones, just as surely as he had known seconds earlier that he would score the last goal.

"I said, 'Harry, I'm done,'" he says. The same man who had been full of preternatural levels of confidence for six weeks had now run completely empty. "I would have been petrified to play the last 34 seconds. I told Harry, 'Please put someone else in.' I was mentally and physically done. I got off the ice, and that was it.

"Thirty-four seconds left. I was not afraid for the guys on the ice. I knew they were going to win the game, and the Russians weren't going to get a chance. But I knew I was done. I couldn't help them."

Sinden, once again reading the situation instead of trying to impose his will on it, took Henderson at his word.

Esposito, on the other hand, told Sinden, "Harry, there's no way in hell I'm coming off the ice, and you know it!" Sinden didn't argue.

He put Ellis back on, then Pete Mahovlich.

"Harry sends me out for the last 34 seconds," Pete Mahovlich jokes, "because I was such a good defence player—*ha*!"

"Pete had been an excellent defensive player throughout the series," Frank says in his brother's defence. "Harry got the right guy, again, and Pete did the job."

"Like most coaches in that situation, after Paul scored you're not celebrating; you're getting ready for the 34 seconds to go," Sinden says. "The Soviets had gotten a lot of odd-man rushes that series, and every time they got an odd-man rush, they either scored or we'd have to make a great save. They never shot wide and had it wrap around the boards, out of the zone. They made the goalie stop it or they scored. So I tried to get our D to stand up at the blue line. I said, 'Make sure we don't give them an odd-man rush.'

"We had Stapleton and White out there at the end, and they broke it up. The Russians didn't get a shot."

To Sinden's credit, he trusted himself and his players once again.

Bobrov, once again, did not, refusing to pull Tretiak for an extra attacker.

Dryden was so nervous that, of the final seven minutes, he remembers nothing until Henderson's goal sparked his memory—and the 34 seconds that followed.

"It was, without a doubt, the longest 34 seconds I have ever played," Dryden wrote. "It seemed like 34 days, but after everything we had been through, we weren't going to let anything crush us now. We checked furiously and they never got off a decent shot. It was over."

"I don't know how to describe this," Clarke says today, "but the Russians didn't even try. *Didn't try to score*. Didn't pull their goalie. Just let the game go. From their point of view, I suppose, they'd already been wildly successful. But I know what *we* would have done: we would have attacked like madmen.

"But that last goal took whatever they had out of them. They played the last 34 seconds like they just wanted to get the game over and get out of there.

"The heart—in the end, that was the difference."

WHEN the horn blew, the players jumped over the boards to hug Dryden—and anyone else still standing.

"You know who was the closest guy to Kenny when it ended?" Phil Esposito asks, laughing. "Me! And when I was hugging Kenny, Patty [Stapleton] was tucking the winning puck into his glove, the SOB! I never knew that dirty bastard still had the puck for years!"

They had won.

It was over.

They were heading home.

32

DAYS TO REMEMBER

The Canadians lined up to shake hands with the Soviets—a ritual they had not missed since the ignoble capper in Montreal.

One of the films about the series depicts Phil Esposito, Gary Bergman, and others after the game, lying on the ice, having a beer, looking at the stands.

"Never happened," Brad Park says. "All bullshit."

What actually happened was more poignant.

"The series ended with 3,000 Canadian fans standing tall," the late Brian Glennie remembered, "full of pride, eyes filled with tears singing 'O Canada' like I've never heard it sung before or ever will again. I shall cherish that moment forever."

"As we skated off the ice after the last game," Gary Bergman recalled, "I stopped for one more look around that old barn. I realized that never in my life would I be prouder or have more respect for a group of men than I did at that moment."

Even Bobby Orr, who never played a shift in the series, said, "What that team did, I don't think there has been a greater feat in sports. It was an unbelievable comeback against a great Russian team. I've never seen anything like it."

IN contrast to the press conference after the first game, when Harry Sinden flatly confessed, "They outplayed us everywhere. We offer no excuses whatsoever," this time he said, "It may have been the greatest [game] ever played." It had lived up to his pregame prediction that it might be just that. He didn't have to add who won it.

It was true: the world had never seen a better hockey game, because the world had never seen hockey played like this before: the intensity, the pressure, and the unprecedented stakes, with the best of two hockey universes becoming one for 60 minutes, and reinventing the sport in the process.

While reactions offered in the heat of the moment often seem silly years or even days later, we can say today, a half-century later, that Sinden was right: Game Eight still stands as the greatest hockey game ever played.

The Canadians not only played their best hockey of the tournament, but because they learned more than the Soviets, they played arguably the best hockey played by any team, at any time, anywhere in the world.

Mark Mulvoy covered the series, and just about everything else, for *Sports Illustrated*. "I've been to every important major sports event 15 times," he says. "The Super Bowl. The World Series. The World Cup. The Olympics. And I'm telling you, there was nothing like these eight games. Nothing. *Nothing!* Never seen anything like it. They had it all. Importance. Tension. Getting to see the sport's two dominant teams play for the first time. Everything. Haven't seen anything like it since."

Perhaps the highest praise came from the father of Soviet hockey himself, Anatoli Tarasov: "The Canadians battled with the ferocity and intensity of a cornered animal."

"I remember Tarasov saying that 'we, the Russians, can compete with the Canadians in strength, shooting and skating,'" Paul Henderson says, "'but we can't compete with their hearts.'

There's something to that. If you watched the games in Moscow, you saw it."

Nobody showed more heart than the team's unofficial leader, Phil Esposito, the grizzled warrior. He was genuinely moved when Henderson told him, in the locker room right after the game, "I've never seen anyone play like you did tonight." Esposito set up or scored four of Canada's six goals, including its last three. He was everywhere, skating full speed for a staggering 46 minutes of a fast-paced 60-minute game. To this day, almost everyone who's seen it believes Esposito's third period was the best period anyone's ever played.

In explaining the peak performance of his life, Esposito simply says, "I refused to leave the ice." Perhaps more important, he refused to lose, and refused to let his teammates lose, too.

"I think he played the best four games of his life," Clarke says. "He was simply phenomenal. He was a leader in the locker room, but more so on the ice. He had a hell of a career—speaks for itself—but he was never better."

"I could never reach that level again," Esposito admits.

IN Team Canada's locker rooms the praise flowed as freely as the beer.

While the players and coaches cheered, embraced, and carried on, the sense of high achievement surged through them. But the feelings of triumph and unbridled joy, as powerful as they were when they finally indulged them, soon gave way to profound relief and gratitude—the kind you see on the faces of people who've just survived a sinking ship. After living in danger for a solid month, the players were finally setting foot back on solid ground. They were safe.

"The so-called high after Game Eight, it was not a frenzy of exhilaration," Park says. "It was relief—*total* relief. There was no whooping it up, no yelling and hollering. We'd avoided the gallows—and not by much! We got a Game Eight pardon. The governor called at a minute to midnight. We were free—and for good."

In the corner of the locker room, Dennis Hull sat next to Yvan Cournoyer, both slouched against the wall, drinking their beer and taking it all in. Cournoyer didn't realize it until he watched the tapes years later, but he had been on the ice for all three of Canada's third-period goals, scoring the second one. He finished the game with a plus-5 on even-strength scoring chances, tying Rod Gilbert and Jean Ratelle for the team lead that night.

"Yvan was outstanding," Clarke says. "You expect that from him, but he rose to another level."

Hull, who had not won a Stanley Cup in his eight-year NHL career, turned to Cournoyer, who had already won five of his 10 Stanley Cups, and asked, "Yvan, is this what winning the Stanley Cup is like?"

Cournoyer turned and, feigning surprise, asked Hull, "You don't know?"

"That bastard!" Hull says, laughing at the memory.

But then Cournoyer looked Hull in the eye and gave him the news he'd hoped to hear: "Dennis, this is bigger. This is for your *country*."

"I was so glad to hear that," Hull says today. "That made me feel pretty special, that a guy like Yvan would say that. Still does."

Bobby Hull had won the Cup in 1961, but now Dennis had something his older brother did not.

Even after winning five more Stanley Cups during his Hall of Fame career, Cournoyer stands by his statement. "Playing for the Stanley Cup for us was for the principle of winning, to show you were the best. But this series, it was more. It was for your country. For me, it felt like the Olympics. After I put on the sweater of my country, I felt different. Now, when I watch the Olympics, I know how they feel."

"Think about that for a second," Clarke says. "Eight games is somehow equal to winning a Stanley Cup, which takes a hundred."

"I will always remember the celebration in the locker room," Phil Esposito says. "The laughter, the tears. *I had tears in my eyes.* It was beautiful.

"I remember looking over at Paul. He looked *so worn out*. He was out there flying, *possessed*, just a few minutes ago, and now he looks like he's played 20 games in a row and couldn't play another. He'd used it all up."

Minutes after Henderson scored his historic goal, the departure of his magical powers, amassed in such quantities for more than a month, was obvious to his teammates. He was drained.

"And Paul?" Clarke says, continuing his unsolicited praise for the team's top performers, man by man. "I'm sorry, but you do not score three goals to win three straight games by luck. Might happen once by luck. Three times? No way. You're dialed in. And Paul wasn't hanging out at the far blue line, waiting to get a goal. He played a complete game every night, both ends, just like we'd talked about.

"In that series Paul was simply that good of a player. I benefited from him, Ronnie benefited—but man, wasn't that a line? Three players who complemented each other, and Harry never broke up that line. It worked because we weren't selfish. Other lines did the same later in the series, but it took them a while."

The three "sixth liners" who went out for a beer in August, promising each other they would work their way into the lineup, finished as the best line in the best series ever played.

ONCE again breaking with the traditional NHL protocol, the players were soon joined by their wives.

"It was the most draining of any game I've ever watched in all of Brad's career," Gerry Park says. "That last game, I've never experienced anything like it—and I'm not sure I'd want to again. When it was over we went down to their room, but the guards were standing before the doors to keep us, the wives and families, from getting to the guys! What was the point of that?

"No, not this time. We'd had enough. We girls all put our arms around each other, then started the cheer, '*Da, da, Canada! Nyet, nyet, Soviet!*' and just started rocking back and forth, then we went right through the line and pushed through the door to where the guys were.

"They looked so drained, but so happy to see us."

═

THE players took their time getting to the showers. When they left their locker rooms, walking past the thousands of telegrams and postcards covering the ten-foot high walls for the last time, the players and their wives got on the bus to attend a formal reception with government officials from both countries and the Soviet players—but only a few showed up. For all the hullabaloo made when the Canadians failed to shake hands after Game One, the Soviets returned the favour—but this time no one noticed.

The reception was everything the game was not: slow, scripted, boring, and completely sapped of spirit.

"There were a few speeches," Rod Gilbert recalled, "how we learned from each other and all that bullshit, but there was no interaction after the speeches. And out they went. Their coaches didn't want us interacting with their players, afraid we'd tell them how much money we're making.

"There. That's the communist system."

Back at the hotel the vodka ran like water. The party went all night, with thousands of Canadians singing and chanting together, accompanied by Pierre Plouffe and his bugle, which had escaped capture.

At some point Brad and Gerry Park, Dale Tallon, and a bunch

of Canadian friends slipped out with bottles of champagne to find Red Square. Along the way, Gerry Park recalls, they walked down into the subway station to give the old ladies they'd seen sweeping all week, with their brooms of bundled twigs, some champagne to thank them. But the second they gave them a few glasses, their supervisor materialized out of nowhere and confiscated the champagne for himself.

"I can remember that so well," she says, "the faces of the women."

The Park party proceeded to Red Square, where they found the guards marching in front of Lenin's Tomb at 2 a.m. "They were changing the guard," Park recalls. "Those guys were focused, just like the guards at Buckingham Palace. And we're shooting our champagne corks right past their noses. I give 'em credit. They didn't blink."

"I don't speak Russian," Tallon says, "but you could tell they were saying to each other, 'These guys are crazy!' Eagle and everyone warned us not to do something stupid like that, so I was worried we'd get our heels tattooed and tossed into the hoosegow."

"We didn't get in trouble," Park adds. "But I don't know why. Maybe they figured it was best just to let us go, and get us the hell out of their country the next morning. And they were probably right."

DAWN came too soon for the players. They had to be on the bus to catch an early flight to Prague, so most of them hadn't slept. Very few were hungover, however—because they were still drunk.

They hurried to stuff their dirty, smelly clothes into their suitcases, often with the help of their wives, who would be staying behind for two days before flying out themselves.

"The guys had to get up *so* early," Gerry Park recalls. "But most of them never went to bed. I remember just throwing Brad's stuff in a bag. He didn't care!"

When they boarded the plane, they found a couple unexpected passengers: Soviet head coach Vsevolod Bobrov, who would be scouting the game, and their least-liked official, Josef Kompalla. During the series, the officials had penalized Team Canada for 147 minutes and the Soviets for 84. That's a 63-minute differential, or the equivalent of playing an entire game short-handed, with almost all of that gap, incredibly, occurring in the last three games. No one had called more penalties than Kompalla. The pair's presence on the plane provided fuel for the conspiracy theorists, who suspected a quid pro quo, but by then most of the players cared more about getting sleep than revenge.

While they were settling into their seats in Moscow, the reporters' stories were coming off the presses back in Canada. Most of them managed to flip-flop just in time to get in front of the parade again.

Maurice Smith of the *Winnipeg Free Press*, who had written after the fifth game, "no way now that Canada's National Hockey League stars are going to win their series," took a different tack. "You've got to hand it to the National Hockey League stars. They didn't beat the Russians because they possess far greater skills, they won because of sheer determination and pride in their professionalism."

The *Montreal Star*'s Red Fisher confessed he emitted a few "cries" during the game because "there was a lot of guts on the ice here last night." The *Globe and Mail*'s Jim Vipond opined that the comeback victory was "a tribute to their Canadian heritage."

But the *Montreal Star*'s John Robertson—the only prominent columnist who had picked the Soviets to win the series (6–2) and promised, "If Canada wins four games I'll eat this column with Russian dressing at centre ice in the Forum on any day Sam Pollock would care to name"—was nothing if not consistent. The morning after Game Eight, Robertson put aside the historic comeback to get to his central point: "What I'm complaining bitterly about is the way they abdicated an infinitely greater responsibility—as Canadians carrying Canada's image to untold millions who are going to judge us as people by what they see on television."

Ken Dryden took exception to these columns. "According to the printed reports, there is a debate raging in Canada over the behaviour of the Team Canada players in Moscow," he wrote. "A number of writers suggested we disgraced our country. Well, as far as I'm concerned, many of our reactions were quite understandable; in fact, I don't believe we reacted any differently than we would have in an NHL game. We were told to play our game—and we did. The Russians, of course, did not play like an NHL team, thereby offering a sharp contrast. If you are a critic of the NHL style, then you have a right to criticize us. If not, then you are taking a cheap second guess at something you've never questioned before."

Most of the groggy players didn't know about these reports being loaded into the printing presses, and probably wouldn't have cared if they did. They knew only that they had salvaged the game, the series, and their self-respect. They were grateful to be leaving Moscow for their home country, even with the detour to Prague, a much more welcoming city than Moscow.

"There was a great relief in winning," Ratelle recalls, "and there was a great relief in leaving."

"I'm gonna tell you something nobody knows too much," Cournoyer says. "In the plane from Moscow, we all got up and sang 'O Canada.' We *all* sang. I never forget that feeling."

When they finished, some with tears in their eyes, a few of the players resumed celebrating, while others fell asleep during the three-hour flight—none harder than Paul Henderson.

Sinden, battling a vicious hangover himself, reflected on what had just happened. "How did we beat them?" he wondered. "I don't have the answer. But as bitter as I am about their lying officials, I have to take my hat off to the Russian players. But ask yourself this: How did the Russians lose when they can skate as well as us, pass as well as us, and out-condition us?

"I started thinking about this today on the flight, and the thought kept coming back to me that we won because we knew how to play the big game . . . Canadian pros definitely are more accustomed to playing in games with more at stake than the Russians. Just look at the way we won the last three games, games we couldn't afford to lose. We won them all in the closing minutes. At the start of the series you would have said that Russia would win any games decided in the final minutes" because of their great conditioning.

"They were stronger physically, but we were tougher mentally. Our mental conditioning—the kind of toughness that comes only from playing in something like the Stanley Cup—is the thing that, in the end, proved the difference."

RED and Joy Berenson stayed behind in Moscow for another day.

Walking downtown the day after the finale, they saw a newspaper broadsheet displayed in a glass case at one of the bus stops.

"The front page showed a picture of a druggie in a big park in Toronto, giving himself a shot in the arm," Berenson recalls. "The picture next to him was a picture of [Soviet leader Leonid] Brezhnev holding a baby. That was the comparison. It was brutal."

Pointing to the front page, they asked their translator what the headline said.

"At first they didn't want to read it to us because it was so derogatory," Joy recalls. "They finally told us it said: 'The Canadians cannot handle their freedom' and 'They will never be invited back again.'

"They had to run us down every chance they had."

"Everywhere we looked," Red remembers, "there was something questioning who we were, what are values are. It made a simple fact very clear: you were not at home."

On their Air Canada flight leaving Moscow, filled with fellow Canadians feeling equal parts jubilant, raucous, and homesick, as soon as the plane had gotten just 10 feet (3 metres) off the ground, the pilot—who knew how they all felt—got on the PA system and said, "Welcome to Canada!"

"The plane erupted in cheers," Joy says. "People were crying. And everyone started singing 'O Canada'—and I mean everyone. I've never heard it sung like that."

WHEN the team landed in Prague, Sinden, assessing his troops getting off the plane, wisely cancelled practice. There was no point. They went out again that night, basking one last time in the now-easy camaraderie they had worked so hard to establish.

The next day, when Dennis Hull was walking up to the rink, "this tall, handsome man was chatting me up. He spoke some English and wanted to know what it's like in Canada and the U.S. And I tell him, 'You know, buddy, I'd love to chat but I've gotta get ready for a hockey game.'"

Inside, Hull recalls, "Harry lined us up on the wall because we'd been out all night. He walks down the line and points to one guy and says, 'You look like you can play,' and the next, 'You look like you need the night off.' And that's how Harry picked our lineup for our last game."

Sinden rostered players who hadn't gotten much playing time, including Bill Goldsworthy, Wayne Cashman, Rod Seiling, Mickey Redmond, Don Awrey, Dale Tallon, Marcel Dionne, and Brian Glennie, plus some stalwarts like Phil Esposito and Brad Park, the only two players to dress for all 14 contests, including the camp scrimmages in Toronto.

Paul Henderson remembers asking Sinden, "'Please put

someone else in.' I had no interest in playing in Czechoslovakia. I had nothing left in the tank."

September 30 probably marked the only night in seven weeks in which the players Sinden dressed were just as happy to be playing as the ones in the stands were to be sitting out.

The most important name on the score sheet that night, however, was Stan Mikita, who had lived in Czechoslovakia until he was seven. His parents made the heart-wrenching decision to send him to Canada to live with relatives.

"I played with Stan in Chicago," Hull says, "and plenty of times I heard the other team call him 'you stinkin' Commie' or something equally creative. He'd only gotten in two games in the series because the game the Russians were playing just didn't fit his style of skating six miles an hour and stickhandling through everyone."

Mikita still had brothers and sisters in Prague, and the home crowd knew his story well.

"It was the first time they'd ever seen him," Hull says. "When they introduced him, it must've been a five-minute standing ovation. Honest to God, I had tears in my eyes. That was special."

When Hull lined up for a faceoff, he received another surprise: the man who'd been asking questions in the parking lot now stood there waiting to take the faceoff: Václav Nedomanský.

"'Sonuvabitch!'" Hull recalls thinking. "'That's the guy who was chatting me up. I've been had!' Then he goes right down and dangles through everyone."

Hull had a hunch he'd be seeing Nedomanský again, and he was right about that. Nedomanský became the first Czech player to defect, playing five seasons for the Detroit Red Wings and paving a path for the great Czech stars to follow.

The Czechs had upset the Soviets a few months earlier in the World Championship, but the Soviets were the better team. Still, having reached their emotional peak two nights earlier and not gotten much sleep since, Team Canada couldn't hold its early 2–0 lead, which flipped to a 3–2 deficit.

But once again, the Canadians found something extra to avoid an embarrassing loss. With 13 seconds to go, Clarke won the faceoff in Czechoslovakia's zone back to Park, who fired on net. The puck came back to Park, but this time he faked the shot, then snapped it in front of the crease to Serge Savard, who banged his own rebound to secure a 3–3 tie, with four seconds left.

The tour was complete. Without realizing it, in four short weeks the Canadians had seen the Brave New World of hockey, filled with Swedes, Russians, and Czechoslovakians, a world they had not even known existed a month earlier.

After the game, Canada's locker room lacked the air of catharsis felt in Moscow. But it had something else, something they hadn't thought of before.

In "a scene I will never forget," Sinden wrote, it gradually dawned on the players, slowly and quietly taking their pads off, that they would not be together as a team again. "No one said anything, but you could sense a nostalgic feeling vibrating among the players . . . Then someone started humming a song; I'm pretty sure it was Phil Esposito. Then he started to sing it: 'Thanks for the Memories,' Bob Hope's theme song. And almost like it had been rehearsed, every guy stood in front of his locker, stopped for a few minutes, and joined in as loudly as he could. It lacked quality, but it had heart.

"And right down to the end, the last thing they would do together as a team abounded with the greatest attribute of this squad: heart."

THE original plan was to split the team into two flights on the way home, the way the team had done when it travelled across Canada and Europe, at the NHL's request. But Alan Eagleson decided that after all they'd been through, he couldn't do that to them. Leveraging his contacts with Air Canada, the Canadian Amateur Hockey Association, and the Canadian government, Eagleson did what he did best: he found a way to get things done no one else could. He managed to find a 200-seat plane and fill it halfway with the players, coaches, staffers, and reporters.

"I'm walking down the hallway of the rink," he remembers, "and I hear these guys moaning and groaning, guys from the CAHA and Hockey Canada, complaining that 'Eagleson's trying to do this and that and can you believe it?' I was so pissed, I popped in and said, 'Look, I've got a plane. I've got the approval from the Canadian government and Air Canada. If you don't like it, don't get on my fucking plane. Go on your own goddamn plane!'"

They shut up and got on the plane.

The team resumed the celebration—and the naps—shortly after boarding, and kept it up through a stop in London to refuel the plane and restock the bar, on the way to Montreal, then Toronto.

Pat Stapleton and Bill White were up to their usual pranks. While one of the team doctors slept, the duo cut the stitching that attached the sleeves to the shoulders of the doctor's sport coat, then waited for him to wake up.

About 30 minutes outside of Montreal, Sinden moved up to John Ferguson's seat to give his thanks.

"There is just no way to measure what John Ferguson did for me and for this team," Sinden wrote. "He was the only guy who never said die . . . a beautiful person. John and I really didn't have to say anything to one another. What we felt didn't have to be transmitted by words."

But Sinden said them anyway, and as he did, "I saw his eyes filling up, the tears forming in the corners. I got all choked up and had to walk away. I went to the back of the plane and wanted to cry. If I were alone, I would have."

When the plane landed, the team doctor stirred awake, stretched out, and watched his sleeves fall off his coat. He was so embarrassed, he stayed on the plane while the others got off to avoid looking silly in front of a throng of fans.

Prime Minister Trudeau had flown in from Ottawa to greet the players. Because of some technical difficulties, the pilot asked the passengers to exit out the back, where Trudeau would be waiting for them.

"But," Park recalls, "Eagleson says, 'Hold it! We're not going out the back of the plane, we're going out the front! You tell Trudeau to move.'"

This started a back-and-forth between the pilot repeating his instructions and Eagleson refusing to obey.

"Finally," Park says, "someone says, 'Shut up, Eagle. He's the fucking prime minister and you're not!' That ended that. We went out the back."

"Right there," Ratelle says, "we should have known then that there's something wrong with that guy."

When the players walked off the plane, they were met by thousands of fans cheering for them in the pouring rain. They boarded a fire truck to drive around the airport and wave at the fans, who were going berserk.

"We really had no idea of the impact that the series had back home," Dale Tallon says. "We didn't know. All we knew is we were gangsters, the bad guys, from Montreal to Moscow. We kinda liked being the good guys again!"

"They say 85 percent of all Canadians were watching that game," Eagleson says. "My question is: Who the fuck were the other 15 percent?! I've never met anyone who didn't remember that series!"

"No customs that night!" Savard says. "Just pick up your bags and go. I've got to get home, fast as I can, because I want to see the plane land in Toronto!"

The remaining players who travelled to Toronto mounted a stage in the rain in front of City Hall to address another huge crowd. When Park saw his mother, he jumped into the crowd and brought her up on stage.

"All the guys had had their share," says Gerry Park, who was watching on TV from her parents' home in Winnipeg. "But when you think about all the bashing they took—it was just horrible, so demoralizing, so hard. It was like everybody had turned against them. Your neighbour wouldn't talk to you. So alone.

"So when they came back, and they were treated like conquering heroes—well, after everything they'd been through, I thought, 'Fair enough. They deserve it. They earned it.'

"I think what made it so special was losing the games in Canada. If the series had been a cakewalk like it was supposed to be, it wouldn't have been special. We wouldn't have remembered it. And they wouldn't have had to come together, a bunch of guys who'd never played together before.

"And that's it: being so down, down, down, then getting back up to win the ultimate goal. That was pretty cool. Watching on TV, I can still remember what a good feeling it was, and what a different feeling from when we flew to Moscow. You don't get many stories like that."

When the impromptu ceremony ended and everyone dispersed, the Toronto players headed to their homes, and others who would be flying out of Toronto the next day stayed at the Sutton Place, where the entire adventure had started seven weeks before.

"Clarkie and I roomed together that night," Stapleton recalled. "We woke up, went to the airport, and flew back to Chicago and Philly. And that was it."

Having never expected the series to mean so much, the organizers didn't plan a celebration, either.

"This turned serious real fast," Park says, "but it started as a lark. Guys win the Stanley Cup and they get to enjoy it all summer. They plan it out, and each guy gets the Cup for a couple days and has a party. We finish the biggest comeback in sports history, and we have no time to enjoy it with each other and the people who supported us. The next day, we're headed to our homes—and training camps. It was back to business.

"And that's a shame."

33

WHAT IT CHANGED, WHAT IT MEANS

Hours after the Esposito brothers landed on Canadian soil, the mayor of Sault Ste. Marie asked them to come home so the city could throw a big parade for them.

"I call Tony," Phil recalls, "and he said, 'I'm going back to Chicago. I don't want any parades. I don't want anything.' And I said, 'Well, I can't go if you don't go.' And he said, 'You conned me into this and I don't want to think about it again!'"

Phil's power of persuasion over his younger brother had reached its limits.

"The next day," Phil says, "I was on the ice with the Bruins. Two nights later, I played in a preseason game. It was over."

Those players who reported to Montreal, Toronto, and Vancouver were surrounded by fans and media dying to talk about the series. The Hendersons' young daughters had to put a sign up on the front door that said, "We Have No Autographs Left." His life would never be the same.

But those who played in the States felt like they'd fallen off the grid.

"Three days after we beat the Russians," Bob Clarke recalls, "[the Flyers] played an exhibition game in Richmond, Virginia.

They were all celebrating back in Canada, but I didn't know about any of it until after the season. I had no idea."

WHEN the players rejoined their NHL teammates near the end of the normal fall training camps, most Team Canada players could see they had gained an edge.

"Coming back to the NHL after playing the Russians," Pat Stapleton said, "it felt like slow motion! *That* was noticeable."

Stapleton's teammate, Dennis Hull, had a similar sense. "When I came back I was in the best shape I'd ever been in."

He played like it, finishing with a career-high 90 points—21 more than his next-best season—which would have been enough to win the scoring title most years before the Esposito-Orr combination started rewriting the record books.

The previous fall, Philadelphia head coach Fred Shero had wanted Clarke to replace Eddie Van Impe as the team's captain, but Clarke had declined. "We've already got a good captain," Clarke told him. "So I won't be."

But a year later, when Clarke returned from Moscow, Shero told him, "You're *going* to be the captain."

"He wasn't asking," Clarke recalls.

When Clarke asked Shero if he'd told Van Impe, the coach said he hadn't, but he would do it soon.

"I'll tell him," the 23-year-old Clarke said, showing exactly why Shero had wanted him to be captain in the first place. "When I approached Eddie, he said, 'It's the right decision. I'm glad.'"

That season Clarke would finish second in scoring behind only Phil Esposito, and first in voting for both of the league's MVP awards—the Hart Trophy, selected by members of the media, and the Lester B. Pearson Award, voted on by his peers.

"Playing with the guys I played with on [Team Canada], and at that level," Clarke says, "it elevated my game, and my expectations for myself. I don't know if I ever would have reached that level without Team Canada."

Almost everyone, however, found that they could never reach quite the same emotional peak again, even in the Stanley Cup Final.

Most of the players' reputations rose with Team Canada, especially lesser-known players like Gary Bergman, Pat Stapleton, Bill White, Dennis Hull, and J.P. Parisé, to name a few. Others who already were considered top players gained new respect from their peers and fans for demonstrating such toughness and team spirit under pressure, including Yvan Cournoyer, Rod Gilbert, and Jean Ratelle.

Bobby Orr's absence from the series revealed that Harry Sinden could successfully coach without him, Phil Esposito could play a leading role without him, and the Rangers' Brad Park, his top rival as the NHL's best defenceman, could play with anyone. In fact, Park would rightly be named the series' top defenceman, Esposito the top forward, finishing with 52 shots in eight games, more than two a period. The next closest was Maltsev, with 32.

"I tell this to Phil whenever I see him," Gretzky says. "The greatest game I ever saw anyone play, ever, was Phil in Game Eight. He was controlling the play, every shift—and I think he barely came off!—and really controlling the entire series. Looking back, that's what stays with me: just how good Phil Esposito played. He was the true heartbeat of the team.

"On the last shift, you knew Phil wasn't coming off, and he battled to get the puck and put it on net, and of course Henderson banged it home. We did it! I don't know if any goal has ever made me happier. Henderson changed the *mindset* of an entire country, from being disappointed and down to exuberant and proud. And that's how we felt. That's how we *all* felt. I might have been jumping up and down by myself in Mrs. Rizzetto's living room, but I didn't have to wonder what my dad was feeling, or my classmates, or my teammates. I knew all of Canada felt this way!"

But not everyone benefited from a Summit Series bump the following season. Jean Ratelle had to take pills for a bad back for six weeks, thanks to the Intourist beds that were too soft and too short. Due to a groin injury Paul Henderson had sustained during the series, he would play only 40 games that season.

For leaving the team in Moscow, Gilbert Perreault, Rick Martin, and especially Vic Hadfield would be reminded of it throughout their careers. Whenever Hadfield played in Canada, he was booed lustily—by the same fans, it must be said, who had booed Team Canada in Winnipeg and Vancouver. To his credit, Hadfield never ducked those games, taking his medicine with good humour.

Just a few days after Sinden returned to Canada, a 20-minute phone call with the Boston Bruins was enough to make him their new general manager, at $80,000 a year—almost five times what he had made as their Stanley Cup–winning coach two years earlier. For a man who had been out of hockey, then out of a job when the construction company went bankrupt, it's fair to say Sinden had bet on himself and won. He thrived as general manager for 28 years, adding the titles of president and chief executive, and was inducted into the Hall of Fame as a builder in 1983.

As founder of the NHL Players' Association, Eagleson dramatically increased the players' power and pay, then helped create the Canada Cup, a competition among the top six hockey nations that was held five times between 1976 and 1991. But in 1994 the FBI charged him with 34 counts, including embezzlement and fraud, for skimming money from NHL contracts, player disability settlements, and Canada Cup revenue. Canada followed with eight counts of fraud and theft. Eagleson served four months of an 18-month sentence. He was disbarred and removed from the Order of Canada and the Hockey Hall of Fame. In 2005, Canada granted Eagleson a pardon, clearing his record.

"I know what I did, I paid a price," he says today, "and I can live with both those things."

The Summit Series players remain divided on Eagleson. Some insist he should not be invited to reunions because of what he did later, but no one denies his essential role in the Summit Series.

THE series would change the game in countless ways. One of the simplest was the way it broke down the barriers the league had built up to keep the players apart.

"NHL players are fans, too," Clarke says. "They watched the series and saw what we did. So players on opposing teams would often come up to you and say something about it," a simple gesture that would have been unthinkable a year earlier.

The Summit players had been raised in a system built to breed distrust among opponents. "But when we came back, it had changed," Rod Seiling says. "During warm-ups, when I tapped Phil on the pads on his way by, my teammates would say, 'What the hell are you doing?!' I said, 'Man, I just went to war with him, so get lost!' But if I'd tapped him on the pads the year before, you'd have an all-out brawl!"

In 1974, before a game in New York against the rival Bruins, Park raced to the hospital for the birth of his second child, a son named Robert. He got to Madison Square Garden right when the game started. When he hopped on the ice for a faceoff a few minutes later, "Both Phil and Bobby [Orr] come up to me and ask me how my wife is and how my baby is. That was wonderful. Before '72, that never would have happened. Hell, they would have been pissed that I'd made it back in time to play!"

Their friendships have extended far beyond their playing careers.

"I will walk forever with those guys," Esposito says. "I think we're as close as any team in hockey." That they were together only seven weeks speaks to the intensity of those days and the strength of those bonds. They can't always recall the details of their first Stanley Cup playoffs, but they can recount these games down to the minute, and tell you with confidence who their linemates were in Game Four.

"There is something special about this team that's very hard to describe," Cournoyer says. "We were only together for a short time, but every time we meet, it's like we were teammates for life. When I shake hands with Phil Esposito, I shake hands with a teammate from '72, not a Boston Bruin. We don't talk about all the playoff games. We talk about '72."

Perhaps more surprising have been the friendships that have developed between the Canadian and Soviet players during official reunions in 1987, 2002, and 2012, as well as unofficial meetings.

"Over the years, we've spent a fair amount of time with them," Park says. "We have a great deal of affection for them. And we have a pretty good understanding of what they went through. Their lifestyle was pretty tough.

"In '87 we had a little three-game series called 'Relive the Dream.' We played in Hamilton, Montreal, and Ottawa. But they were kind of kept apart from us, because [Viktor] Tikhonov, a real SOB, was their coach.

"In Montreal we had a little function upstairs after the game, and [Valeri] Vasiliev and I were getting along pretty good, and then they decide to leave. On the sidewalk, Vasiliev was walking 20 feet in front of me, and Tikhonov comes up behind him and slaps him on the back of his head! Man, I covered that 20 feet in a heartbeat, grabbed Tikhonov's arm, and said, 'No!' He wasn't expecting that.

"So I told our guys, 'After the game in Ottawa, we're going to hijack these guys.' We told them to stay on the bus at their hotel, and let all the coaches and officials get off. A few of us jump on their bus and tell the driver to follow the Team Canada bus. We take 'em to a strip club, and they had the best time. We footed the tab. They loved it."

"A few years ago I picked Tretiak up at the Montreal airport,"

Yvan Cournoyer recalls. "We had five hours to kill, so I brought him home. I passed him a bathing suit, and we had a swim in our pool. I could never have believed in '72 I would have this guy in my pool. And my bathing suit fit him—and it was red!"

During the 2002 reunion in Moscow, Savard recalls, "We had a dinner at the arena, and then they put just the former players in a room for a couple hours. We talked about everything—what everyone was doing, what we remember. And every time we see those guys, it feels like you knew them forever. How can that happen?"

The speakers at the reception immediately following Game Eight, who talked about learning and friendship, were spouting, as Rod Gilbert said, "bullshit." Nobody was thinking in those terms then. But years later, when the players look back, they see that learning and friendship were two of the Summit Series' greatest products—though probably not in the manner the speakers envisioned.

THE Summit Series was that rare sporting event where both teams could be said to be winners. Team Canada showed it was, in fact, the best team in the world—and did so despite clearly inadequate scouting and preparation; unfavourable timing, rules, and referees; and the absence of Bobby Orr and Bobby Hull. After the national media ripped the players for being soft, entitled, and selfish, they proved themselves to be the exact opposite of all those things, while demonstrating uncommon hockey intelligence, resilience, and poise under incredible strain. In the process, they brought their nation together as it had never been unified before.

If the Soviets fell a period short of pulling off an earth-shaking upset, they achieved just about everything else they could have hoped for, and then some. Eight games transformed the Soviets' mocking critics into respectful devotees of their revolutionary approach to everything from conditioning to offensive play.

In the years that followed it would be the Soviets' methods, not the Canadians', that would be copied worldwide. At my hockey school the next summer, both coaches had visited the Soviet Union that spring and returned to teach us what they had learned, on and off the ice. The revolution started that quickly.

"Phil said immediately after the series that the game of hockey will never be the same," Ellis recalls. "He was sort of praising both teams—and of course he was right."

When the Summit Series ended, Clarence Campbell, president of the NHL, displayed a rare flash of humility when he told *Sports Illustrated*, "This should teach us that we don't know everything about hockey."

Even Toronto's Harold Ballard agreed. "If we're smart, we'll go home and begin to apply some of the lessons we learned from the Russians. The sad thing is that we may not be smart enough. Too many people will say, 'See, our guys are better,' instead of saying, 'Okay, let's make our guys better.'"

Philadelphia's Fred Shero was the first NHL coach to travel to Moscow to learn their methods, while American college coaches like Bob Johnson and Herb Brooks were figuring out how to combine the Soviets' training and offensive concepts with the North American emphasis on physical, individual play.

When I once asked Brooks about the Western Collegiate Hockey Association—college hockey's oldest league, featuring Minnesota, Wisconsin, North Dakota, and the major Michigan teams, a group that won 10 of 11 NCAA titles between 1973 and 1983—he said, "Our preparation and training were at the forefront. We had a group of real outstanding coaches—smart and open-minded. It was just a real tough league, and we had a jump on everyone else."

Brooks, of course, applied that knowledge to his 1980 Olympic team, where he led his American college kids to upset the Soviets in the famed "Miracle on Ice."

More than a few Summit alumni found this quite amusing.

"The U.S. beat basically the same team that we played," Ron Ellis says, "partly because the Russians made the same mistake we did: they underestimated them." He smiles. "Big mistake."

The 1979–80 season happened to be the one in which the NHL welcomed Wayne Gretzky and the Edmonton Oilers, who would become the embodiment of the new hybrid style. The lessons from the Summit Series were now baked into the NHL and the players burned in the memories of the next generation.

"When Messier and I were just 19-year-old teammates, and one of us made a great play in practice, we'd tell the other guy, 'Well that was mighty Yakushevian of you!' That was the highest compliment we could give. Years later, Mark and I went to Russia to do an event with Yakushev himself, and we told him this, and he loved it. I don't think he ever imagined two Canadian kids would remember him so well."

The same league that had been 99 percent Canadian in 1972 is now home to players from 22 nations. The three countries Team Canada played 50 years ago produce 20 percent of today's NHL players, without whom the league could never have doubled from 16 teams in 1972 to 32 teams today. Of the approximately 1,100 players who played in an NHL game during the 2021–22 season, more than half, about 57 percent, were born outside of Canada.

The Summit Series produced many winners, but none bigger than the sport itself, whose scope expanded almost overnight. After hockey fans around the world saw just how good hockey could really be, they demanded more—and they got it, in the form of five Canada Cups and three World Cups of Hockey, which produced incredible games and six titles for Team Canada.

In the 1990s NHL players joined their nations' Olympic teams, and the results were striking: between 1992 and 2002, four different nations won the gold medal—in order, Russia, Sweden, the Czech Republic, the very countries Team Canada had faced in 1972, and Canada itself. With Finland winning five Olympic medals since 1998—including the gold in 2022—and the United States narrowly missing out on two gold medals, hockey's Big Six have become almost coequal leaders of the sport.

And yet, if Canada lost its status as the sport's only superpower in 1972, the 50 years since have re-established Canada as the best among equals, winners of three of the last four Olympics featuring the top professionals, plus six titles in the "best-on-best" competitions mentioned earlier. Canada has had to share the stage but not the crown. It is still the world's greatest hockey superpower.

All this has improved the sport itself. The game has never been stronger.

IN 2000, the Dominion Institute (now known as Historica Canada and noted across the country as the producer of the Heritage Minute series of short films) asked 5,700 people to name the most significant event in Canadian history.

Confederation topped the list, as you would expect, but the Summit Series ranked fifth, and World War II sixth. You get the idea. The series' place in the Canadian conscience has only grown.

If not the most important, you could argue that the Summit Series was the most memorable event on that list. Instead of a Revolutionary War, with its shot heard 'round the world, Canada gained its independence from Great Britain slowly and quietly over the course of a century. Canada suffered no civil war, and as important as its contributions were to both world wars, the effort and credit were shared.

But the Summit Series stands apart. It is a distinct moment in history, with the stakes clear to everyone, culminating in a decisive, indisputable triumph that captivated the entire country, and one that is Canada's alone.

Even Phil Esposito's speech, delivered spontaneously from the heart, full of frustration and determination just minutes after another crushing defeat, ranks as one of the most famous speeches in Canadian history.

"Listen," Esposito says, "when I hear a guy on the news say that the greatest speeches ever given were Lincoln's Gettysburg Address and Winston Churchill's 'blood, sweat, and tears' speech, and then he says, 'We have a hockey player who made the greatest speech of all time in Canada,' I can't believe it. When I hear things like that, and I hear things like that all the time, it shows you how important this series was to the whole country.

"I'm glad I said yes!"

THERE are many ways to measure the impact of the Summit Series, but the best might be the simplest.

"Ten years after, 15, they didn't talk about this like they do now," Serge Savard says. "I'd never guess we'd be talking about this years later. Oh no. But they do, all the time. This thing was special, and it's still special. To me, it's the emotion. That's why everybody says it's the biggest memory they have. No one can elevate themselves emotionally that high by themselves. And you can't do it very often, either. We were lucky to experience this. I put the series ahead of everything else I accomplished in sports. That's how big it is to me."

"I won 10 Stanley Cups, but they don't talk about those," Cournoyer says. "But every week they talk about the '72 series. When I play golf they tell me where they were when we scored—every time! We thought we did something great, but we never thought it would last so long. We talk more about it now than we did then! Every time I look at the film, even now I get a chill. You don't forget that."

Canada also seems to have a disproportionate number of

citizens, now about 49 years old, named Paul and Pauline. "I meet them all the time," Henderson says.

A few hours before I interviewed Rod Seiling in the summer of 2021, he happened to be walking his granddaughter's dog through the park.

"Guy pulls up in his car," Seiling said, "and he says, 'You're Rod Seiling, aren't you?'

"I say, 'Yes, I am.'

"Then he shouts, 'Team Canada '72!' And he drives off.

"How much better can you get than that? We hear it all the time, to this day. It's amazing.

"There are three dates every Canadian our age remembers: when JFK was shot, when they first landed on the moon, and the Summit Series. It gave Canadians an identity, something we had been lacking really since the start. It was something to be proud of, and maybe all the more so because of the initial letdown. To come back from the dead, to give them hope, to make them proud to be Canadians, to be proud of the flag—it was new, in a lot of ways, and all the more fulfilling."

In 2012, Ken Dryden joined the Summit Series 40th anniversary tour—which ran from St. Catharines, Ontario, to Vancouver—mainly because he felt he had to. He was pleasantly surprised, however, that the largely unscripted events prompted him and his teammates to leave their canned comments behind and give fresh, spontaneous answers.

"It turned out to be a real discovery for me," he says. "I had learned more about the series that first night than I had the 40 years before."

That's how Dryden ended up talking on stage about the practice in Winnipeg, when he found that his missing skate had been used to prop the door open, and Red Berenson quipped, "Well, Dryden, that's the first thing you've stopped all week."

Cournoyer, one of seven other players on the stage, "thought that was hysterical—the funniest thing," Dryden says. "When we went to the next stop he kept telling me how funny it is. When we get to the stage in Vancouver, Yvan says, 'Kenny, you've got to tell the story about the skate!' So I tell the story.

"My sister lives in Victoria, so she was there with both her daughters and both her sons-in-law. Of course, *she* thinks it's hysterical, too. I'm sure the fact that it was me humiliating myself was very appealing. She has that kind younger-sister devilishness, but something less benign than devilish."

A few months later, as Christmas approached, a box arrived at Dryden's home—big and heavy. "I have no clue whatsoever," Dryden recalls. "I can't figure it out from lifting or shaking it, and as I'm opening it I have *no* idea what it is.

"First thing I see looks kind of like marble, and it's white. Then I see cuts in the marble, like blade cuts in the ice—then a couple of decorative pucks, and the last thing I see is the plaque: 'It's the only thing I've stopped all week.'

"Her daughters' husbands work in the trades and did all the work, but they were looking for the skate so long and they couldn't find it—and finally sent [the base] without it. So it's still in my office without the skate.

"That's the trail of the moment from Winnipeg back in 1972—and they all love it.

"Oh, it's great. It's inspired!"

When I asked Dryden to consider the entire experience, and what it all means, Dryden paused to think—a common response from him. When he finally spoke, his thoughts came out in fully formed paragraphs, and he was able to roll his mind out in one clean sequence. He knows what he thinks about this, and feels.

"Maybe the proudest part is that we *did* hang in there, and you do so because you have no choice," he said, warming to the question. "Because it's who you are. Because you've had lots of experiences to draw on, and if you do hang in there, you know good things can happen. And you have faith in that.

"People often ask, 'What's your favourite moment in hockey?' And you start out by saying we won all these Stanley Cups—and I've heard the answer many times before, and I've probably said it, too: they're all like your kids, and you can't choose your favourite among them.

"I would love to be able to say that. But no, that's not it. You do feel differently about them. Some Stanley Cups I can hardly remember. The one I'm supposed to remember the most is my first one, when we came from nowhere to win it, and I was a rookie with six games' experience. Jean Béliveau said that was his favourite Stanley Cup, and he won 10 or something.

"But it isn't. Not for me. It's 1976.

"And this is why: after we won it again in 1973, the Flyers won the next two Cups. So we'd lost what we'd had, and for a couple years. You can't call it a fluke. So it's as if we were on a mission, and it's fun to be on a mission. And when you feel that way, it takes on a kind of mood and atmosphere and sense of shared purpose. And it felt like we were on a mission from the moment we lost the year before [in 1975] to the final period of the fourth game in Philly [in 1976], when we finished the sweep."

Dryden paused again to let those paragraphs set before composing the final part of his answer.

"And then there's the '72 Summit Series. It's my favourite hockey memory, and I can't argue with it. It's how I feel.

"And perhaps that's surprising, because I had some really bad moments in that series, and I played much less of a role in that series than I had in the Stanley Cups, where Scotty [Bowman] played only one goalie the whole way. But you have the feelings that you have and you can't argue with them.

"In part it was because the Summit Series took place on a higher plane, a level of competition that had more meaning even than what we had thought had the most meaning, the Stanley Cup playoffs. But this had meaning beyond that.

"If we'd won eight straight, like we were supposed to, I think I'd hardly remember it. But that's not how it went.

"The entire series, start to finish, took only 27 days. Yet it combined in the same experience the lowest lows and the highest highs I'd ever had—and you almost never have that experience, that much up and down, in the same month. I never did, before or since. You had to experience the worst of it, you had to *deal* with the worst of it, and you had to find a way to see something that might be better. You take a step toward that, but then you feel that slipping away and leading you into something even more horrible, and then you have to find a way out of that, and then something else. And with each setback, you can either give up or you can invest more of yourself, then more, and more, as it demands.

"But you know the more you put into it, the more crushed you'll feel if you fall short. So the temptation is to hold back—and we didn't do that. We went all in.

"The combination of all those things—that's it. That's why it means more to me than anything else I've done. The lowest moment of my career was that first night. Game One. And the highest was Game Eight. As good as it gets.

"I knew it was big and it mattered to us at the time, but I wouldn't have thought about it in those terms—about the future—that it was going to be historic. I was not that conscious of it. You get on with things.

"But you get to a certain point and you realize just how much it matters. In the context of all the other things you've done, it still stands out. And you have certain feelings, and you can't order those feelings, you can't direct them, you can't argue against them, and you can't argue for them. You can only accept them as they are. And for me, I know, this was it.

"And the only way you know how big it has become is by looking back."

Appendix

ROSTERS AND STATISTICS

Team Canada 1972—Numerical Roster

No.	Name	Pos.	NHL Team
1	Ed Johnston	G	Boston Bruins
2	Gary Bergman	D	Detroit Red Wings
3	Pat Stapleton	D	Chicago Black Hawks
4	Bobby Orr	D	Boston Bruins
5	Brad Park	D	New York Rangers
6	Ron Ellis	RW	Toronto Maple Leafs
7	Phil Esposito	C	Boston Bruins
8	Rod Gilbert	RW	New York Rangers
9	Bill Goldsworthy	RW	Minnesota North Stars
10	Dennis Hull	LW	Chicago Black Hawks
11	Vic Hadfield	LW	New York Rangers
12	Yvan Cournoyer	RW	Montreal Canadiens
14	Wayne Cashman	RW	Boston Bruins
15	Red Berenson	C	Detroit Red Wings
16	Rod Seiling	D	New York Rangers
17	Bill White	D	Chicago Black Hawks

18	Jean Ratelle	C	New York Rangers
19	Paul Henderson	LW	Toronto Maple Leafs
20	Pete Mahovlich	LW	Montreal Canadiens
21	Stan Mikita	C	Chicago Black Hawks
22	Jean-Paul Parisé	LW	Minnesota North Stars
23	Serge Savard	D	Montreal Canadiens
24	Mickey Redmond	RW	Detroit Red Wings
25	Guy Lapointe	D	Montreal Canadiens
26	Don Awrey	D	Boston Bruins
27	Frank Mahovlich	LW	Montreal Canadiens
28	Bob Clarke	C	Philadelphia Flyers
29	Ken Dryden	G	Montreal Canadiens
32	Dale Tallon	D	Vancouver Canucks
33	Gilbert Perreault	C	Buffalo Sabres
34	Marcel Dionne	C	Detroit Red Wings
35	Tony Esposito	G	Chicago Black Hawks
36	Richard Martin	LW	Buffalo Sabres
37	Jocelyn Guèvremont	D	Vancouver Canucks
38	Brian Glennie	D	Toronto Maple Leafs

Head Coach: Harry Sinden • Assistant Coach: John Ferguson

Team USSR 1972—Numerical Roster

No.	Name	Pos.	Club Team
1	Victor Zinger	G	Spartak Moscow
2	Alexander Gusev	D	CSKA Moscow
3	Vladimir Lutchenko	D	CSKA Moscow
4	Viktor Kuzkin	D	CSKA Moscow
5	Alexander Ragulin	D	CSKA Moscow
6	Valeri Vasiliev	D	Dynamo Moscow

7	Gennadi Tsygankov	D	CSKA Moscow
8	Vyacheslav Starshinov	C	Spartak Moscow
9	Yuri Blinov	LW	CSKA Moscow
10	Alexander Maltsev	RW	Dynamo Moscow
11	Yevgeni Zimin	RW	Spartak Moscow
12	Evgeni Mishakov	LW	CSKA Moscow
13	Boris Mikhailov	RW	CSKA Moscow
14	Yuri Shatalov	D	Krylya Sovetov
15	Alexander Yakushev	LW	Spartak Moscow
16	Vladimir Petrov	C	CSKA Moscow
17	Valeri Kharlamov	LW	CSKA Moscow
18	Vladimir Vikulov	RW	CSKA Moscow
19	Vladimir Shadrin	C	Spartak Moscow
20	Vladimir Tretiak	G	CSKA Moscow
21	Viacheslav Solodukhin	C	CSKA Moscow
22	Vyacheslav Anisin	C	Krylya Sovetov
23	Yuri Lebedev	LW	Krylya Sovetov
24	Alexander Bodunov	RW	Krylya Sovetov
25	Yuri Liapkin	D	Khimik Voskresensk
26	Yevgeni Paladiev	D	Spartak Moscow
27	Alexander Sidelnikov	G	Krylya Sovetov
29	Alexander Martynyuk	RW	Spartak Moscow
30	Alexander Volchkov	C	CSKA Moscow

Head Coach: Vsevolod Bobrov • Assistant Coach: Boris Kulagin

Note: In North America, CSKA Moscow was commonly referred to as the Central Red Army, or simply the Red Army, while Moscow-based Krylya Sovetov was popularly known as the Wings of the Soviet, or the Soviet Wings.

Team Canada 1972—Statistics

Name	GP	G	A	Pts	PIM
Phil Esposito	8	7	6	13	15
Paul Henderson	8	7	3	10	4
Bob Clarke	8	2	4	6	18
Yvan Cournoyer	8	3	2	5	2
Brad Park	8	1	4	5	2
Dennis Hull	4	2	2	4	4
Jean-Paul Parisé	6	2	2	4	28
Rod Gilbert	6	1	3	4	9
Jean Ratelle	6	1	3	4	0
Gary Bergman	8	0	3	3	13
Ron Ellis	8	0	3	3	8
Gilbert Perreault	2	1	1	2	0
Bill Goldsworthy	3	1	1	2	4
Frank Mahovlich	6	1	1	2	0
Pete Mahovlich	7	1	1	2	4
Bill White	7	1	1	2	8
Wayne Cashman	2	0	2	2	14
Serge Savard	5	0	2	2	0
Red Berenson	2	0	1	1	0
Stan Mikita	2	0	1	1	0
Guy Lapointe	7	0	1	1	6
Mickey Redmond	1	0	0	0	0
Don Awrey	2	0	0	0	0
Vic Hadfield	2	0	0	0	0
Rod Seiling	3	0	0	0	0
Pat Stapleton	7	0	0	0	8

Goaltending	GP	W	L	T	Min	GA	GAA
Tony Esposito	4	2	1	1	240	13	3.25
Ken Dryden	4	2	2	0	240	19	4.75

Did not play in Summit Series games: Marcel Dionne, Brian Glennie, Jocelyn Guèvremont, Ed Johnston, Rick Martin, Bobby Orr, Dale Tallon

Team USSR 1972—Statistics

Name	GP	G	A	Pts	PIM
Alexander Yakushev	8	7	4	11	4
Vladimir Shadrin	8	3	5	8	0
Valeri Kharlamov	7	3	4	7	16
Vladimir Petrov	8	3	4	7	10
Yuri Liapkin	6	1	5	6	0
Boris Mikhailov	8	3	2	5	9
Alexander Maltsev	8	0	5	5	0
Vyacheslav Anisin	7	1	3	4	2
Vladimir Lutchenko	8	1	3	4	0
Yevgeni Zimin	2	2	1	3	0
Yuri Blinov	5	2	1	3	0
Vladimir Vikulov	6	2	1	3	6
Valeri Vasiliev	6	1	2	3	6
Gennadi Tsygankov	8	0	2	2	6
Alexander Ragulin	6	0	1	1	4
Viktor Kuzkin	7	0	1	1	8
Alexander Bodunov	3	1	0	1	0
Yuri Lebedev	3	1	0	1	2
Alexander Gusev	6	1	0	1	2
Alexander Martynyuk	1	0	0	0	0
Viacheslav Solodukhin	1	0	0	0	0
Vyacheslav Starshinov	1	0	0	0	0
Yuri Shatalov	2	0	0	0	0
Yevgeni Paladiev	3	0	0	0	0
Alexander Volchkov	3	0	0	0	0
Evgeni Mishakov	6	0	0	0	5

Goaltending	GP	W	L	T	Min	GA	GAA
Vladislav Tretiak	8	3	4	1	480	31	3.88

Did not play in Summit Series games: Alexander Sidelnikov, Victor Zinger

Acknowledgements

As I wrote in the Author's Note, this book was not my idea. Pat Stapleton, one of Team Canada's unsung heroes, called me in 2017 to discuss the possibilities, which naturally intrigued me. He then came to meet with me and his former teammate Red Berenson for a couple days to talk it all through, and the more we talked, the more we liked the idea. Pat and I talked on the phone or in person just about every week for two years, becoming good friends in the process. He was relentlessly upbeat and supportive. I miss him answering the phone: "Hockey heaven, Strathroy Division!" He would often close by saying, "My life is better because you're in it." My life certainly improved when Pat Stapleton was in it, and there is no question that without Pat Stapleton, this book would never have happened.

After Pat's passing, his teammate Brad Park gamely agreed to become my liaison with Team Canada, and he was every bit as good-natured, helpful, and encouraging as Pat had been—no small statement. I hope our frequent talks continue. The title for this book comes from Park, who told me in an interview, "This was the greatest comeback in the history of sports," and I thought he was right. Brad gave me the inspired idea to interview the wives, starting with Gerry Park.

My next thanks goes to their teammates, without whom this book wouldn't be very much. With Pat and Brad opening doors, the players were uniformly generous, helpful, and interesting, providing information, insights, and especially stories never published before. Perhaps most important, they were honest, and fearless.

In Toronto I interviewed Ken Dryden, Yvan Cournoyer, Serge Savard, Brad Park, and his best friend, Rod Gilbert, and I visited again with Pat and Jackie Stapleton in Strathroy. I returned to Toronto to talk with Ron Ellis at his employer's, the Hockey Hall of Fame, and drove to Marcel Dionne's amazing memorabilia shop in Niagara to see him and the Mahovlich brothers, Frank and Pete, for a few hours. Later I flew to Boston to meet with Harry Sinden and Jean Ratelle, then Tampa for a marathon session with Phil Esposito, and Philadelphia for another long talk with Mr. Flyer himself, Bob Clarke. In my hometown of Ann Arbor, I met with Red Berenson several times to get his story and helpful overviews of the whole experience, and also to talk with his wife, Joy, for the women's perspective.

Naturally, quite a few interviews I conducted over the phone, including, in alphabetical order, Jocelyn Guèvremont, Paul Henderson, Dennis and Janet Hull, Gerry Park, Rod Seiling (and, by proxy, Sharon Seiling), Jackie Stapleton, and Dale Tallon. Alan Eagleson lent his encyclopedic knowledge of the series, while former *Sports Illustrated* editor-in-chief Mark Mulvoy gave me some great quotes, insights, and ideas I couldn't get anywhere else.

In all cases the coaches, players, wives, and other subjects afforded me lengthy follow-up calls to make sure I got it right and provided some additional information the second and third time around.

When I felt I had enough original material to create a book proposal, I relied on my agent, Jay Mandel at William Morris Endeavor, to help shape it into something we could ship to publishers. Thanks also to his assistants Alex Kane and Jessica Spitz.

Brad Wilson of HarperCollins Canada was immediately interested in the idea, convinced publisher Iris Tupholme of its merits, and worked to turn it into the book you have in your hands. His patience, good cheer, and enthusiasm for the project never waned. Thanks also to art director Alan Jones and photo editor Monika Schurmann, who navigated the sea of pictures the series has generated, pulled out the best for our purposes, and secured their rights. Noted author Tim Rappleye put me in touch with Anatoli Tarasov's grandson, Yuri Karmanov, who provided some great photos. Under the guidance of production editor Natalie Meditsky, copyeditor Lloyd Davis went above and beyond, doing more fact-checking than I've ever received from a copyeditor. Thanks also to proofreader Patricia MacDonald. Sales director Michael Guy-Haddock, director of marketing Cory Beatty, marketing manager Neil Wadhwa, and publicity director Lauren Morocco all made sure this book got into your hands.

I hired a quartet of first-rate researchers to dive into some of the books on the subject, the many websites, articles, and other information online, and help answer specific questions. Clara Boudette, Emily Simanskis, and Chris Vinel all did great work on often short notice, adding fuel to their already bright futures.

One of the unique aspects of this book was the application of contemporary analytics to games now a half-century old. I asked Evan Hall, videographer for the University of Michigan's hockey program, to break down all eight games using modern methods to view the performance of each player and the team itself through a new lens, swapping the rough measurement of shots on goal with the more sophisticated plus-minus scoring chances when full strength, a far more telling measure, especially in a series where the Soviets rarely shot until they had a high-percentage chance. His great work adds a new dimension to an old story.

Because this story has so many layers, I needed a strong team of readers to help me keep the story straight while keeping it moving. I hit the jackpot with John Kryk, the NFL columnist for the *Toronto Sun,* his longtime sidekick Steve "Dr. Sap" Sapardanis, a former goalie at the University of Windsor, David Harlock, who played in the NHL and the Olympics, and former NPR and CBC radio producer David McGuffin. These three combined their great passion for the series with an unflinching eye for inconsistencies. Jon Paul Morosi, Neal Boudette, and Kris Manery also provided helpful feedback. All errors, of course, are mine alone.

My last thank yous are my biggest: my wife, Christie, and our son, Teddy, whom she now drives to mini-mites at ungodly hours with Stompin' Tom Connors singing "The Hockey Song" and "Hockey Mum." As Connors says, "You are a superior class." They have not only tolerated my trips to the "writer's cave," but have provided their unconditional support and love throughout. Nietzche said if you know your "why," you can fight through any "how." They are the best "why" I could ever have. I love you with all my heart.